Teaching Kids to Read For Dummies

Book series to take seriously

If you're rushed for time in your library (and even if you're not), check out (figuratively and literally) popular children's book series. If your child loves a series but you can't find it on the shelves, ask your library to borrow from other libraries. Here they are, the series to take seriously:

- *A to Z Mysteries* by Ron Roy (Random House)
- *Amelia Bedelia* by Peggy Parish (HarperCollins)
- *Animorphs* by Katherine A. Applegate (Apple)
- *Arthur* by Marc Brown (Little, Brown and Company)
- *The Bailey School Kids* by Debbie Dadey (Scholastic)
- *Captain Underpants* by Dav Pilkey (Blue Sky Press)
- *Clifford, the Big Red Dog* (Cartwheel Books)
- *Dr. Seuss* books by Dr. Seuss (Random House)
- *Goosebumps* by R.L. Stine (HarperCollins)
- *Harry Potter* by J.K. Rowling (Scholastic)
- *Junie B Jones* by Barbara Parker (Random House)
- *Magic Tree House* by Mary Pope Osborne (Random House)
- *Nate the Great* by Marjorie Sharmat (Yearling Books)
- *The Secrets of Droon* by Tony Abbott (Scholastic)
- *A Series of Unfortunate Events* by Lemony Snicket (HarperCollins)

Your child's first essential sight words

Your child has to know some words by sight. She doesn't have to have instant (or sight) recognition of thousands of words, but she should have sight recognition of the words that turn up again and again in regular text. Here are the 50 most common words of all (the ones you should help her get to know):

the	he	at	but	there
of	was	be	not	use
and	for	this	what	an
a	on	have	all	each
to	are	from	were	which
in	as	or	we	she
is	with	in	when	do
you	his	had	your	how
that	they	by	can	their
it	I	word	said	if

To-do list for parents of pre-readers

You can prime your child for reading in a lot of ways. Here are some of the best:

- Read him a lot of books from a lot of genres (like fiction, non-fiction, jokes, recipes, cartoons, rhymes, and poems).
- Get stories on cassette tape for him (from the library) and buy him a sturdy cassette player.
- Listen to stories, songs, and rhymes on tape as a family (especially on car trips).
- Improve his gross motor skills with a lot of outdoor play (especially games with balls).
- Improve his fine motor skills with blocks, Legos, puzzles, threading (beads onto string), play dough, painting, drawing, coloring, and finger painting.
- Talk to him without simplifying your vocabulary.
- Show him how to draw lines and curves in preparation for real writing.
- Show him the letters of the alphabet and help him trace and draw them in different mediums (like sand, sugar, shaving foam, and chocolate pudding).
- Help him make letters out of play dough.
- Draw letters for him and laminate them. At first, guide his finger to trace the letter. Then just let him loose with markers. The ink rubs off, so he can use the letters again and again.
- Talk in letter sounds. Say things like, "*Milk, mug, magic, mice.* Can you think of another *m* (pronounced *muh*) word?
- When you go shopping, spot letters in shops and on signs. (Give your child a notebook that you've written letters in. He can cross letters off as he spots them.)
- Join the library and go to story times.

Sounds to start your reader off with

Reading is largely a matter of knowing sounds and how to put them together. To get your child warmed up, start him off with these sounds:

- The sound of the first letter in his name. Say things like "*Martin, milk, money, memory.* What else?"
- The sound of the first letter in the names of family members, friends, and pets.
- The sounds of the rest of the letters of the alphabet. Pick two or three letters at a time. Talk about them; hunt them out in shops, books, and newspapers; and trace and write them. Do this letter activity for a few days and then pick another two or three letters and do the same again.
- *sh, ch,* and *th* make special sounds. Talk about them with your child so that he can distinguish them from other letter sounds.

Copyright © 2004 Wiley Publishing, Inc. All rights reserved.

Item 4043-2.

For more information about Wiley Publishing, call 1-800-762-2974.

For Dummies: Bestselling Book Series for Beginners

Teaching Kids to Read

to Read

FOR

DUMMIES®

Teaching Kids to Read

FOR

DUMMIES®

by Tracey Wood, MEd

Wiley Publishing, Inc.

Teaching Kids to Read For Dummies®

Published by
Wiley Publishing, Inc.
111 River St.
Hoboken, NJ 07030-5774
www.wiley.com

About the Author

Tracey Wood was born in England. She went to teachers college in Leeds and graduated with an honors degree in Psychology and Education. She taught in a special school for four years and loved it. But sunnier climes called, and she left England for a backpacking vacation in Australia. Twelve years later, she was still enjoying the warmth of Australia and had traded her backpack for a husband and two kids.

In Australia, Tracey earned a Diploma in Special Education and a Masters degree in Education. For several years, she ran a high school special education unit and then started her own reading clinic. In the 1990s, Tracey moved to the San Francisco Bay Area. She ran a reading clinic; helped in her kids' school; led two scouting troops; instructed for the Red Cross; created her Web site, ReadingPains.com; and wrote her first book, *See Johnny Read!*

Still on the move (with her husband's job), Tracey recently left the USA for Toronto. She wrote much of this book on the long drive. She is grateful to her kids for giving her a notepad and for filling her in on the parts of *Harry Potter* she missed hearing on CD while she was busy scribbling.

Dedication

Two weeks before the birth of my first child, a friend came to my classroom to wish me luck. "Not long now," he said. "Everything's going to change for you soon. When the baby comes, you'll really know what's what." It's been over ten years since then, and now I have two middle-sized children. They give me endless material to write about; make me happy and sad and other things between; and break, lose, or eat many of my belongings. This book is dedicated to them. What my friend said all those years ago was true. Because of you, my incredible kids, my greatest joy, I think I have a better grasp of "what's what."

I am under strict instructions not to mention my husband. So I'll have to be quick: Agent X, you read nearly all of my words, even when you were really sick of them; fixed my e-mail blunders; and helped me overcome my fear of the new printer (that does 63 more things than the old "on or off" one did). All the love and heartfelt appreciation I could write, please take a truck full of it, as said.

Publisher's Acknowledgments

We're proud of this book; please send us your comments through our Dummies online registration form located at www.dummies.com/register/.

Some of the people who helped bring this book to market include the following:

Acquisitions, Editorial, and Media Development

Senior Project Editor: Tim Gallan

Acquisitions Editor: Natasha Graf

Copy Editor: Laura K. Miller

Assistant Editor: Holly Gastineau-Grimes

Technical Editor: Marey Richins

Editorial Manager: Christine Meloy Beck

Editorial Assistants: Melissa S. Bennett, Elizabeth Rea

Cover Photos: © Tim Krieger/Alamy

Cartoons: Rich Tennant, www.the5thwave.com

Production

Project Coordinator: Adrienne Martinez

Layout and Graphics: Jonelle Burns, Amanda Carter, Andrea Dahl, Denny Hager, Stephanie D. Jumper, Michael Kruzil

Proofreaders: Dwight Ramsey; TECHBOOKS Production Services

Indexer: TECHBOOKS Production Services

Publishing and Editorial for Consumer Dummies

> **Diane Graves Steele,** Vice President and Publisher, Consumer Dummies
>
> **Joyce Pepple,** Acquisitions Director, Consumer Dummies
>
> **Kristin A. Cocks,** Product Development Director, Consumer Dummies
>
> **Michael Spring,** Vice President and Publisher, Travel
>
> **Brice Gosnell,** Associate Publisher, Travel
>
> **Kelly Regan,** Editorial Director, Travel

Publishing for Technology Dummies

> **Andy Cummings,** Vice President and Publisher, Dummies Technology/General User

Composition Services

> **Gerry Fahey,** Vice President of Production Services
>
> **Debbie Stailey,** Director of Composition Services

Contents at a Glance

Table of Contents

Introduction

You're thinking of teaching a child to read. What a great idea! Now you just need exactly the right blueprint. So here it is, the guide that gives you all you really need to know in terms that you can feel at home with. That's a pretty big claim, so let me qualify it.

This book is written with two people in mind: you and the child you're thinking of teaching. Why is this book right for both of you? Well, *Teaching Kids to Read For Dummies* is easy to follow, pick and choose from, and come back to. It gives simple, practical activities that work. It explains strategies in easily managed, bite-size pieces, and you just need paper and pens for an immediate start. You can learn and do everything that I suggest in this book quickly. You get simple ways to measure your success as you go. You always know what to do next.

And the child you're thinking of teaching? This book can meet his needs, whether he's 2 or 12, fast paced or steady, an absolute beginner or someone who's begun but could use a little help. In this book, you find out how to make activities suit every individual child, how to make activities age appropriate, how to add more challenge or support, and how to make gender allowances (if that's relevant). I talk about the unexpected twists and turns that a child's thoughts can take, too, so you don't get the kind of surprise my 7-year-old daughter gave me a few weeks ago. Sighing profoundly about schoolwork, she confided, "Sometimes I purposely get things wrong if the work's really boring."

Have I mentioned that I'm a mom? Well I mention it now because it has a lot to do with the tone of this book. In my pre-mom years, when I was a childless schoolteacher, parents were always asking me for help. What books should their child be reading? How could they make reading fun? Why wasn't their child all that interested in books? I would give advice but inwardly be puzzled that parents seemed to find it so hard. What was the problem, I wondered; why were such capable and concerned parents so adrift? Then I had children of my own and it wasn't long before I was stopped in my smug tracks. Suddenly, I was asking for a lot of help. How could I keep my children quiet in public places? Why did my kids fight so determinedly? And a penny dropped about all those parents I'd helped before. A lot of skills, like teaching a child to read, seem like child's play in the hands of the experienced. The rest of us have to learn them. So now I offer you my specialized but empathetic guidance. All the down to earth, honest information you need to give a child a happy and solid start with reading is in these pages. Welcome to *Teaching Kids to Read For Dummies!*

About This Book

Whether you're just thinking of teaching a child to read or you're all set to go, whether your child is a complete non-reader or has already started to read, and whether you're apprehensive or know quite a bit about teaching, this book is for you. You can surf through it or immerse yourself chapter by chapter, as you need. This book has so much information that you're sure to get the guidance you're looking for. And whatever your needs and interests, you'll love "The Part of Tens," where you get quick lists, each with ten items, of all the important and fun stuff.

Foolish Assumptions

Because you're reading this book, I assume . . .

- ✔ You'd like to help a child read but need plain-talking, down-to-earth guidance.
- ✔ You have interest and enthusiasm but not unlimited time.
- ✔ You'd like pointers as you go to let you know what to do next and whether you're doing things right.

I don't assume that you have a background in education or any special knowledge of phonics or grammar. If you follow the advice in this book and are willing to make an effort, you can teach your child to read or improve your child's reading skills.

Conventions Used in This Book

To "he" or not to "he"? In this book, I clean up that sticky dilemma by using "he" and "she" interchangeably. You can be sure this book is for and about all our kids, and after you're used to the idea of switching between "he's" and "she's," you'll probably end up thinking all other books should do it, too.

Lots of books about reading are full of educational jargon. This book isn't. It gives the jargon, sparingly, and warns you in advance so that you don't have to read it if you don't want to. Don't let the jargon scare you — it's there in case you need to impress someone or you feel so confident with this book that jargon only scares you the tiniest bit.

As well as bits of jargon, you're going to see sidebars in this book. Sidebars offer bonus or additional information that you don't *have* to read (unless the sidebar police are in your area).

How This Book Is Organized

This book has six parts:

Part 1: Preparing Your Child for the Road Ahead

Because I know you're itching to get started and can figure out a lot of preparatory reading activities for yourself, Part I takes a quick look at all the wonderful songs and games that prepare children for reading and then launches straight into the alphabet. Here you can find out how to teach single letter sounds and letter partnerships (like *ch* and *sh*), why vowels are particularly important, and how to *bl* e *nd* (get the idea?) letters together. I also talk about the best time to get your child started on reading so that you don't worry that you're being too pushy or too laid back.

Part II: Building Words from Letters and Sounds

You've heard the short vowel thing before but didn't really pay much attention. Why would you? It's neither interesting nor useful to you . . . until you're trying to remember how you learned to read when you were a kid so that you can help a kid now. *Now* short vowel sounds interest you, and when you get to see a child learning them, you're engrossed. (Or is that just me? Do I need to get out more?)

Part III: Advancing to Sight Words and Long Vowel Sounds

Anyone with school-age children has heard about *sight* or *most common* words. In this section, you're told what all the fuss is about and how to get one step ahead. Teaching a child instant recognition of sight words helps her make quick and noticeable progress, so most parents and teachers should be interested in this section. You can also learn about long vowel sounds. A lot of writers get carried away with sounds and tell you about voiced sounds, whispered sounds, and yelled-at-the-top-of-your-lungs sounds (I lied about the last one), but I don't do that. Speaking as someone who can barely remember to feed dinner to her kids, never mind recall all those sounds, I limit the sound-jargon in this section to the word *long*. I explain what a long vowel sound is in simple terms. Then I give you two easy-as-can-be spelling rules so that you always know a long sound when you see (or hear) one.

Part IV: Scary Stuff Beginning with S: Soft Sounds, Suffixes, Syllables, and Silent Letters

Some things cause kids problems. Do I put a double *p* in *slipping* or not? Do I write *slept* or *slepped?* Is it *gem* or *jem?* In this section, you get helpful pointers so that you sound like you know what you're talking about when your child asks tricky questions. And if that doesn't work, I give you some good stalling- and avoiding-type answers to tide you over until you find the real answers.

Part V: Reading, Reading, and More Reading

This part shows how to make sure that your child really *does* enjoy reading. If that sounds strange to you, you're one of the lucky parents whose child has never thrown a book at the wall in frustration. Here's where you learn to make sure this book toss doesn't happen (or happen again) with *your* child. Discover how to choose books that are just right for your child (not too easy, not to hard), find out how to have fun reading out loud together, know how to correct his errors graciously and find out what will keep him reading when you're not there. I also touch briefly on what to do if your child is having trouble reading and where you can go for further help.

Part VI: The Part of Tens

The Part of Tens is where all the most important information gets boiled down to wonderfully easy lists. Here, you get ten word families, ten phonics rules, ten things that help your budding reader, and ten reading resources.

Icons Used in This Book

You occasionally see little pictures, called *icons,* next to blocks of text. Here's what the icons mean:

You see this icon next to information that's really worth hanging on to.

Here's something that you *don't* want to do. It's easy to make mistakes, so this icon warns you of the landmines.

Here's your jargon alert. Skip ahead or brace yourself!

This icon means I'm offering a golden nugget of handy advice, probably learned firsthand.

When you seen this icon, I'm presenting an activity that you and your child can do together.

Where to Go from Here

If you're ready to leap straight into action, go to Chapter 3, "Tigers and Teachers: Listening to Letters." This chapter shows you how to begin matching letters to sounds. If you're working with a child who already knows some sounds and words, go to Chapter 8, "Reading short *a* Words." Make sure that Janey correctly sounds out the short vowels because if she doesn't, she's going to run into problems later, and then go to Part III to get started on sight words and long vowel words. A few lessons on sight words can give your child's reading fluency a real boost, and they give you a good way to have fun and see quick results. If you're not in that much of a rush, you may enjoy the traditional journey through this book, starting at Chapter 1 and working through, chapter by chapter. The chapters in this book let you pick and choose, but they also follow a logical progression.

Part I

Preparing Your Child for the Road Ahead

In this part . . .

Well, you've done a lot of thinking and talking about how you're going to teach your child to read, and now it's time for action. Oh boy. Where do you start? What do you do *exactly*? Should you use some sort of easiest to hardest progression? Don't worry, this part has the answers. It moves you gently from sounds to letters to words. You can find out how to get the hang of things like long vowel sounds and blended letters, and it's chock full of fun activities to steer you clear of the phonics-is-so-dull pitfall. I talk about the best time to get your child started on reading, too. Should you be hiring a (stern) tutor, putting a clamp on the TV, or dishing up Dostoyevsky? This part gives you inspiring, practical, and manageable answers.

Chapter 1

The Wonder and Power of Reading

*N*ot long ago, I lived in a house nestled in a quiet wooded hillside. Sometimes, I sat in the garden soaking up the great outdoors, but more often, I'd be gathering the clothes and kitchen implements my children had sneaked outside. My children lived in a fantasy world of wizards and spells inspired by the children's books they read every night. They found all sorts of unlikely capes and wands to help them enact their parts. As I gathered their broomsticks and bowls of potion, I often felt guilty. The man next door, retired with grown children of his own, liked to head outside, too; quietly, with coffee and newspapers. My kids' tremendous hullabaloo must shatter his peace, I thought. One day, my neighbor stood on his verandah and saw me. He beckoned me over. "I've been wanting to talk to you," he said. "I call your girls the princesses. They play such fantastic games! I love listening to them. They're so spirited and imaginative, you should be very proud." Yes, exactly, I thought! What a discerning neighbor! What fine kids! What a mom!

Reading is wonderful and powerful. It can turn little girls into princesses and back gardens into enchanted forests. When your child can read, he gets to experience and work through all sorts of situations, fantastic or real. He can live other lives and go to other places. He gets a broader view of life. And, as if this broad perspective weren't enough to convince you of the importance of teaching your child to read, there's the more mundane, but no less important, truth that good readers get better jobs.

Understanding the Process

Here's where it all starts! I'm about to plunge you into the world of sounding-out, sight words, suffixes, and much more. You get masses of information and advice, but it's going to be fun. This chapter gives you a quick overview of everything that's coming up. Here, I squash this whole book down into a few pages, leaving out whopping chunks so that you have to read the rest of the book!

You're a good reader. You're reading this book, so you must be. You probably don't remember when or how you started to read. It was all so long ago and, as far as you know, it just happened. Well, that's where my vantage point comes in handy for you. I know that reading didn't just happen for you, at all. Even though I wasn't there, I know that you put together a whole collection of skills to reach that final end:

- ✔ You got the hang of sounding words out.
- ✔ You learned some words so well that you knew them by sight.
- ✔ When you looked through books, you used a lot of contextual cues to fill any gaps you had.
- ✔ You stuck with books because you were a successful reader and had fun reading.

So, now I've told you a bit of your life history. And better still, you're more ready to help your child learn to read than you were a couple of minutes ago. How's that? Well, now you know that to be a reader, your child has to acquire some reading skills and have fun doing it.

A lightning tour of sounding out

Sounding out is the backbone of reading. You can sound out most text, so children have to learn how. You may think that sounding out (called *phonics* in schools) starts with "*a* is for *apple,*" but that's not strictly true. In school, children *are* taught that "*a* is for *apple,*" but before that, and largely at home, you've already started your child on phonemic learning. At home, when you sing songs and chant rhymes and poems, you're building *phonemic awareness.* You're showing your child that words and sentences are made of different sounds, and you're helping her hear those sounds. And that awareness is the most important precursor to reading. When your child identifies the small sounds in words and sentences, she's wired up to attach those sounds to letters later on. Great, isn't it? All this time, when you've been talking, singing, and rhyming, you've been your child's first, and perhaps most important, reading teacher.

If you play the sounding-out version of "I Spy with My Little Eye" with your child, give yourself a pat on the back. By saying things like, "I spy with my little eye something beginning with *muh*," you're focusing your child's attention on sounds. I rank this activity as the number one game for helping your child with phonemic awareness. Check out Chapter 3 for more on phonics.

A peep at sight words

In this book, I also give you a quick overview of how your child gets to know some words by sight. A few years ago, learning words by sight meant using a "look and say" method. Parents or teachers showed kids flashcards and, as long as the children saw the flashcards often enough, they were expected to remember those cards. But it turned out that the "look and say" method wasn't as great as people had thought. In fact, it wasn't very effective at all. Kids couldn't remember dozens of words only by the way they looked. None of us can remember large amounts of information unless we have some help. We need little memory joggers, and the information we're trying to absorb must mean something to us, too. So, the sight words I talk about in this book aren't "look and say" words, they're words you get to know by sounding out and using contextual cues until you have instant recognition of them. I go into detail about sight words, and give you some fun activities to play with your child, in Chapter 11.

Sight words occur so often in any text that your child has to get to know them by sight. Otherwise, he's constantly stopping and starting when he reads and doesn't understand a thing he's reading. Sight words are words like *they* and *were.* They're all over the place, so you should introduce your child to them before you dive into any stories.

A word or two about contextual cues

Readers use contextual cues all the time, at the same time as sounding out and getting to know sight words very well. The term *contextual cues* looks pretty imposing, but, in fact, it describes something so simple that you do it almost unconsciously. Using contextual cues to read means using pictures and the meaning of the text that you've read so far to figure out any words or bits of text that you don't know. Your puzzle-solving brain does this process pretty instinctively. So, don't be alarmed by the juicy term contextual cues — it just means reading around a thing, and hole-filling, which your brain naturally does.

Getting the better of jargon

You're probably downright annoyed by most reading jargon. Words like *digraph* and *syntax* don't resemble any words used by average parents, yet teachers sometimes throw them into regular conversations. Well, just so you can keep your cool, unruffled image intact, here are a few nasty terms with the nastiness taken out of them:

- **Phonemic awareness:** *Phonemic awareness* is knowing the sounds in words. Before kids learn that letters represent sounds, they must first hear those sounds. Rhymes and songs help your child hear the different letter and word sounds. If you read "Humpty Dumpty" to your child, he hears that *Humpty* and *Dumpty* sound alike, as do *wall* and *fall,* and so do *men* and *again.* He hears that words aren't randomly put together but are made of units of sound.

- **Phonics:** After your child has had a lot of fun with blind mice and contrary Mary, it's time to show her that we represent the sounds we say with squiggles on paper, called letters. When you show her that single letters, and combinations of letters, represent sounds, you're using *phonics.* You may begin by showing your child the first letter (and sound) in his name and how other words start with the same letter, like *Paul, pen, paper,* and *picture.*

- **Sight words:** If you were to count the words in a typical piece of text, you'd find that the same words, words like *they* and *were,* crop up again and again. In fact, those words appear so frequently that a group of 220 of them make up about 70 percent of all typical text. Because these words pop up all over the place, your child should know them by sight. They're *sight words.* In schools, you see lists of these words. They may also be called most frequent or most common words.

- **Decoding:** *Decoding* is breaking words up and reading one bit at a time. If your child were reading the word *letter,* he'd read it in two parts — *let* and *ter.*

- **Encoding:** *Encoding* is breaking words up and writing one bit at a time. With the word *letter,* your child would say the two parts (*let* and *ter*) to herself and then write them.

- **Grammar and Syntax:** These two terms mean much the same thing. *Grammar* and *syntax* are about knowing how sentences go together grammatically — knowing your *is* from your *are;* understanding how to use words in the right order; and getting tenses right. If you talk properly to your child, he gets the hang of most of this grammar and syntax stuff. That's why we parents are forever saying things like, "I *brought,* not I *brung!*"

I talk more about these terms throughout the rest of this book, but don't let that put you off!

What next?

When a child starts to read, she needs to understand how to sound out, recognize common words by sight, and read around and between the lines. How can your child master these three things? You can help her practice

> ✔ Sounding out
>
> ✔ Getting to recognize sight words quickly
>
> ✔ Doing *guided reading* (meaning she reads, you guide)

You have all that you really need to know about the process, for now. If you want to know more about words like *grammar, comprehension,* and *decoding,* check out the nearby sidebar, "Getting the better of jargon." But if you've had your fill of terms like phonemic awareness, move on to the next section, "Getting Excited about Reading."

Getting Excited about Reading

What's exciting?

Rhymes, recipes, songs, jokes, stories, the Guinness Book of Records, comics, computer games, board games, puzzles, activity books, letter tiles and blocks, video tapes, cassette tapes, and themes. What do I mean by themes? I'm talking about themes like bugs, space, ghosts, fashion, fairies, dogs, cats, horses, battles, lizards, dinosaurs, engines, trains, cars, sports, pop culture, heroes, and television characters.

Got your tapes?

This year, my family moved from California to Toronto. My husband and I weighed the pros and cons of taking a plane journey or a car trip. We really didn't *want* to be locked in a car with our kids for several hot and tedious days, but we thought we should give them the geographical experience. So we plotted a route that took us through Yellowstone National Park and the Grand Canyon.

When we arrived at Yellowstone National Park, we came upon a *Closed* sign at the camping site.

Then, at the Grand Canyon, my kids declared that it was too hot. They took about twelve steps to take a peek over the edge then got back in the car. Our trip had all the makings of a disaster. But it wasn't a disaster at all. Why? Because my (foresighted) husband had compiled a treasure chest of 25 CDs with raved-about children's stories on them. We were all completely entranced for the entire two or three thousand miles and enjoyed stories together as a family that we would usually have left our kids to listen to alone.

Kids are interested in so many things that you can easily get them excited about reading. You can immerse your child in things she's interested in, and then you can either share them with her or be close by, enjoying your own great read. Anything and everything you do matters. But make choices to fit your life and be consistent. Set time aside every day for being a reading family. You don't have to read a book each day, if that's too much for your schedule, but maybe you could visit the library every week so that you always have books in your car. Maybe you could play tape stories before bed. And maybe you could make sure that you have a good book on your own bedside table.

Picking the Right Time to Start Reading

Each child is unique. Some start reading earlier than others, some do it with more ease than others, and a few seem to do it early with hardly any help at all. You have to feel your way when it comes to picking the best time to introduce your child to sounding out and identifying words by sight. Even so, you shouldn't wait too long to begin. Most kids start to read around a general time, and here are some hard facts about when that is:

- ✔ Most children start to read between ages 5 and 7.
- ✔ Children make their best progress with reading in kindergarten and first grade.
- ✔ If your child hasn't started to read by age 7, you need to give him extra help.
- ✔ Some children start to read before age 5, but only some.

I often talk at schools. When I've finished giving my riveting presentation, I invite parents to ask me questions. I always get asked this question: "My child doesn't seem to understand the letters, what should I do?" When I ask the child's age, the parent usually tells me her child is 4 years old.

Parents of 4-year-olds get especially worried. If you're a parent of a 4-year-old (or younger), show your child the letters so that she's familiar with the way they look. Have her trace over the letters so that she gets a feel for writing them. Practice talking about the first sound in words and grouping words with the same sound together, like *box, bag,* and *butter.* Enjoy a lot of stories, rhymes, and songs. If your child does all the things I've just mentioned with ease, she's probably ready for you to start showing her how to blend letters together to make words. But don't rush her. If she loses interest along the way, take a rest. Instead of hurrying ahead, prepare fertile ground for starting again a few months down the track. Here's a list of easy things you can do:

- ✔ Play sound games like "Simon Says" and "I Spy with My Little Eye."

  Simon Says is a listening game. You give your child instructions and she listens for the odd one out. She has to follow all instructions that start with "Simon says" but *not* instructions that don't start with "Simon says." Say things like, "Simon says put your hands on your head; Simon says turn around once; Simon says rub your tummy; Scratch your knee." If your child scratches her knee, you get to say "Ah ha! *Simon* didn't say it!" All players stay in the game, even if they get caught out. And you speed up your instructions as players get better. For more fun, have kids who are caught out run once around the garden (or to a tree, door, or suchlike) and then rejoin the group.

✔ Sing songs.

✔ Chant rhymes.

✔ Read books (to her), and more books, and more books.

✔ Listen to tapes of songs and stories.

✔ Read alphabet books.

✔ Play with alphabet puzzles.

✔ Let her see you reading your own books, magazines, or newspapers.

Making Friends with the Alphabet

Singing songs, chanting rhymes, and reading stories to your child probably seem like chicken feed to you. You take all that stuff in your stride. But you may not be so sure of how to introduce your child to the alphabet. Exactly what should you do? How can you make it sound like fun? Should you buy any of the thousands of "foolproof" products you see advertised?

In Chapters 3 and 4, you're going to read a lot about the alphabet. For now, let me give you the secret of the alphabet, in a nutshell: Your child probably recognizes letters as being letters. He's watched *Sesame Street,* has seen a lot of letters, and knows that they're called letters. He can probably name some, too. But he probably hasn't gotten the hang of the fact that letters represent the sounds we speak. This understanding of the alphabet really helps your child master reading.

Teach your child that letters are the written form of words by explaining it as I just have and by consistently using a letter's sound, when you can. If you see the word *bread,* say something like, "That word is *bread,* and this letter is *buh* (pointing to the *b*). *Buh* starts *Brian* and *bacon,* too. Where else would you see it?" Chat like this for a while and then make a *b* poster.

A *b* poster is a poster full of things that start with the letter *b*. Start by buying a blank poster and then gather your materials. You can simply use markers, or you can add pictures cut out from magazines, too. Chat to your child about *buh* things (*belt, Ben, bench, black, bun, beans, breath*). Have him draw them. Help him write *b* at the top of the poster or next to every picture he draws. Add *borders* to make the poster look extra good and pin it on your wall.

To teach your child the alphabet, you need to

- Chat about rhymes. ("I put my *coat* on the *boat*," "I saw a *pig* wearing a *wig*," or "I can *dig* because I'm *big*.")

- Point out everyday letters, like the first letter in street and shop signs, headlines in newspapers and magazines, and words in books.

- Play with magnetic letters, letter tiles, letter cards, or letters you've written individually on pieces of card. Say, "Find me *duh*, like in *David, Donna,* and *dentist*."

- Take an interest in your child's letter books, puzzles, and games.

You don't need to buy elaborate learning materials because your child can understand letters, and enjoy the experience, with everyday chat and simple play.

 If you do buy alphabet books, some are better than others. Funny ones with clear pictures are especially good, but kids like straight forward *apple, balloon, cat* type books, too. I love the book *Phonics 1: Alphabets* by Mandy Ross and Neal Layton. *Alphabets* uses funny rhyme and alliteration ("Molly has a monster on her mat") and has cute-as-can-be illustrations. My favorite page reads, "Unwin has an umbrella bird in his underwear." (The illustration, by the way, doesn't have the hapless Unwin actually wearing the underwear at the time of the bird incident!)

Building Words

Oh my golly, you're going to be hearing a lot about building words! You're going to get the complete lowdown on word building in this book, starting with single letters and building up to whole chunks of sound in Part I. In Part II, you get the knack of blending and, when you find words that don't sound out easily, you get how-the-experts-do-it tips.

Word building begins with single letter sounds. You teach your child the sounds of the alphabet and are especially vigilant with the vowels. Every word has a vowel in it, so your child needs to get the hang of vowels. Vowels change their sound, too. They can have a short sound (like *a* in *hat*) or a long sound (like *a* in *hate*). You explain the short sound to your child first and, much later, you get into the long sounds.

Blending is when you glide one letter into another to end up sounding out a whole word. *Blends* are different, though. They're special clusters of letters. Blends are made of two or three consonants that blend together. Blends are letters like *sl, st, cl, dr,* and *pl.* You can find out about both blending and blends in Chapter 5.

Suffixes, Silent Letters, and Other Stuff

This heading may alarm you. You've already been through terms like phonemic awareness, and now here I am with suffixes, and it's only the first chapter! Don't panic! When you come to *suffixes* (or word endings) like *ed* and *ing,* you see that they're pretty consistent and well worth looking at. When does an end *e* get lopped off before adding a word ending? When does a last letter get doubled before adding an ending? What's the story with adding *s* or *es?* I explain all these little puzzles in Part IV, where I also help you sort out silent letters, too. I've crammed Part IV of this book with useful tips.

What do I mean by the other stuff in this section's heading? The other stuff that you find in this book includes stuff like soft sounds, syllables, and vowel+r sounds. I expect that you've never thought of it before, but when the letter *r* follows a vowel, the sound that you make isn't a simple combination of the two.

Reading with Your Child

When you reach Part V of this book, which talks about reading books, it feels like you've walked through the uphill part of your journey and only have to put one foot in front of the other from here on. You don't have to put in any great effort, and you get a clear and lovely view. This book gives you all the tips you need to make reading fun. You see how to choose books wisely and read them to and with your child. I answer questions like, "How should I correct his mistakes?" And you get advice about establishing a fluid style of reading, rather than the stop-start style that puts so many kids off. I also have some recommended reading, too. I don't give you a thousand single titles, though. I have information on a few reliable book series that should keep you stocked for quite some time. And I don't ignore gender differences. I certainly don't tell you to select only girl books for a daughter or boy books for a son, but I let you know the titles that have higher appeal for each gender.

Mirror, mirror on the wall

Before you begin on the chapters about reading, you should take a quick and honest look at your own reading behavior. Are you being a "Do as I Do" type or a "Do as I Say" type? Your child spends a lot of time copying what you do, and you can't get away from the fact that parents who read spawn children who read. To give your child her best chance, make time to read with her *and* show her that you're a reader, too. And, in case you think scanning the odd Web site counts, it doesn't. It's a start, but you should be introducing your child to varied, and frequent, reading experiences.

Choosing the right books

In this book, you hear about two kinds of reading:

- ✔ The reading that you do with your child, where you read to him or you read together
- ✔ The reading that he does all by himself

When you read *with* your child, the world's your oyster. You can get right into award-winning fantasies; almanacs of the unusual, icky, or stupid; and nature books with photographs that leave you wondering how on earth the photographer got them. Enjoy books with your child and go wherever your child's interest takes you. If you're too exhausted at the end of the day to get enthusiastic about dung beetles or dinosaurs, share in the reading by simply hanging out with your child. Read your own newspaper or book while he looks at the Stegosaurus for the umpteenth time.

The reading that your child does by himself is different than the reading you do with him. When he's reading all by himself, his books obviously have to be easy ones. He wants to be able to read them with little or no help from you, and your guidance really counts here. To guide him, you help him select books, you spot new words before he gets frustrated by them, and you praise him. In this book, you read a lot about being supportive and encouraging, and I say a lot about the importance of giving your child choice and ownership of his activities.

You may find yourself taking too much of a lead role when you start introducing your child to reading. You get caught up in the fun of teaching (at least, I hope you do), and then you do a lot of preparing, talking, and instructing. Why wouldn't you? Being active and in control is fun. But, here's the rub — your child wants to be active and in control, too, so you're stealing all his fun! Keep this fact in mind if you want to be a great teacher.

By now, you're probably thinking that there must be more to it than that. My child can't read alone just because I help him select books and weed out the new words. True. The big, industrial-size nuts and bolts of reading are phonics, sight words, and guided reading. You can find out more about guided reading in Chapter 23.

Where would I be without the library! (Catchy, huh?)

Yesterday, I was sitting in a café with my children. It was eerily quiet, so I grabbed a paper bag and wrote this sidebar. The reason it was quiet was that we'd just been to the library. One of my kids was engrossed in *Goosebumps* (which, I may add, lead to her creeping into my bed in the wee small hours), and the other was huddled over a teen magazine, not wanting me to see the *Problem Page* she was absorbed in. I wrote these words of wisdom on my paper bag.

I make at least one visit per week to our local library. I sign out books, magazines, comics, videos, and stories on tape. I have to. I'm not expecting the discipline fairy to drop in on my kids any time soon, so I'm taking matters into my own hands. You see, my kids are rarely subdued when I tell them off; they're locked in a never ending competition over who gets more of everything, is best at everything, or should go first at everything; and they often erupt into fist fights. So I have a constant *situation* on my hands. I respond by surrounding my kids with goodies from the library. I get armfuls of stuff, and then we can temporarily appear like a nice, well-behaved family. But should you ever run into me when I'm not buckling under the weight of a few dozen books and have my kids in tow, back off! I'm a library member on the edge!

When to Get Help

If you ever reach a time when you're worried, or maybe just vaguely uneasy, about how your child reads (or doesn't), Chapter 24 gives you both the comfort and information that may help you feel better. I've crammed the most important things you need to know about reading difficulties into this one straightforward chapter. You get practical advice, a glimpse at when and how most kids start to read, and pointers about where to look for extra help.

And you know that feeling of worrying over a problem and then getting immense relief when you get down to action? Well, this book cuts down your time between the worry and the action. It helps you plan a step by step response of bite-size pieces. And, in case you think you may skip this part of the book because your child's a high flyer, I should tell you that some of the information in Chapter 24 is useful to *all* parents. Every parent gets to experience the parent-teacher interviews. You can bet your life that at one parent-teacher interview in your school-parenting career, you may want to ask for help or register a complaint. Chapter 24 helps you be an effective advocate for your child, steering clear of the bull-at-a-gate or rambling whiner approaches.

Chapter 2

The Pre-Reader: Leading Up to Letters

*T*he other day, I was doing my typical harried sprint through the grocery store when something caught my attention in the fruit and vegetables section. A woman was selecting her vegetables while conducting a non-stop dialogue with her child, who was sitting in the child seat of her shopping cart. "Daddy doesn't like eggplant," she explained. "It's a good vegetable and I like it, but it's the one vegetable your Daddy won't eat." On and on she talked. At the breakfast cereals, I heard her again. "This cereal is coated in honey. It tastes good, but I'm not so sure about all that honey on your teeth." I rounded the corner and distantly heard her elaborating, "Your teeth are very important . . . " I got to the check out line. Two minutes later, she was right behind me. "This food will cost us a lot of money. But we have so much food that we probably won't need to come back here for a few days." I paid for my groceries and could still hear her as I headed for the door. "We still have to get our eggs though. We'll have to go to . . . " Her child was transfixed.

I felt tired just thinking of her stamina. But maybe she'd read the statistics. Studies of preschool children show that the preschool and kindergarten years may be the most significant years for learning in your child's *entire life!* Wow! Are you feeling pressured yet?

The Big Question: At What Age Do Most Kids Start to Read?

Most kids start reading between ages 5 and 7. Girls usually start a bit earlier than boys. Statistically, boys start to talk later than girls and are more prone to ear infections, too. Make sure that your child hears you well and can see letters and symbols clearly, too. To roughly gauge how your child's senses are working, play a lot of listening games and use activity books with activities like "Spot the difference."

Have your child's hearing and vision tested, and if you're worried, get a second opinion.

Some indicators of possible hearing difficulties are:

- A lot of ear infections
- Excessive shouting and talking loudly
- Not answering you
- Mishearing words

You can have some difficulty spotting hearing problems because all kids shout or ignore their parents when they think it's a good idea. But if these indicators happen consistently, and if your child seems innocent of the "I don't hear you because I don't want to hear you" trick, you should definitely get his hearing checked by a professional.

Some indicators of possible vision problems are:

- Head tilting
- Squinting
- Rubbing eyes frequently
- Headaches
- Dizziness
- Tiredness
- Holding books at an unusual angle or distance

Many children have minor problems with vision and hearing. Most kids with vision problems improve quickly after they follow a program of eye exercises. Kids with hearing difficulties often improve when the tubes in their ears grow bigger and stronger all by themselves. Professionals have a lot of simple exercises and gadgets that can help your child. If you're worried, see a professional as soon as you can and try not to let your mind get stuck in worst-case scenarios.

Surrounding Your Child with Words

You do all the right things. You read stories to your child, give her books to look at, have a lot of play and song time, and don't use baby language. But is it enough?

You naturally worry about whether you're doing enough because your child is in the middle of her premium years. So, consider this fact: Your child can become a better reader if she has a wide vocabulary, if she's able to follow a sequence of events (a story), and if she can hear the similarities and differences in words. When you read and sing to her you're providing her with the lot! Make sure you surround your child with books, comics, stories, and songs on tape. Enjoy them with her. Revel in the way children of this age become completely engrossed. Your child may love growling like a dog, scampering like a rabbit, and being a cat. If you can afford the extra milk, go along with your cat's habits and preferences — you'll look back on them fondly in years to come!

Sharpening Your Child's Listening Skills

Recent studies of preschool and kindergarten kids show two important things:

- ✔ These are the best years for learning to read.
- ✔ Learning to read starts in the ears.

You've probably realized how important preschool and kindergarten years are already. At this time, your child is inquisitive. He doesn't have the inhibitions that older kids have. He's brimming with enthusiasm. He can get right into a story, too. He can imagine himself as a lead character in the stories that you read to him and eat, drink, and behave in character. In school, he's on full throttle right through kindergarten and first grade. After that, he gets a little more self-conscious and a little less enthusiastic. Studies of children's reading show that your child is likely to make his quickest and most enduring progress between ages 5 and 7.

You may be wondering about the ear thing. When I say learning to read starts in the ears, I'm not talking about your child having clear hearing (though that's critical, too), but about him being able to hear sounds within speech. Reading is a process of matching written symbols to sounds, so your child has to be able to distinguish those sounds in the first place. The accurate term for this discrimination is *phonemic awareness*.

Using alliteration and rhyme

"The time has come," the Walrus said,

"To talk of many things:

Of shoes, and ships, and sealing-wax

Of cabbages and kings,

And why the sea is boiling hot,

And whether pigs have wings."

Lewis Carroll, *Through the Looking Glass* (Dover Publications)

Everybody knows about rhyme, alliteration, and the simple sayings that help you remember a whole heap of information that you'd otherwise forget. Nearly every person I know goes through the "30 days hath September" rhyme to figure how many days are in each month, and these kinds of rhymes are no less important for kids. Your child doesn't have to remember the days of the month like you do, of course, but he does need to hear sounds and recall other similar sounds. Use great books, like the Dr. Seuss books, to enjoy rhyme and pattern. Later, when your child needs to identify sounds in words, he has a rich store to draw upon. The whole concept of manipulating sounds isn't new to him, and he's equipped with the skills he needs to become a good reader.

Using song and play

A few days ago, I went to a Veterans' Day service at my kids' school. The teachers had done a great job of preparing the kids. A talented girl sang like a lark, we got to see a moving slide show, and some students recited some impressive poetry. But my favorite thing, as usual, was seeing the kindergarteners perform. They sang Louis Armstrong's "What a Wonderful World," complete with all sorts of actions to go with the song. The kids acted out nearly all the lines, and most of them remembered all the words.

Movement and role-play help kids learn. Little kids, especially, need to do big things with their bodies. Sitting still and doing little movements is hard for them — they need to spread themselves out and really get into it. And, given a topic in terms that they understand, they put all of themselves into the role. When you're wondering what to do in preparation for reading, play *Heads and Shoulders, Knees and Toes; Simon Says;* and *If You're Happy and You Know It.* If you're not familiar with these titles, you just need to know that they're games and songs that involve listening to instructions and doing actions. You can use a lot of kids' song-and-game tapes (a must-have for the car!), but you can probably remember a few from your own childhood. Keep a well-stocked dress-up box, too. When your child wants to enact stories that you've read to him, he loves to don hats, capes, and armor. Girls usually enjoy clicking around in high heels and showing off their jewels and gowns in fashion shows.

You've probably heard about different learning styles, multisensory learning, and multiple intelligences. Though some may call me a little crude in my next assertion, I'm going to make it anyway. These terms describe the timeless truth that your child learns better if you provide her with varied activities. If you change your pace and style and let her move around and be busy with interesting things, she can do well. Of course, good teachers have been teaching like this for years.

If you speak English as a second language and don't feel confident with reading in English, don't worry. You can read your child books in your native language and play games in your language, too. Reading skills transfer. If your child does well in your native language, she can probably do well in a second language, too.

Sharpening your listening skills

Children need to become good talkers, as well as good listeners. Then they're full of great ideas that they can organize so that everyone else understands them. Help your child develop into a good conversationalist by being a good listener and a good sounding board. You may be tempted to finish your child's sentences for him and interrupt him, too, so discipline yourself! Keep these points in mind:

- ✔ Make eye contact with your child when he's talking to you. Even if you're busy doing other things, project a general sense of I'm-still-listening-to-you. If your child gets the feeling that he's worth listening to, he's more confident when he talks.

- ✔ Don't interrupt. Little kids especially can ramble on, and on, and on. Even so, it's still his turn to talk!

- ✔ Here's the really hard one for parents — try not to put words into his mouth.

- ✔ Let your child practice explaining things by giving him simple choices. "Should we go to *a* or *b*?" "Do you want to eat this or that?" "Do you want to wear *x* or *z* today?"

- ✔ If your child isn't a great talker, encourage him to say more by paraphrasing what he said to you. *Paraphrasing* means giving his words back to him in a shorter, tidier form. Say things like, "So, you thought it would be a good idea," "So, you didn't get to the shop with Grandma after all," or "So, you felt a bit shy." You're telling him that you heard him and that you're interested in hearing more.

Getting Cozy with Computers

What did we do before computers? I know I got by well enough in my pre-computer days, but I can't seem to remember exactly how I did. My kids can't even begin to imagine computerless days. They're completely comfortable with computers and happily interfere with mine or anyone else's.

So, what's the best way to start your child out in the microchip world? You should probably make your start an easy one. Start with CD-ROMs, like *Reader Rabbit,* because you can't mess things up too much with CD-ROMs, even if you're a complete beginner. Borrow from your library before you buy, too, because CD-ROM's are pretty expensive. Check out the *Living Books* series, which has a set of interactive stories, like "Harry and the Haunted House" and "Sheila Rae the Brave." Your child can listen and read, and she can find all sorts of effects when she clicks on different parts of the screen picture.

Here are a couple of other CD-ROM titles worth checking out for pre-readers:

- *Magic School Bus* (Microsoft)
- *JumpStart* (Knowledge Adventure)

Avoiding computer rage and the "World Wide Wait"

Unless you know quite a bit about computers or know someone who does, you can get frozen or lost in a tangle of Internet pop-up ads and messages like "You need a flumizdong to view this screen, would you like to download one?" I, for one, am terrified of absentmindedly or naively clicking on something that gives my address to cranks across the globe or sends me a warped or pornographic virus (is there such a thing as a pornographic virus?). So I can sympathize completely with those people who want to just use the word processor and hope that their kids learn all they need to know in school. If I'm describing you, you may want to think about these options:

- Stick with CD-ROM's. The Internet can be slow, frustrating, and technically incomprehensible to anyone who doesn't have a diploma in being a computer know-it-all. CD-ROMs give your child computer know-how, and you don't get into a muddle with them. On CD-ROM's like *Encarta* (an encyclopedia), your child can get almost as much information as he could from the Net, and certainly as much as he needs.

- Get connected to the Internet, but avoid the "World Wide Wait" and the possibility that your child may find unpleasant sites by having a computer whiz download good sites for you. Certain pieces of software let you download whole sites so that your child can browse freely and quickly. Computer buffs know what they are and how to get at them.

- Get connected and bookmark good sites for your child.

I recommend these CD-ROMs for older kids:

- ✔ *My First Amazing World Explorer* (DK Multimedia)
- ✔ *I Spy* (Scholastic)
- ✔ *Encarta Encyclopedia* (Microsoft)
- ✔ *Up to the Himalayas* (Victory Multimedia)
- ✔ *The Way Things Work* (Dorling Kindersley)
- ✔ *Where in the World is Carmen Sandiego?* (The Learning Company)

Taming the TV

You can do one of three things about TV:

- ✔ You can refuse to have it in your house and instead have your child be an irritating presence in the houses of friends and neighbors who do have TV.

- ✔ You can take the road of least resistance and let your kid watch all the TV that she wants until she's notable only for a conspicuous lack of personality.

- ✔ You can do like you do with other things and use television viewing selectively.

Hard choice, huh?

TV can be an excellent tool. Where would we be without *Sesame Street* and *Mr. Rogers?* If you're selective, you can make sure that your child views excellent programs. But as she gets older, you have to have an iron resolve. The awful programs that teach her how to be arrogant and rude may become a source of constant battle for you. You may hear an awful lot about "everybody else" and feel like you're always having to justify yourself to your child. I'm afraid that I'm still stuck in this phase, so I have limited wisdom to share! Just stay strong and the TV can become a help to you as you teach your child to read.

Don't let your child watch TV all day, of course, but select and enjoy good programs with her. Your library has a lot of good videos to borrow, too. And though the couch potato choice can be a bad one, it depends on how you go about it. Watch TV for only an hour or the length of a video. Watch selectively. If you watch stories with good plot and style, your child picks up useful things. When she reads, she's able to predict parts of the plot, she has a broad vocabulary, and she understands concepts like motives and cause and effect. She needs these things to fill in the gaps in her own reading.

Get into the habit of video taping favorite shows so that you can limit TV time and watch when it suits you.

Trying First Letters and Names

The first word you show your child should be his name. Naturally, this word is the best place to start. Show your child his name, write it for him to trace over (in a tray of sand, sugar, or rice, on large pieces of paper, and on white-boards), and have him write it all by himself when he's ready. Next, show him family names. Show him every letter of the alphabet in the same show, trace, and write order. You can name the letters, but make sure that you sound them out, too. Take one letter at a time and focus on its sound. You find out much more about the best ways to get to know letters in Chapters 3 and 4. For now, you just need to know that

- Your child's name is probably the first word you show him.
- Show him the words *mom* and *dad* and the names of siblings and other relatives, too.
- Show him the letters of the alphabet, one at a time, taking a few days or weeks with each.
- Briefly tell him the name of the letter, but put the main focus on its sound.
- When he writes letters, have him start by tracing over the letter you write.
- Trace letters in different materials, like sand and sugar.
- Have your child practice drawing lines and circles because letters are made of these shapes.

When you practice these exercises, your child can write his own name in no time at all. It's exciting, the first real thing he's done with letters and words! But, of course, it isn't the first thing he's done with letters and words at all. You've been using words with him forever, and he already understands a lot about language. Your child can start tracing letters just as soon as his small hands and limited fine motor coordination let him. He may be slow to form the letters, and he's certainly a bit on the clumsy side, but he's ready to form the circles and lines that make letters as soon as he can move his fingers through a sand box.

Letters are simply a bunch of lines and circles, and your child can make these shapes when he's about 3 years old. Start with lines. Move on to circles. Then try joining lines and circles together.

Making and creating

Years ago, one of my great joys was to empty my kids' pockets. When I uncovered stones, feathers, sticks, and secret notes, washday was never quite as arduous. Kids love collecting things, often sticky, hair covered, crumpled things that are patently past their best. But that's why kids are such fun. They find joy in small and familiar things — often, things that can be put into scrapbooks, photo albums, and journals. If you have some spare time, make a scrapbook that your child can look through often. Label the inserts. Write simple sentences. Let your child adorn the pages with the bits of feather, stick, and stone that she loves.

If you want to get really fancy with homemade creations, have a go at pop-up books. You may want to check out *How to Make Pop-ups!* by Joan Irvine (William Morrow) to help you put yours together. For a preview that includes a how-to page for making your first pop-up book, visit the author's site at www.makersgallery.com/joanirvine.

Across the Lines and Down the Pages: Teaching a Few Reading Conventions

Before kids even start school, they should know a few book-using conventions. You may want to check the following. Does your child know that

- ✔ You read pages from left to right, going downward
- ✔ We break books into chapters and pages
- ✔ We number the pages
- ✔ The contents page lists chapter names and page numbers
- ✔ Authors write books
- ✔ Illustrators draw the pictures in books
- ✔ The book cover shows the title, author, and illustrator
- ✔ Books can tell true things (nonfiction) or stories (fiction)
- ✔ You shouldn't usually draw or write on books

Controlling the cupboard

If you're like me, you have a cupboard, box, or closet of kids stuff. It has games, crayons, books, and song tapes in it. You use some of the stuff, but a lot of it lasts about ten minutes, the minutes immediately after you bought it. Kids do need stuff, but here are a few strategies that may help you get the better of your cupboard:

✔ The mainstays of a good cupboard are paper, crayons, pencils, and markers.

✔ You can use these things to help your child develop good fine motor coordination: blocks, big beads for threading, fit-it-into-the-space type blocks and puzzles, modeling clay, zippers, and buttons (to do up and sort).

✔ You can put songs on CD and tape to good use. You should keep them in a sturdy box so that they don't get trodden on.

✔ Puzzle books are good, in moderation. Give them out one at a time, or your child may do a bit of each book and then not like them because they're marked and don't look nice and new anymore!

Chapter 3

Tigers and Teachers: Listening to Letters

In This Chapter

▶ Discovering why letter sounds are so important

▶ Finding ways to practice the sounds

▶ Getting to know phonics jargon

I'm driving my kids to their first day at a new school. We're running late, again. They're determined to squabble, again. I'm sure I've forgotten some pink or yellow form. When I turn into the school drive I see cars at a standstill. I feel my temper rising. Then I see a sign. I expect it to say "No stopping," "No dawdling," "No idiocy," or something along those lines, but instead it reads "Kiss and Ride Lane." The sign gives me the patience to wait in line to drop my kids off and get my kiss. I love this school already.

Someone thought hard about the words "Kiss and Ride," and it paid off. I had a great first impression of my kids' school. When you talk to your child about sounds and letters, you need to think hard about your choice of words, too. This chapter explains why you should lead your child from sounds to letters and not the other way around.

I use the phrase *sounds and letters* although I think *letters and sounds* has a nicer ring to it. I place the words in this order because the most important message for you to take from this chapter is that children learn to read by identifying sounds first, *then* matching those sounds to letters.

Figuring Out Letter Sounds

Start out by teaching letter sounds, rather than letter names. Your kid needs to know these sounds long before she needs to know letter names. The very first text she reads is going to be made of simple sounds and no mention of letter names will be made for quite some time. Most people don't realize this, so kids often start school knowing their letter names well, but having no grasp of sounds. These children find it hard to switch from names to sounds. Sometimes their teachers wish they hadn't learned letter names at all.

And anyway, your child will hear letter names early on, thanks to *Sesame Street* and our general conversation, but she may not hear so much about sounds. To give her a good start, make sure you chat often about letter sounds and not just their names.

If you tell your child that every letter makes one or more sounds, you're right. But another way of saying the same thing is to tell your child that we use letters to represent the sounds we say. The concept is the same, but in this version you're asking your child to build upon what he already knows. You're moving from the known to the unknown, presenting new information in a more concrete, less abstract way.

Explain how the written word works by telling your child that

- ✔ Writing is the way we put spoken words on paper so we can share them.

- ✔ Words are made of chunks of sound.

- ✔ These chunks of sound are represented by little squiggles or letters.

Listening for chunks of sound

Now I'm going to tell you how to demonstrate the concept that words are made of chunks of sound. In the next activity, you say words to your child in chunks, and then ask him to merge the chunks together to make the words. Because your child is used to hearing words, his natural inclination is to merge sounds into words. When he gets used to the idea of sounds being in words, then you can narrow his focus onto individual sounds. Next in this chapter, I include activities to help your child isolate each sound. When he's good at that, the transfer to letters is a cinch.

Activity: What's the word?

Preparation: None. Just have this page in front of you and follow the easy steps. Use the dialogue (in bold) if you want to.

1. **I'm going to say a word, but the word is in pieces. Listen to the pieces and you can hear the word. Listen, say "c" "a" "t."**

    Pronounce the sounds and not the letter names. Repeat it a little quicker, with the individual sounds merging together more. Do it three or four times.

2. **Can you hear the word I'm saying? Try this one, "p" "i" "g."**

    Repeat it quicker and with the individual sounds merging together more.

3. **How about this one, "h" "e" "n."**
4. **Let's do a few more**
   1. **P o t**
   2. **M a t**
   3. **H i t**
   4. **N u t**
   5. **T i p**
   6. **W e t**
   7. **N e t**
   8. **S i t**
   9. **H o t**
   10. **B e g**
   11. **H o p**
   12. **S a d**
   13. **M o m**
   14. **T e n**
   15. **Y e s**
   16. **L i d**
   17. **D i g**
   18. **P e n**
   19. **M a d**
   20. **M o p**

After your child practices all these words, she's taken a big step up the reading ladder: She's figured out that words are made of chunks of sound.

Listening for word beginnings

Knowing that words are made of chunks of sound is a great beginning for a child who's learning to read, but she still needs to know more. Your child needs to read those chunks of sound in the right order, moving from the very first sound to the next and so on. The next activity draws your child's attention to the beginning sound in individual words, because that's where she needs to start on every word she reads. Ask her to listen to you say some words then have her repeat the first sound back to you.

Activity: What's the first sound?

Preparation: None. Just have this list in front of you and follow the easy steps. Use the dialogue, in bold, if you want to.

1. **Listen to the words I say. Tell me the first sound you hear.**

2. **Bottle. What does *bottle* start with?**

    Computer. What does *computer* start with?

    Sofa. What does *sofa* start with?

    Book. What does *book* start with?

    Popcorn?

    Alec?

    David?

    Garden?

    River?

    Toast?

3. When you've gone over these words, take turns thinking up new words. Your child may enjoy thinking up words and checking out your listening skills.

You can soup up this activity by imitating TV game shows: time your child, read the words progressively faster, have him ring a bell when he knows the answer, complete rounds, or have him sprint somewhere after a round.

Listening for word endings

Now that your child has mastered the idea of listening for parts of words, he can fine-tune his listening skills in readiness for all the chunks of sound he'll come upon in real reading. He can tune into word endings. Middles come later, because they're more varied; for now, endings are good to listen out for. In the first small words your child reads, endings are pretty close to the beginnings!

Activity: What's on the end?

Preparation: None. Just have the following list of words in front of you and follow the easy steps. Use the dialogue, in bold, if you want to.

1. **You're going to listen for endings now. Tell me what sound each word ends in. Let's practice. If I say *dog,* what's the ending? What about *goat?* And *trick?*** Repeat the word if you need to, and give your child time to answer. If he's not sure about the sounds, think up more words and practice some more.

2. **Here are some more words**

* **Drum**

* **Top**

* **Smell**

* **Run**

* **Skip**

* **Truck**

* **Leaf**

* **Seal**

* **Ant**

* **Shop**

* **Team**

* **Bean**

* **Jeep**

* **Heat**

* **Peel**

* **Seat**

* **Meat**

* **Seed**

* **Wet**

* **Men**

Building Skills with Rhymes, Songs, and Alliteration

Your child is now pretty good at listening to the sounds inside words and can hear beginning and ending sounds. But other listening skills help good readers, too.

Rhymes

Besides being great fun, rhymes are really useful because they give us a mental catalogue of like-words that we can refer to when we have to figure out new words. If, for example, the word *sly* is rattling around your brain, trying to find a place to lodge, you can catalogue it with *my, by, sty,* and *pry.* You don't know about the cranial files and indexes that are getting the job done, but the mental association is made. You can make sense of *sly* because you already know *my, by, sty,* and *pry.* Teachers understand this, so they make sure that beginning readers spend a lot of time rhyming. It's good to give your child the mental gymnastics of playing with rhyme, so here's a listening activity to build up an auditory sweat!

Activity: Find the rhyme

Preparation: Talk about rhyme and give a few examples. They can be silly and impossible, just as long as they rhyme (my kids used to like calling me "Tracey, Tracey silly facey"). Follow these easy steps and use the dialogue in bold if you want to.

1. **We're going to play a rhyming game. Let's think of some rhyming words.** Talk about a few pairs of rhyming words, for example, *cat* and *hat, pin* and *win, hot* and *pot.*

2. **Let's get really clever. I'm going to say a word that needs to find its rhyming partner. After that, I'll say two more words and you choose the partner.**

3. **Lets listen to the first one together. Here goes.** *Lamp.* **Listen again,** *lamp.* **Which of these next words is the partner?** *Light, stamp.*

4. Help your child get the right answer (stamp) and move on.

   If your child needs help with this activity, do the next questions together. If he's racing forward, have him answer them by himself.

5. **Now you can listen for some more partners (answers are in bold print):**

Sink	**Pink,** crown
Nest	**Vest,** elephant
List	Skunk, **fist**
Swing	Bottle, **king**
Hand	**Stand,** money
Star	**Far,** equipment
Spell	**Smell,** chimney
Stop	Kitten, **mop**
Smoke	**Joke,** bucket
Skirt	**Shirt,** bear
Skate	**Late,** spoon
Street	**Sweet,** map

Square	Plum, **stare**
Clock	**Sock,** zip
Grass	**Class,** snip
Ant	Step, **plant**
Drum	**Plum,** wet
Plug	**Bug,** jam
Smell	**Fell,** truck
Ten	**Men,** slip
Chin	Dog, **thin**
Truck	**Luck,** job
Dad	Joke, **mad**
Blast	**Past,** mop
Bun	**Fun,** dinner

Songs

Songs are even more useful than rhymes. It's so easy to remember a song and everyone enjoys a good warble, including (and often especially) the tonally challenged. Songs help your child remember a huge amount of information and they give him lots of opportunity to manipulate and play with letter sounds too. Here's my all time favorite letter song.

Activity: Abby loves apples song

Preparation: Sing this to the tune of "Skip to my Lou." Remember to talk in letter sounds and make up alliterative verses. Like this:

Abby loves apples a a a

Abby loves apples a a a

Abby loves apples a a a

Skip to my Lou my darling

Bobby plays baseball b b b

Bobby plays baseball b b b

Bobby plays baseball b b b

Skip to my Lou my darling

Colin copies Carol c c c

Dingoes in the dungeon d d d

Eggs in the elevator e e e

Fingers in the fountain f f f

Don't get hung up on correct spellings in this game. If, for example, your child sings, "Colin kisses Carol," the word *kisses* is fine even though it starts with *k* and not *c*. Your child has correctly used a *cuh* sound and the only difficulty is if you're singing with a group of children. They'll all be too busy rolling on the floor laughing about *kissing* to sing any more (especially if you have an unfortunate Colin or Carol in your group).

Alliteration

Tigers and teachers dancing on the deck. What fun alliteration is! You've already sung a few alliterative lines and now you get to think up more groups of words and make absurd combinations. In the next activity, you ask your child to listen hard for a sound pattern, and then make up alliterative rhymes that follow that pattern.

Activity: Follow the pattern

Preparation: None. Just have this page in front of you.

I like beans and books, but not cushions.

I like cats and cars, but not dogs.

I like dragons and donuts, but not vegetables.

I like vases and vinegar, but not shoes.

I like shops and shells, but not maps.

I like mops and magnets, but not lemons.

I like lettuce and lips, but not bags.

I like bags and belts, but not windows.

I like water and weddings, but not fingers.

I like fish and fun, but not tents.

I like toys and torpedoes, but not nuts.

I like nets and nights, but not sweaty feet.

Just like before, if your child says something like, "I like shops and sugar," don't worry about *sugar* starting with an *s* and not *sh*. He has the right idea. He heard a *sh* sound and replied with a *sh* sound. Later on, when he's got a lot more reading under his belt, he'll figure out that sugar isn't spelled like it sounds.

The Latest Word on Phonics

Phonics simply means teaching letter sounds. For some hands-on examples of how to do this, take a look at activities in the sections "Figuring Out Letter Sounds" and "Building Skills with Rhymes, Songs, and Alliteration" earlier in this chapter.

Phonics in the old days

A cat

A cat sat.

A cat sat on a hat.

The hat got flat!

TECHNICAL STUFF

"Phonemic awareness" and other teacher-related jargon

Teachers often use terms that only they know about. They don't mean to baffle us, but they're so familiar with some terms that they assume everyone else is too. They don't stop to explain their words and have no idea they're talking in gobbledygook. Some of the worst gobbledygook I've come across in schools has to do with language programs. *Language* these days doesn't usually mean French or Spanish, like it did when I was a kid; it means reading and writing. And language programs have all sorts of complicated names that teachers expect you to just know. They may say that your child is doing *Lindamood-Bell, LIPS,* or *Orton Gillingham* and act surprised if you answer "What the heck?" These terms are second nature to teachers but a mystery to everyone else. These programs tend to focus on phonemic awareness with various bits of this and that to distinguish themselves from the rest.

Any mention of phonics really has to include an explanation of *phonemic awareness*. If you're chatting to friends, you can talk about phonics and no one thinks you're stuck in the Middle Ages, but if you talk to teachers, you need to flaunt the term phonemic awareness. Educators can get pretty heated up about terminology, and phonics has recently taken a back seat to phonemic awareness. The distinction is made because a few teachers feel that phonics implies teaching single letter sounds and nothing else. Of course that never really happens, but who am I to argue? Phonemic awareness is said to be a more accurate term for describing the way sounds should be taught. Sounds should be taught before any mention is made of letters. Then, and only then, children should be shown that letters represent sounds (and are not isolated symbols that "make" sounds). It's all a bit nitpicky, but you should know about these nits if you're preparing to spruce yourself up and impress a teacher with your outfit and grasp of technical stuff!

You probably read something like this when you were in school. Thousands of children were taught to read with phonetically controlled text like the preceding poem, and thousands still are. Phonetically controlled books use words that kids can sound out. They use the same words and sentence patterns often. Harder words (that can't be easily sounded out), like *what,* are introduced gradually. Phonetically controlled books sound a bit (well a lot) dreary to adult ears but when kids read these books they feel they're really reading. I use more phonetically-controlled reading books than regular reading books because kids can actually read the books themselves, and they love that. When people point out that phonetically-controlled reading books aren't as stimulating as real books, they're right, but they're talking from the perspective of fluent readers. Kids who are just starting out with reading, at least the ones I see, have no beef with cats and hats. They don't mind starting off small and soon progress to the more exciting phonetically-controlled books, like the Dr. Seuss books.

Phonics and recent phonics offshoots

Teachers generally agree that phonics is a must, but they quite often disagree on how it should be taught. You can find lots of phonics programs, most claiming to have the best style or track record. They're probably fairly similar (but don't point that out to anyone who's been arguing and splitting hairs for years!). The best measure of any program is whether it's easy for you to follow and looks appealing to your child. If you decide to use a commercial phonics program, be prepared to be actively involved.

Your child makes the best progress when you guide him and give him your time and attention. Sure you can leave him to work alone for short spells, but don't fool yourself that you can leave him to work by himself for long periods and get the same results as if you sat with him. Dozens of studies have shown that *direct instruction,* where you talk and interact with your child, is the most productive way to teach, and even good computer programs are subject to this principle. Sit with your child in front of the screen and he benefits from your attention and occasional input and direction.

Phonics versus whole language

Over the years, phonics has sometimes had a bad rap. Not long ago the whole language way of teaching children to read was considered to be the best way. Phonics was said to be dull and limited. The *whole language* way, where kids are immersed in fun literature so they soak up reading skills, was preferred. Some educators still argue for one or the other style but most recognize that it's really not a case of one approach versus the other. Children need to learn phonics but should be immersed in lots of great stories and reading and writing activities too. Then they get to learn the rules *and* soak them up from the real thing. Like learning to dribble and pass a soccer ball in training drills and playing actual games, too.

Chapter 4

m or *n?* *b* or *d?* Looking at Letters

*T*hese days, I can't see some things. Fine print, sewing thread, telephone numbers, and sell-by dates are all beyond my range of vision. Luckily, I have keen-sighted kids who can be bribed or coerced into seeing things for me. They see everything and, unsolicited, alert me to my half-clean coffee mugs or gray hairs. But I guess I should be thankful. They need those good eyes to spot differences, similarities, and directional features in letters. Is capital *s* the same as lowercase *s?* Does *b* face to the left or right? Is it *d* or *p* that hangs down under the line?

Your child has probably seen letters since he could first focus his eyes. On wallpaper, posters, T-shirts, and his own blocks, puzzles, and cloth books. If he has older siblings, he's probably spent many happy hours chewing or scribbling on books that you inadvertently left within his seek-and-destroy radar. Still, he may not have taken in the fine detail. So if you haven't stocked up on letter puzzles, blocks, and alphabet books, now's the time. Make sure that letters surround your child, and then narrow your focus to a few letters each week. Attach them to the sounds your child already knows. Choose up to five letters each week, and show your child how they work. Use the activities in this chapter to chart your way, and over the course of five or six weeks, cruise happily through all 26 letters.

Getting Started with Letters and Sounds

Ideally, you should spend a little time each day, maybe 20 or 30 minutes, helping your child get to know how letters represent sounds. You don't have to plan a military-style operation; instead, find everyday opportunities to point your child's attention from sounds to written letters while having fun. Here are a few examples of simple conversations that help your child make the sound-to-letter association here:

- ✔ **Look at the margarine, see the** *m* (pronounced "muh") **for margarine? See if you can find some other** *m* **things in this aisle.**

- ✔ **Look at the "stop" sign. See the big** *s* (pronounced "sss") **at the front? What else do we know that starts with** *s?*

- ✔ **Let's play a game until we get to Grandma's. Let's see if we can spot ten things that start with** *g* (pronounced "guh"), **like Grandma.**

- ✔ **I see a** *b* (pronounced "buh"). **Can you find it?**

As well as spending about ten minutes each day on these games, build bedtime reading into your routine. Read good stories to your child and take time to look at the letters in reading books. Look for the letters you've been talking about and count how many you can find.

Try to have a few different people read to your child. Especially if you have a son, try to have a male read to him. Some boys never get to see men reading. They see them playing sports, acting, and singing but not picking up books or newspapers.

The letter of your name

Here's a good starting exercise for making the sound-to-letter association. This activity focuses your child's attention on the first letter in his own name, and you can repeat it with any other word or object that comes to mind.

If your child's name starts with a long vowel sound (Ivor, Amy, Enid) or an unusual pronunciation (Austin), choose a different letter to start with. Maybe *m* for *Mom.*

Follow these steps and use the direct dialogue (in bold) to get your child started on letters:

1. **Think of the sound at the beginning of your name.**

   If your child's name is David, he'd say "duh."

2. **Think of some other things that start with that sound.**

   He thinks of dance, dress, dough, and dandelion.

3. **I can write that sound on paper. Watch how I make it, and then you can make it.**

Slowly write a large *d,* and have him trace over it. Write several for him to trace over. Have him write it on a whiteboard, in sand, in a tray of salt — even on paper!

You must choose how you have your child write letters. Many teachers begin teaching letters as circles and lines because smaller, relatively uncoordinated fingers can write that way much more easily. For these teachers, *d* becomes a circle and a line. If you prefer to start with correct letter formation right from the start, make sure you're using the same style that's used in your child's school. Ask her school for a handwriting guide so you can see how to form each letter (where you begin and end and which direction you go in).

4. **Let's see if we can find the letter in some books.**

You and your child can have great fun looking at books together and seeing if you can spot the letters you're focusing on. But be forewarned — we adults don't notice changes between fonts, but children do because they only know one style of print. And they don't see that style in books. You'll notice this confusion the most with the letter a. The a you find in books doesn't look like the a you write for your child, and the g is different, too. Point this difference out to your child, and see whether you can spot any other tricky font settings to watch out for (like serif font, which has tiny flat lines added onto the tops and bottoms of letters). Tell your child that some letters in books — especially a and g — don't always look exactly the same as those you write out for him.

If your child eagerly wants more, investigate another letter, but don't overdo it. Don't give him more than five letters at a time. Practice each letter until your child identifies them quickly, and then gradually add more.

Hear it, see it, write it

The first thing your child should know about letters is how they sound. Any time you do a letter activity with your child, move from hearing to seeing to writing.

B is for Ben

A friend of mine spent many happy hours teaching her two sons their letters. The boys grew up and forgot the lessons, but their nostalgic mom (who, by the way, became a teacher) kept the proof. Ben, her youngest son, was so proud when he discovered his initial that he wrote it all over the place.

On chairs, tables, and walls, he quietly wrote with permanent marker. Though his mom was hopping mad at the time, she cooled down enough to keep a few tiny mementos. Keen eyes can still find B's in corners and on the undersides of tables at my friend's house. The scribe is now 21 and 6 foot 3!

The natural progression of skills goes from hearing to seeing to writing, moving from easiest to hardest. Your child can hear a sound relatively easily; she finds it a little harder to hold that sound in her mind and spot the corresponding letter; it's hardest of all for her to recall the letter and write it without any visual prompts.

Until now, your child has listened to a lot of sounds and has started to spot the corresponding letters. He should be doing a whole lot more of this spotting by now. You want to use letter games, puzzles, and simple workbooks with him. Do practical activities, too. Much of the rest of this chapter contains a lot of simple instructional activities. They're fun to do, and you should aim to brush up on them for 10 to 30 minutes every day until the skills come as second nature to your child. To do these activities, simply follow the steps and use the dialogue in bold.

When you buy games, puzzles, and simple workbooks to help your child understand letters, choose lowercase letters. Your child uses lowercase letters long before he needs to think about capital letters, so you waste your time introducing him to capitals until he instantly recognizes lowercase letters. By then, your child will pick up capitals more easily.

When children practice looking hard at letters so that they can spot similarities and differences, experts call it *visual discrimination*. You may hear the term *visual perception* used when talking about the same reaction, but strictly speaking, *discrimination* involves spotting differences, and *perception* has to do with processing and understanding what you see.

Activity: Spot the first letter.

Preparation: Make or buy a set of letters. In this activity, your child hears the word you say, remembers the first sound, and spots the right letter for that sound from a small group you offer him.

To begin, use a few letters that look and sound very different, like *m a s d t*. Build up to more letters still with distinctly different sounds and shapes, like *m a s d t l c f h*. Last of all, use a random bunch of letters.

1. Give all the letters, or just those you've tackled so far, to your child.

2. **In this game, you'll be looking at some letters and finding the sound that you hear**

3. Spread the letters out.

4. **I'm going to say a word. You listen for the first sound. See if you can spot the letter that makes that sound.**

5. **Here we go!** *Book.* **Can you see the letter?** *Money.* **Can you see the letter?** *Wallet.* **Can you see the letter?**

6. Keep making up words until your child has found about ten, and then swap over — he tells you a word, and you find the letter.

Most children like giving you a hand. Find your letter pretty slowly so they can help you out.

Activity: Find the same letter.

Preparation: Have a poster-size piece of paper and bright markers, a blackboard and chalks, or a whiteboard and good markers. If you're good at enlarging and copying, you could use your word processor to make sheets. This activity is purely visual. Your child finds a given letter in a small group of letters.

You can do this activity with a set of letter cards instead. Lay the letters down in the same order as you would if you wrote them in the activity.

1. Draw lines across your paper so your writing stays level and your child can easily read from left to right without losing his place.

2. Write a neat, fairly large letter on the left of your first line.

3. Write four different letters, plus the letter you started with, on the right of the first line, about five letter widths from the original letter.

4. Keep writing until you have ten lines, placing the letter you want your child to find in a variety of positions in the lines. (Make that letter the first letter in some lines, the second letter in others, and so on.)

5. Put the paper and pen in front of your child.

6. Let him have a quick look at the letters.

7. **Look at the first letter. Follow the line across to the other letters. Can you see the same letter?**

Children very often find staying on the same line difficult. This is called *tracking,* and it's a skill that gets better with practice. To help your child follow the line he's on, have him track with his finger, a ruler, or a pen.

Activity: Write what you hear.

Preparation: Provide your child with paper and pencil, blackboard and chalk, or whiteboard and markers. Think of words that have a distinct first letter. In this activity, your child really has to think because you read out words and he has to write down the first sound he hears in each word. If he's uncertain, provide letters for him to choose from; if he's confident, he can go without them.

1. **In this activity you have to listen carefully to a word and then write down the letter you hear at the beginning. Here we go:**

2. **Candle; Table; Door; Egg; Picture.**

3. Keep saying words until your child has done about 20. This task is tricky, so be sure to tell him that and show him you're proud of him.

Giving your child a reason to read

As I tapped out this chapter on my computer yesterday, my kids came rushing in from school. They couldn't wait to get to me. They had fantastic news to share. The new *Captain Underpants* book had come out, and one of them had a copy from the school library. "And guess what it's called, Mom!" they yelled, *"The Big Battle of the Bionic Booger Boy!"*

Admittedly, *Captain Underpants* isn't exactly fine literature, but what a great book for looking at *b's!* It reminded me that reading to your child every day is a must. Even if your child's only at the stage of figuring out the *b* sound, you have to show her that good things are in store for her when she can read all by herself. If she knows that identifying single letters will eventually let her read exciting, funny, interesting books that just wait out there for her right now, she'll stick with the alphabet enthusiastically.

Activity: What's missing?

Preparation: Have a set of ten single letters. Use letter tiles if you have them, or cut a few index cards in half and write a letter on each half. Give your child paper and pencil or a whiteboard and markers. You two can have a lot of fun with this memory game. You show your child three letters at a time, and then you take one away. He has to write down the missing letter. Here's how you play:

1. Give the letters to your child.

2. **In this game, you have to lay three letters down. Look carefully at them.** Give your child time to look.

3. **Now I'm going to take one away.** Remove one card.

4. **Can you see which letter is gone? Write the missing letter down.**

5. Do about ten turns, and then celebrate your child's success.

This activity describes the easy version of this game. To make the activity harder, jumble the letters around. For a hardest-of-all version, lay five letters down each time, instead of three.

Using Books and Paper to Understand the Sounds of Letters

Three kinds of books can help you and your child when you're looking at letters and their sounds:

    ✔ **Reading books:** You can pore over these books to find sounds and letters.

    ✔ **Workbooks:** You can buy these books from bookstores or school supply stores.

    ✔ **Homemade books:** You have the most fun with these books because you and your child get to make them yourselves!

The first kind of book explains itself; just curl up somewhere comfortable and enjoy the story together. Workbooks and homemade books need a little explanation.

Workbooks

When you buy workbooks, don't feel that you have to plow through each and every page or every item on a page. Few workbooks are 100 percent user-friendly, and you don't need to struggle with pages that confuse or frustrate you. Don't use the pages that cause you problems. Stick with the straightforward pages, and perhaps find another use for the too-hard pages.

You can use those workbook pages that seem a bit too hard for your child in all kinds of creative ways. If the difficult pages have good pictures, cut the pictures out. Do a _match the letter to the picture_ activity. Write letters on small pieces of paper and ask your child to find the letter that goes with the picture. When he's done that, take the pictures away and rearrange the letters. Ask him to do the same matching activity in reverse — he reads the letter and then finds the picture to go with it. Finish up by asking him to look at the picture and write the letters for himself.

Books that ask children to listen for long vowel sounds

One problem that surfaces a lot in workbooks happens when the book asks your child to think about long vowel sounds when he's only just starting out on short vowel sounds and hasn't heard of long sounds. For instance, he may be asked to choose a letter to match one of the pictures of a horse, monkey, and eagle. He says the names of the pictures to himself but finds that "eagle" begins with a long _e_, an unfamiliar sound. He hasn't come upon the long _e_ sound yet, so this task is a nasty one for him. Books that throw in long vowels before the child has learned them drive me crazy. Avoid these pages. Come back to them after your child has moved forward and has heard all about those harder sounds.

A _short vowel_ typically comes by itself in a short word. It makes a short sound. _Long vowels_ come in words with other vowels in them, too, and they sound different. For example, you can find short vowels in _bag, dog,_ and _hit_ and long vowels in _hope, meet,_ and _nail._ You can hear the difference between the vowel sounds when you listen. I explain more about short and long vowels in Chapter 7.

Writing letters in sand and sugar

After your posters hang on the wall and your homemade books pile up, you needn't stop there. My kids used to like having a tray of sand, rice, or sugar (the amount your child can lick up may horrify you) to draw letters in. Making letters from buttons or pasta shells is fun, too. To soup up the activity, you can add a guessing game. Try to guess which letter your child draws and ask him to give you clues. Take turns. For a challenge, try asking only yes/no questions (your child can only answer you with "yes" or "no").

In the activity "What's missing?" earlier in this chapter, you used the same set of pictures and letters for three different activities. First, your child read a letter and found the picture to match. Next she looked at a picture and found the matching letter. Last of all, she looked at a picture and wrote the matching letter for herself. Teachers typically use this sort of resourcefulness. They find several different variations of a task. They not only get to recycle their materials but also give children practice and repetition to consolidate the message of the activities. This is teaching at its best — you should always try to think of more than one use for the same materials.

Homemade books

Here's something you may want to get right into. It's not for everyone, but some people love putting together homemade books. Even if you're not particularly arty, make at least one book with your child. It's not that hard to do, and he'll probably like showing his very own book to other people. Making books is simple. Just choose a letter, or a different letter for each page, and draw or paste pictures or drawings that begin with that letter on the letter's page. Staple the pages together and make a nice cover. You two can have fun with great big books, or you can make posters, if you prefer. Cutting posters into shapes looks good and can be simple. Cut the posters into shapes, like a bat for *b,* a cat for *c,* and a door for *d.* If, like me, you're a conspicuously bad artist, you'll soon be able to think up things you can draw solely out of basic shapes. On each poster, glue or draw your pictures and add to them as you find more. Your *b* poster, for example (shaped like a bat), would include things like balls, blocks, bulldozers, bread, butter, bagels, branches, blimps, balloons, brushes, baseball players, blonde hair, and beaches.

Identifying the Consonants

The consonants are all the letters that aren't vowels. Your child doesn't need to know this distinction yet, but you should mentally separate them from the vowels because the vowels are a special group. They're trickier to get to know than the consonants because they each make more than one sound. A few of the consonants have more than one sound, too, but you can be absolutely certain that all the vowels do. So enjoy the consonants with your child first. They give you the opportunity to chat, play, and enjoy her development.

You can involve your child in a number of activities, using just consonants. For each letter you focus on, think of things that start with the same sound, like

- ✔ Names (family, friends, TV characters) — Mark, Mary, Melanie
- ✔ Food — melon, meat, mandarins
- ✔ Names of objects — maps, mittens, money
- ✔ Sports and games — mountaineering, motocross, marbles

You can also look out for the letter you choose on things around you:

- ✔ Signs on walls
- ✔ Billboards
- ✔ Books
- ✔ Newspapers

When you come to consonants that have more than one sound, for example *c* (which can sound like *c* as in *consonant* or *c* as in *cycle*), focus on the easy *short* sound for now, as in *consonant*. You can read more about *long* sounds and *short* sounds in Chapter 7.

Getting to Know the Vowels

I often meet children who can't tell me what the five vowels are. They have a rough idea, but can't tell me the whole *a e i o u* sequence. I'm always a bit surprised by this fact. Maybe they can get by without knowing exactly which letters are vowels, but I'm not sure you should let them. For one thing, every word has a vowel in it, so it makes sense that your child should know the vowels. For another, your child will soon have to pay these letters special attention because they always represent more than one sound.

When you mention that almost every word has a vowel in it somewhere, you can say to your child, "I bet you don't believe me, do you?" Get a book, or better still, a page of writing that he can mark, and tell him you can prove your statement. Have him do a vowel search.

Why it's important to know the five vowels well

Vowels change the most in reading (consider how the letter *a* sounds in *all, at,* and *ate*), so if your child knows which letters are vowels, he knows which letters to watch out for. Introduce him to these special five and ask him often, "Which letters are vowels?" You ask him for their names when you do this, but that's okay. Keep the focus on sounds, as you have for all the letters, but have him recite the *a e i o u* sequence as an extra. This bonus knowledge will be useful when you progress to harder reading.

Few vowels; many sounds

A is for *apple.* It's also for *ape* and *all.* When you come upon words like these, what should you tell your child? Tell him that he should remember the vowels as the famous five. Everyone knows them because they have an important job. Like all the letters, they represent a sound — but they're not limited to one sound. All the vowels represent at least two sounds, so *a* represents *a* as in *apple, a* as in *ape,* and a few more sounds, too.

For now, the important sound to remember is *a* for *apple.* Teachers often call that version of *a* a short sound (can you hear that *a* is shorter than *ay?*), and you and your child really need to get to know this one. You need to get to know *e* as in *elephant, i* as in *igloo, o* as in *octopus,* and *u* as in *up,* too. These are all *short* vowel sounds.

If your child gets bogged down in words like *ape* and *acorn* for the letter *a,* redirect his attention. Say that it's true that these words start with *a,* but for now, the *a* sound — as in *apple* — is most important. When you come to words like *again* and *around,* do the same sort of thing. These words start with an *uh* sound, but you should pronounce them with *a* as in *apple.* You get to save a lot of explanations for later. It's the same with the word *a* as in *a man,* too. You want to start off pronouncing *a* the short way, as in *apple.* Later, when your child's reading, she'll naturally convert to saying *uh,* and this conversion will be easy.

How to get really well acquainted with the five vowels

The five vowel sounds are quite similar, so a few visual cues can really help a child remember which letter makes which sound. Some commercial programs have come up with a good way to make the letters stick in a child's mind; they turn letters into characters (without altering the letters' shapes). The programs put these characters into rhymes, songs, and stories. Naturally, your child can remember songs and stories more easily than isolated letters. You can borrow this excellent idea by turning the vowels into your own characters.

If you want to explore the commercial programs that turn letters into characters, take a look at *Letter Land* or *Zoo Phonics.* You can find both products on the Internet, but you may want to team up with friends to buy them. The basic picture cards aren't too pricey, but often the buying doesn't stop there because the company requires you to buy several items. *Letter Land* originated in the United Kingdom and has since spread across the globe. *Zoo Phonics* is a Californian product.

You can easily turn the vowels into characters for your child, and it's well worth doing. Even terrible artists can draw simple characters. (I promise!) In Figure 4-1, I give some ultra simple models you can use. After you have made the vowels into characters, make up stories and adventures to suit them. Draw a whole series of pictures. Make posters, books, and models. The adventurous, colorful vowels become much easier for your child to remember than plain, ordinary letters. Using Figure 4-1 as your guide, draw on those vowels to make

- ✔ Allie (who loves acting)
- ✔ Eddie (the mouse who scares elephants)
- ✔ Inky Pen (who leaves a spot of ink wherever he goes)
- ✔ Ozzie (who swims on and on and on)
- ✔ Up Man (who points both arms up for us because he thinks we won't remember where up is).

If you want a very active way to fix the vowel sounds in your child's memory, here's a vowel drill cleverly disguised as a fun game.

Activity: The come-alive-cards game.

Preparation: Have 20 blank cards. The cards can be index cards cut in half or blank flashcards you buy at a school supply store. Write each of the five vowels three times on three separate cards until you've made 15 letter cards. Leave the remaining five cards blank. This game uses the five vowel characters (Allie, Eddie, Inky Pen, Octopus, and Up Man). The objective is to act out the card. The blank cards are wild cards, and you make up a unique action for them. Most kids like to make the wild card action running to and from somewhere. By the way, you get to run with them — that's what they find so exciting and silly!

1. Deal out all the cards, face down, so you each have an equal pile.

2. Take turns turning over a card.

3. Both of you must act out every card turned over, not just your own. When you or your child turns over Allie, give her a round of applause; for Eddie, hold your hands together (mouse-like) in front of you; for Inky Pen,

pretend to scribble; for Ozzie, wave both arms (and legs if you like); and for Up Man, hold your arms up. You may want to spend a few weeks in heavy training for this particular game, especially if your child chooses something like a run to the tree in the backyard for the wild card action!

Allie

Eddie

ink

Figure 4-1:
The five
vowels
made into
five
characters.

octopus

up

Making Time for Letter Names

After your child has a great appreciation for letter sounds, he can easily get on top of the letter names. I say _easily_ not because knowing letter sounds helps with getting to know the letter names, but because your child is already familiar with letter names. He has heard and seen letter names from general conversation, kids TV, preschool, or any other social organization he belongs to. He'll probably know a few alphabet songs, too. I don't suppose that many kids in the English-speaking world can't sing the alphabet song that goes with the "Twinkle, Twinkle, Little Star" tune. If you're not familiar with this song and haven't tuned in to _Sesame Street_ lately, you have the perfect excuse for being a couch potato for a while. Programs like _Sesame Street_ give your child a lazy, comfortable way to soak up the letter names.

I expect I've raised a few shackles by encouraging couch potatoism. Just to set the record straight, educational programs are worthwhile and fun. They shouldn't take the place of direct instruction, though. In other words, don't sweat if your child gets hooked on educational TV, but make sure you spend time with her doing active, fun games and activities that draw her attention to sounds and letters.

Calling All Capitals

Your child should concern himself with capital letters only after he's become completely comfortable with lowercase letters. After he has the lowercase letters down, he can get to know capitals and their job — beginning sentences and special names. Your child can identify many of the capitals easily because they're larger versions of lowercase letters (C, K, O, P, S, U, V, W, X, and Z). Other capitals are only a bit different to their lowercase partners (F, I, J, M, and Y). Some look nothing at all like their lowercase counterparts (A, B, D, E, G, H, M, N, Q, R, and T), so they take a bit more practice.

When you spend time getting to know the capitals, sort them into groups of difficulty. You just need to be conscious that your child will grasp some of the letters easily because those letters look just like the lowercase versions of themselves, although she may find getting to know some of the other letters more difficult because those letters look totally new. Don't try doing all the hard ones at once. At any one time, use several easy letters and just a couple of hard ones. Match the letters to pictures, sounds, and their lowercase partners. Stick a magnified set of uppercase letters on your refrigerator. After your child goes to sleep, move a letter into the special star place (an area that you make special with decorations — all the bells and whistles) for your child to find in the morning. He has to guess why that letter's special. Here are some reasons a letter may be special:

- ✔ You put something starting with that letter in your child's snack- or lunchbox.
- ✔ You're serving a breakfast that starts with that letter.
- ✔ You plan to have a favorite meal for lunch or dinner that starts with that letter.
- ✔ You plan to visit someone or somewhere that starts with that letter.
- ✔ Today's weather starts with that letter.
- ✔ Today you plan to buy something that starts with that letter.
- ✔ It's the first letter of a favorite item of clothing.
- ✔ It's the first letter of a family member's name.
- ✔ A pet's name starts with that letter.

Chapter 5

Blending Letters Together

In This Chapter

▶ Understanding what counts as a blend

▶ Finding blends at the beginnings and ends of words

▶ Getting your child's tongue around blends

▶ Shopping for tools to create blend activities

*I*f you start reading this book at this chapter, you may think that I've grown tired of writing a book about teaching children to read and have decided to write a cookbook, instead. Well, even though I boast about my shortbread, you could more aptly call any book I wrote about cooking a leaflet. Luckily for you, I'm not sharing my limited culinary skills in this chapter. The blends I talk about here aren't food combinations and you won't be required to wash your hands, though you can if you want to. The *blends* in this chapter are two or three letters that blend one into the next to make a sound. I explain exactly which letter combinations count as blends, which don't, and how to get your tongue around them.

Blends and Non-Blends: What's the Difference?

When is a blend not a blend? When it's made of a vowel and a consonant. Though all letters blend together to make words, only pairs or trios of consonants count as *blends*. The letters *an,* for example, aren't a blend. They merge together (and so do letters like *at, it,* and *ut),* but because they're not both consonants, they don't count as blends. I don't know who decided this rule, but the idea of calling two or three side-by-side consonants blends is a good one. These blends sound different from chunks (like *an, en,* or *it),* and they make your tongue move differently when you say them. So give them their own special place in the reading scheme.

The term *blending* describes how your child blends letters together to read whole words later on. Blending is done with all letters, but the blends I'm talking about in this chapter are the chunks of two or three consonants.

Getting Ready for Blends

To blend letters together, your child has to know each individual letter well. (I discuss how to teach letters and sounds in Chapters 3 and 4.) Otherwise, he spends all his time trying to recall single sounds, rather than getting smoother at putting them together. If you think your child doesn't really have automatic recognition of sounds and how those sounds look as letters, recap. Figuring out how to read isn't so much a matter of speed as of accuracy. You'll find slowing down at this early point worthwhile because any gaps in your child's understanding now will only get bigger later.

If you need to recap or consolidate things that you've done, be sure to do it calmly and supportively. You can set your child back a long way by something as simple as a few cross words or an exasperated tone. He really wants to impress you, and he really wants to read. But, like anyone else, he'll feel angry or disheartened if you inadvertently humiliate him.

Blends at the Beginnings

Typical blends include *st, sp, sl, tr, dr,* and so on. Blends come at the beginning and the end of words (*nd, ng, mp*), and there are heaps of them. Table 5-1, "Blends at the Beginnings," may look overwhelming. Bear in mind that I'm throwing a lot of information at you here, but you may find much of that information useful later.

Don't try to use all the words in Table 5-1. Just read them to yourself to get the idea of drawing your child's attention to blended sounds. That's all you really need to do at this point. I've given you more than you need so that you have a good stash of words to refer to later. When your child starts to read and write words, and she's focusing again on blends, come back to this list.

Table 5-1	Blends at the Beginnings
Blend	*Examples*
bl	black, blink, blister, blot, blocks, blender, blimp, blast
br	brown, brag, brick, bring, brooch, bread, broom, break, brain
cl	cliff, clown, clock, clasp, cloak, clap, clip, clamp, clatter
cr	crust, creep, craft, crest, cream, crimson, crab, cry, cringe
dr	drive, drink, draft, drool, drum, drop, dry
dw	dwindle, dwell, dwarf
fl	flood, flick, flash, flame, fleet, flag, flip, fly
fr	frost, freak, Fred, Friday, fry, fruit, frog, fresh
gl	glow, glide, glad, glove, glimpse, glee, glade
gr	grip, grow, ground, grand, grouch, growl, green, Gran, grind, grin, grapes
pl	plan, please, plaster, plow, plant, plug, play, plate
pr	prick, prod, proud, pretty, pry, private, print, pride, prickle, present
sc	scout, scamper, scale, scope, scab, scar, scarf, scum
scr	scrape, scratch, scream, screech, screw, scribble, scrub
sk	skip, sketch, skeleton, skunk, skin, sky
sl	slip, slide, slant, sleep, slope, sloppy, slim, slipper
sm	small, smell, smack, smudge, smile, smart
sn	snail, snap, sneak, snoop, snip, snatch
sp	spill, spin, spank, spade, spoon, spider, spell
spl	splash, split, splinter, spleen, splatter
spr	spread, spray, spring, sprint
squ	squeal, squeak, squid, square
st	stand, stack, stop, stamp, start, stolen, stink, stairs, stay, steel, stem
str	strip, stride, stranded, stroke, strawberry, string, stream
sw	swing, swim, switch, swell, swagger, sweet, sweat, swollen
tr	tread, trip, tree, treat, trap, tribe, trend, trade, true, train
tw	twang, twist, twin, twenty, twig

When you come to the *squ* blend, remind your child that *q* never goes anywhere without u. *U* makes no sound at all, but tags along for the ride.

Training His Ears to Hear Blends

You (and your child) can find blends all over the place in everyday conversation. They're pretty much written as they sound, too, so you don't have to worry about any surprising pronunciation. You just have to get the hang of distinguishing the blends. To start your child off with blends, try this "Five stars" activity. Follow each step and use the dialogue, in bold, or come up with your own dialogue.

Activity: Five stars.

Preparation: Give your child paper and pens, or board and markers, so he can draw.

1. **Listen to these words and see if you can hear the beginning sound. "Start, stem, stand."**

2. Say the words slowly and clearly, and give your child a chance to answer. Repeat the words slowly if he needs to hear them again.

3. Continue with slow, clear pronunciation: **Is *stop* a *st* (pronounced "stuh") word? Is *step* a *st* word? What about *frozen*?**

4. **Can you tell me some other *st* words?**

5. Keep saying the key words slowly and clearly: **Listen to these new words. *Twist* starts with *tw: prize* starts with *pr: frost* starts with *fr*.**

6. **Can you remember what *twist* started with? What about *prize*? And *frost*?**

7. **Now let's play a game. See if you can win five stars off me. I'll tell you three words. If you tell me the beginning sound, you draw a star. When you have five stars, you're the champion. Here we go:**

   twist, twin, twenty

   spin, spit, spell

   drink, drool, drum

   blend, blast, blister

   proud, prick, pretty

8. When your child gets five stars, have a celebration. Then do this activity, with new blends from Table 5-1, for five minutes each night. Save the three-letter blends (like *scr, spl, spr,* and *squ*) for a grand finale.

Auditory discrimination

If you read other books about reading, or talk to teachers who use big words, you may hear the term auditory discrimination. This term just means listening skills. *Auditory* means hearing, and *discrimination* means telling the difference between. The whole package, *auditory discrimination,* means hearing different sounds. Your child uses auditory discrimination when he hears the different sounds inside words.

To add sparkle, give your child stickers to use. The stickers can be stars, rainbows, or anything else your child finds fun and special.

After your child can hear blended sounds, she'll want to be able to spot the corresponding letters. You can help her get to know the written blends with the next activity. It asks her to select, from a few options you've written down, the blend she hears.

Activity: Choose from five.

Preparation: Have a sheet of paper and five index cards ready. Write 15 words on the paper and a different blend on each of the five index cards.

1. Write yourself a list of 15 words on your sheet of paper. Choose five sets of blends, three words in each set. (For example: 1. black, blast, blink; 2. press, problem, proud; 3. start, stand, stick; 4. drink, drop, dramatic; 5. grab, grit, ground.)

2. Put your list aside and get the index cards. Write the five blends, each on a separate index card (for example: *bl, pr, st, dr, gr).*

3. Give the five blend cards to your child. Have her read them to you, and then spread them out so she can see them all.

4. Read the 15 words to your child in random order.

5. After each word, ask your child to choose the blend that she hears. If she doesn't point to the proper blend card, tell her she's close (a nice way to say *not right*) and repeat the word.

If your child catches on to this activity really quickly, play with ten blends. If she likes writing the letters, have her write her own blends rather than point to blends on cards.

Instead of using index cards for your activities, you can buy blank flashcards from school supply stores. They come in neat boxes for storage and cost no more that ten dollars a box.

The same-or-different game

This game is great, but it takes a bit of preparation. I give you the steps to this game here, and you can decide whether your schedule and fruit bowl are up to it! Remember to do Steps 1 through 6 out of sight of your child (you don't want to make it too easy for him!).

1. Get three oranges, an apple, 20 coins, a pen, and paper.

2. Put two oranges together, and put the apple and remaining orange together. The two oranges together represent *same*. The orange and apple together represent *different*.

3. On the paper, write yourself a list of 20 pairs of words. Some pairs should start with the same blend, some should be different. Use Table 5-1 for ideas. Here are some examples:

   Slide, slipper (same)

   Flag, float (same)

   Crane, crab (same)

   Planet, brick (different)

4. Count how many *same* pairs and how many *different* pairs you have.

5. Write your *same* number on a small piece of paper and your *different* number on another small piece of paper.

6. Hide each number under the correct pair of fruit. Your *same* number goes under the two oranges, and your *different* number goes under the orange and apple.

7. Call your child. Give him the 20 coins. Explain that you will read out pairs of words. If each of the pair has the same first sound, he puts a coin by the two oranges because they're the *same* pile. If each of the pair has a different first sound, he puts a coin by the orange and apple because they're the *different* pile.

8. Read out your pairs of words, slowly and clearly.

9. After you read all the words, and your child has had a chance to decide which pile those words belong in, he counts the coins and looks under the fruit to see whether he gave the right answer. If his number of coins matches the number written on the paper, he's a champion!

You can use other objects instead of fruit, and instead of coins, you can use tokens, pasta shells, or whatever else you can lay your hands on. It's good to play once or twice, and then you should answer your child's pleas for more with a pledge to play again the next day. A couple of games over a few nights really sharpens your child's ear.

Variation: Instead of a written list of word pairs, use pairs of pictures. You need to cut pictures out of old workbooks and put them into pairs (don't say I didn't warn you that this activity takes some preparation!). Your child looks at each pair, says the words to himself, and decides whether he's hearing the same beginning sound.

Sounds charades

I have never met anyone who didn't enjoy a game of charades. People usually only play at Christmas, but you can play whenever you want. See if you can recruit the whole family into this activity and make a good old-fashioned games evening out of it.

To play this version of charades, you have to act out any word at all that starts with a blend, but first you must write the blend down for your child to see. For example, you can act out being a clown, but first you write down *cl*. You can mime eating bread and begin by writing *br.* Some possibilities include:

Frog, branch, space, blink, cliff, drink, truck, grapes, skipping, swimming, gliding, and so on. See Table 5-1 to get more ideas. And if older kids join in, don't show them the blend beforehand. They have to work it out for themselves.

The next activity will keep your child's mind from wandering. Here, she gets to try her hand at a whole heap of words. Using a bag, hat, sock, or box, follow these simple steps. Suggestions for dialogue appear in bold. This game calls for some enthusiasm and a "can she do it?" mood.

Activity: A whole bag of blends.

Preparation: Grab ten index cards, a good marker, your bag (or hat, or whatever), and Table 5-1.

1. Write the blends (not the words) onto your cards, one blend per card.

2. Put all the cards into the bag.

3. **Can you pull out a card and read it to me?**

4. **Can you tell me a word starting with that sound?**

5. **Can you do them all?**

6. Congratulate your child and do the activity again the next day. Play for about a week or until your child can do the activity quickly and confidently.

If you want to use the whole set of blends, start out small. Put ten blends in the bag, and then add to them each night. If your child finds the activity easy and finishes all the words the first time, add more blends from Table 5-2, "Blends on the Ends."

Fun at the School Supply Store

Your child can best get a grip on blends by playing games with them. Remember to have fun — keep a happy tone, set a comfortably fast pace, and play a lot of games. You've probably had enough of writing blend cards for games by now, so give yourself a pleasant break by heading for your nearest school supply store. If you don't know where to find the store nearest you, check the phone book, or you can ask at your child's school. The school secretary usually knows absolutely everything worth knowing about getting school supplies, and if she's not the scary sort, she'll be glad to help you, even if your child hasn't started school yet.

Board games

I can go clothes shopping and come back empty-handed. I can visit Las Vegas and not lay a bet. I can be set loose in Baskin Robbins and not order extra hot fudge sauce and end up feeling queasy. But don't trust me with your wallet (just in case you were thinking of it) in a school supply store. I love buying flashcards and board games, and I usually spot a nice poster or three dozen, too. If you haven't yet indulged yourself in a school supply store, you're in for a treat. These shops always have lovely card games, letter tiles, flashcards, posters, and enough glitzy stickers, pens, and pencils to keep all your nephews and nieces happy for several Christmases to come. Browse around and keep your eyes peeled for board games and flashcards. Board games can really cheer up the introduction of blends. (Let's face it — blends aren't the most stimulating subject matter you'll ever come upon.)

I've spent many happy hours playing a version of Chutes and Ladders with blends ingeniously built into it that I found at my local school supply store. One bonus feature about these games is that many come with blend cards you can use again. I have a board game that cost ten dollars and supplies me with dozens of cool picture cards that I use all the time.

If you're lucky enough to snag some of these cards, here are a couple of activities you can do with them:

 ✔ Show the pictures to your child and ask him to either select or write the blends that go with it. For example, *st* goes with *stamp*. (For kids who select, write the blends on index cards beforehand.)

 ✔ Show the blends and ask your child to find the corresponding pictures.

The pictures I'm talking about range from clowns and trampolines to straw and tractors. I could make my own sets of pictures and blends, but I figure that life's only so long. Boxed games save you a lot of time, and they look and feel nice, too.

Workbooks

While you're browsing for inexpensive and durable board games, check out the workbooks. Find the workbooks section of the store and scan the selection. Don't be put off by the size of the task! You probably see dozens and dozens of books, all with different styles and themes. Where do you start?

Choosing a workbook

Choose a workbook with your child in mind. What does he like? What turns him off? How many pages will seem challenging but not overwhelming to him? Most children like these features:

- Pictures
- Color
- Notebook, not textbook, size
- Easy instructions
- About size 14 font

You'll be glad about these features, too — especially the easy instructions part. Kids hate having to wait for you to work out instructions and may decide to walk off and do something else while you're gathering your thoughts!

If you don't have one, you may want to buy a small whiteboard. You'll soon be asking your child to write words, and she'll have a lot more fun writing on a whiteboard. Book-size whiteboards cost around five dollars in some of the big chain stores.

Planning to be his sidekick

Think of workbooks as tools. Like any tool, they're only as good as the person using them. Your child is a beginner. He doesn't have the skill to read instructions or get around other obstacles that a book may put in his way. It's your job to help. You can't just plunk a workbook down and leave your child to finish it himself. He can only do so much on his own, and solitary work doesn't hold appeal for very long. Set time aside to sit with your child when he works on a workbook. Watch him. Encourage him. That may be all you need to do. More likely, he'll need some help now and again. Guide and support him, and always remember that your job is to help out, not take over. Most of us are raging megalomaniacs at heart and have to consciously curb the impulse to do everything ourselves!

When you help your child by talking to her, demonstrating for her, and playing with her, it's called *direct instruction*. This teaching method is so effective that teachers always try to do some of it with their students. If you've been doing the activities in this book, you can congratulate yourself on having given your child direct instruction.

Altering a workbook so that it works for you

Beginner's workbooks always ask children to match a picture to the right sound. Your child has to draw his wiggly line between picture and sound, and this activity can keep him quiet for several minutes. You probably paid a few dollars for the book and hoped it would occupy your child for hours. But there he stands, after ten minutes, smiling up at you with his completed book in hand. Don't be hard on yourself — it happens to us all.

I have a sneaky way for you to get your money's worth out of that book — take your scissors to it. Cut out the pictures and words. Play matching-up games with them. Can your child match blend to picture, and then picture to blend? If you take away the blends, can he write them for himself? Put your words and pictures away, and recycle them again later. Buy a scrapbook and glue, and let your child do his thing. You can use activities like these to have a few fun and very productive hours.

Recycling a workbook

Solving a puzzle or mystery can give you a lot of satisfaction. Granted, some of us want the solution to come a lot easier than others, but even so, it feels good to crack the case. Here's a simple activity that most children like. It brings out the detective in your child, and you get to recycle a workbook, too! If your child's the puzzle type, he may stick with this activity for up to an hour.

Activity: Find it.

Preparation: Get an old workbook or page of writing. Plan five finding-type activities, using the following directions for your child (or directions you come up with on your own):

- ✔ **Find three words that start with *st*.**

- ✔ **Find all the *cr* words you can. Count them. There should be four. Put a cross on each of them.**

✔ Find a word that had *br* in it. Color it brown.

✔ Find a very long word that has *bl* in it. Color it blue.

✔ Find the word that has *sw* in it and put a circle around it.

✔ Claire read this page. Put *Cl* at the end of this page to show she read it.

✔ Can you think of an animal that slithers and starts with *sn?* Draw one of these animals somewhere on this page.

✔ The word plate starts with *pl*. Think of a purple fruit that starts with *pl*. Draw it on this page. If you like this fruit, draw two of them!

✔ Draw three things that start with *st*.

✔ Find a word with *st* in it and a word with *fl* in it. Join them together with a line.

Scrapbooks

Scrapbooks are worthwhile teaching tools. They can be totally personalized and therefore more interesting for both you and your child. Who doesn't like poring over photos and remembering snippets of time from mementos and keepsakes? Have your child think of words that begin with blends that have a special meaning for her. Perhaps she's fascinated by snakes, space, or trains? These words all start with blends. Create your own masterpiece by decorating your scrapbook, inside and out. Try having categories. *People* and *food* are always good categories to start with. You can include words like Grandma, Steven, Brooke, and Fluffy; or cream, fruit, bread and crackers.

Blends on the Ends

You're not done with blends yet. You probably spotted it ages ago; a whole army of words have blends on the ends of them. There's *ng* on all those words that end with *ing*, and there's *nk, st,* and a few more, besides. Table 5-2 has a smorgasbord of *nk's* and *nt's* and other such blends to give your child's tongue a workout. Check out the activities after Table 5-2. When you get going with those activities, you can refer back to Table 5-1 and Table 5-2 for more word and blend ideas.

Table 5-2	Blends on the Ends
Blend	*Examples*
ct	fact, pact, insect, direct, correct, inspect, reject, duct
lk	milk, sulk, silk, bulk
mp	lump, jump, bump, hump, stump, stamp, limp, lamp
nd	end, bend, lend, spend, mind, find, kind, hand, band, land, stand, pond
ng	song, long, ring, sing, bring, fling, sting, wing, hang, bang, lung, clang
nk	sink, blink, chunk, skunk, monk, wink, think, trunk, bunk
nt	spent, sent, meant, tent, bent
sk	tusk, mask, ask, risk, task
st	past, last, nest, cost, dust, frost, test, mist, list, best, pest, trust

A simple spelling rule to share with your child for the *ct* sound is that it's always *ct* and never *kt.*

You should pay extra attention to the *ng* and *nk* endings. They're sometimes called nasal blends because they're not as clearly pronounced as other blends.

Activities: Easy to harder.

Kids who are still finding their feet with blend sounds and letters should do listening activities:

1. Read out a group of words with the same beginning sound and ask your child to tell you what the beginning sound is.

2. Read out different words to your child, one at a time. After each word, ask him to tell you what the beginning sound is.

3. Read out a group of words with the same ending sound and ask your child to tell you what the end sound is.

4. Read out different words to your child, one at a time. After each word, ask him to tell you what the end sound is.

5. Make up alliterative sentences that use blends. (For example: *The stupid stag stood on the stamp.*)

Kids who are a little more confident with blends should do looking and finding activities:

1. Write three blends on a whiteboard (or make cards with blends written on them). Read out words and have your child find the right blend.

2. Show your child a blend and ask him to tell you a word with that blend in it.

3. Give your child pictures and have him find the matching written blend.

4. Give your child a written blend and have him find the matching picture.

Kids who are experts with blends should be writing their own blends:

1. Read out to your child words with blends in them. Ask her to write the blends down. Have a written set of blends for her to refer to.

2. Read out to your child words with blends in them. Ask her to write the blends down without a written set of blends to refer to.

With any activity you do, train yourself to think *easy to hard.* Give a few progressive variations of the same activity. Go from hearing to finding to writing. Repeat an activity a few times and comment on your child's increased speed and accuracy. Repetition is important because your child needs several exposures to a thing before it sinks in. Moving from the concrete to the more abstract is important, too. Think in terms of demonstrating a thing to your child, helping him do it, and then leaving him to do it by himself.

Chapter 6

Four Special Sounds in Reading: *ch, sh, ph,* and *th*

I've filled this chapter with things children hold dear. Here your child gets to talk about chocolate, chewing gum, and chips; she can delve into sharks and phantoms; and if her attention starts to wander, a quick look at thumb screws, shackles, and chains will give her a good wake-up call. It's all here. Delve into the *ch, sh, ph,* and *th* words. Enjoy them because they're not hard for your child to get the hang of — they're just a set of new and distinctive sounds represented by two letters instead of one. Your child will have a blast stretching her vocabulary, imagination, and gore with words that include *ch, sh, ph,* and *th*. Think of it: *chase, chilling, shrink, shriek, shake, phone, microphone, graph, thrill, throat,* and *thunder*. These are interesting words! Oh, and think particularly about *th*. A lot of the words that your child first reads start with *th: the, this, that,* and *they* probably feature prominently.

Helping Your Child Hear *ch, sh, ph,* and *th*

By now you're probably aware of the natural sequence for understanding sounds: First the ears get a workout with listening activities; then the eyes take a turn as your child gets to find the right letters from a few choices; last of all, your child finally gets to use those jazzy pencils to write down the sounds he hears.

Keep an upbeat pace and work from the easiest task, listening, to the hardest task, writing. Move from ears to eyes to hand, and play games to repeat and refine the skills you're focusing on.

Chocolate begins with ch

You need to start your child off with listening activities. What could be hard about hearing the *ch* sound? So many cool things start with *ch* that your child's ears are already primed. You need only whisper the word *chocolate,* and you have your child's full attention. Follow through with *chips* and *chewing gum,* and she's all yours. *Ch* is a good sound to hear, and your child will appreciate it in no time at all. Tell her the things you've thought of that start with *ch.* Think of more things together. Set a goal of thinking up 20 words.

Okay, your child can hear *ch.* But can she solve your quiz? Tell her that you're going to test her with a quiz. Say that you're not sure whether she can do it. (You need to set the dramatic stage.) Now your child feels marvelous when she answers your questions!

Activity: The hardest quiz, ever!

Preparation: Look at the questions in the quiz that follows and select those you feel sure she knows. All the answers in this quiz start with *ch.* (Direct dialogue appears in bold.)

1. **You eat these — they're yummy.** (chocolate chip cookies, cherries, chips)

2. **Christian people go here on Sundays.** (church)

3. **This is yummy to eat; it's brown and melts in the sun.** (chocolate)

4. **If you buy something small and give ten dollars to the cashier, what will you get?** (change)

5. **This is a kind of cheese.** (cheddar)

6. **These are reddish fruit.** (cherries)

7. **To make wood for a fire, you get a log and do what to it?** (chop)

8. **This is a game played with a lot of interesting pieces, like knights, kings, and queens.** (chess)

9. **You can eat this as nuggets, or you can eat just the wings or legs.** (chicken)

10. **If something gets stuck in your throat, what might you do?** (choke)

11. After your child gives you all the answers, celebrate. Perhaps some chips or chocolate are in order!

60 or 6D?

I recently caught a flight from Philadelphia to Toronto. Because I hate flying, I braced myself for the closet-sized plane I knew waited for me. But the person at the desk told me some great news. I had seat 60. Seat 60? Wow, if the plane has at least 60 seats, it must be larger than I thought, after all. I glanced at my ticket, and sure enough, I saw seat number 60. I walked to the plane with a light step. Imagine how cheated I felt when I came straight to a closet with wings. (Long and thin with chairs rather than hangers and shelves, but otherwise, a closet.) What went wrong? Why didn't I have the big plane I had expected?

The confusion happened when 6D had sounded like 60 to me. With my questionable eyesight, 6D had looked like 60, too. What does this story have to do with you and your child? When you give your child listening activities, be sure to pronounce your words clearly. When you write letters for him, keep your handwriting neat and simple, too. Lose, for now, any extra slopes and curls you've cultivated over the years. Such attention to detail makes a pleasant flight.

Showing off the sh sound

Sh is a great sound because it has a game built right into it. Just say "shh" to your child and follow up by whispering a shower of *sh* words in his ear. He'll like the novelty of whispering, and you can follow up by seeing how many *sh* words you can both come up with. Can you reach a total of 20? After you're all warmed up from thinking of 20 words, have a go at this quiz.

Activity: The quiet quiz.

Preparation: Just have this page in front of you.

1. **You can sail in this.** (ship)

2. **You buy things here.** (shop)

3. **Circles, squares, and triangles are all what?** (shapes)

4. **You can find these on the sand at the beach.** (shells)

5. **Diamonds do this in the sun.** (shine)

6. **What's a girl's name that begins with *sh?*** (Sharon, Shelley, Shirley, Shana)

7. **What's a boy's name that begins with *sh?*** (Shane, Shaun)

8. **Gardeners keep their tools and lawn mower in this building.** (shed)

9. **This sea animal has a lot of sharp teeth.** (shark)

10. **A knife is what?** (sharp)

If you still have energy to spare, try making cute alliterative phrases and sentences. Start with *sh* phrases and sentences, and then add a few *ch* phrases and sentences to your list, too. Try to make 20. I've included a few ideas to get you started:

- ✔ Shells on the shady shore.
- ✔ Shadows and shelves in the shed.
- ✔ Shopping for shocking shades.
- ✔ Sharon bought shiny shoes at the shop.
- ✔ Sharon shaved Shaun's shins.
- ✔ Shh, the sheep are asleep in the shed.
- ✔ Cheating at chess.
- ✔ Chasing chickens in church.
- ✔ Chomping on chops and chicken.
- ✔ Charlie ate chips in the chilly chimney.

As a final addition to this activity, read the sentences to your child, deleting the last word of each sentence. Can he remember the ending? Better still, read the sentences to someone else, and let your child help that person guess each last word. When your child leaps on you and your spouse at the end of a long day to do this activity (and your child can keep this up long into the night!), you may find yourself having doubts about this exercise. The look of joy on your child's face should put those doubts to rest!

A phase of ph

Although you don't find many *ph* words (unless you look through a medical dictionary, maybe), this little partnership is so weird that it's memorable simply for being weird. Why on earth do *p* and *h* sound like *f*? Who knows? I guess people somewhere must know, but I don't. Tell your child about this weird pair, and she'll be intrigued. Tell her you're sorry that you're not much help in figuring out why this chunk sounds like *f,* but there it is, one of life's mysteries. If you do happen to know every last detail of the origins of *ph* because you have a rare and intimate grasp of Latin, share this insight with your child. Or just play dumb.

I bet you're expecting some activities here. Well, I said that *ph* is weird, and here's where I prove it. I've been thinking of *ph* words for a while now, and here's what I've come up with: *phantom, Phil, phew, physical, phone, phonics, phase, oomph, graph,* and *digraph* (you can read about digraphs in the sidebar "Di's graph" later in this chapter). Not a very impressive list, right?

A person can grow old trying to think of *ph* words. Just tell your child that sometimes the odd couple, *ph,* turns up to make the *f* sound. Then move forward. Get on with your life.

Thinking about th

Th is a nice, but changeable, little sound. It makes the sound of *th,* as in *the,* and *th,* as in *thing.* Many teachers spend a long time showing children the difference between these versions of *th* and telling them about voiced and unvoiced sounds. I find this method a bit dreary and prefer to simply say words with children until they hear the patterns for themselves. Get to know *th* words with your child but don't worry too much about fine distinctions between the two *th* sounds. Later, when your child reads *th* words in context, he can firm up his understanding. Which words can you talk about? What about

> *Think, through, throat, three, thrill, threat, thanks, thump, throttle, the, that, these, thermos,* and *thigh*

Activity: Thinking about *th* words.

Preparation: Just have this page in front of you, read the questions out loud, and have your child tell you the answers.

1. **You sew with this.** (thread)
2. **You use your brain to do this.** (think)
3. **You say this if someone does something for you.** (thank you)
4. **A nurse can take your temperature with this.** (thermometer)
5. **If you have a cold, this part of you may be sore.** (throat)
6. **You go here to see a movie.** (theater)
7. **To keep your soup hot, you can put it in this.** (thermos)
8. **This is something you do with a baseball.** (throw)
9. **This is a small number.** (three)
10. **This is a loud noise that comes before lightning.** (thunder)

You can make alliterative sentences, using *th.* (See the section "Showing off the *sh* sound" earlier in this chapter for some fun ways to play with these sentences.) For more listening games, try turning your alliterative sentences into songs. Get the whole family singing, and bully them into a game of charades, too. Flip back to Chapter 5 for charades instructions.

The case of the unwanted *th* sound

When my daughter was 5, she had a lisp. She asked for thauthe (sauce) and thockth (socks), and she studied thpathe (space) in school. I saw a speech therapist. The therapist told me not to worry and that the critical age for a lisp was 7. My daughter would probably lose her extra *th's* by that age, and if not, I should come back then.

My daughter turned 6, and then she turned 7. She continued to lisp, but she corrected herself when I reminded her. I sent her off to the speech therapist, who told me that my daughter didn't have a lisp. The speech therapist had asked her to read out lists of words, and, predictably enough, my daughter performed perfectly. The speech therapist sent us away with lists of words to practice, but I'd already been doing that with my daughter and knew such practice

wasn't a long-term option. So instead, I convinced my child to read aloud to me every night from a good book. If she lisped, I had her repeat the sentence she had lisped on. At first she grumbled, but she did that for effect more than anything. She enjoyed her reading and loved having me listen to her.

She's now nearly 8 years old. She still loves reading to me, and her lisp is almost completely gone. If your child has any problems with his speech, get working on speech therapy as early as possible, but don't panic about his reading. Unless he has a significant hearing loss, he should be able to tackle reading as well as any other child. Mild speech impediments don't typically impede a child's reading.

Practicing the ch, sh, ph, and th Sounds

By now, your child has done quite a bit of listening. She's tuned into these special sounds, and she's ready for a challenge. Using Tables 6-1 and 6-2, run through the activities in this section with her. Because you can look back at previous section in this chapter to get familiar with how the activities work, I include harder words (especially the words in Table 6-2, which have the special sounds at the ends). Before launching into the words in Table 6-2, explain that the special sounds come at the end of these words.

Activity 1: Hear the sound.

Read a random selection of 20 words from Table 6-1 and ask your child to identify the beginning sound. You can do the same activity, using the words from Table 6-2. Just ask your child to identify the *ending* sound of each word.

Activity 2: Hear the word.

Read 20 words from Table 6-1 (or Table 6-2), but break each word into two chunks. Ask your child what word you're saying. I've chunked the first five words in Table 6-1 for you.

Activity 3: Find it.

Give your child three special sounds cards — *sh, ch,* and *th*. Read 20 words from either Table 6-1 or Table 6-2 and have her pick the sound she hears from the three cards.

Activity 4: Write it.

If your child enjoys writing, repeat Activity 3. Only, this time, she writes the three special sounds herself and then puts a check under the one she hears. You do the same, and then compare notes.

Table 6-1	Words with the Special Sound at the Beginning	
ch words	*sh words*	*th words*
ch-amp	sh-ock	th-an
ch-ap	sh-elf	th-ank
ch-at	sh-ift	th-at
ch-eck	sh-ack	th-em
ch-ess	sh-all	th-en
chest	shell	theft
chick	shin	thick
chill	ship	thin
chimp	shot	thing
chin		think
chip		this
chomp		thrash
chop		thrill
churn		thump
chunk		

Di's graph

You probably cast your eyes over this sidebar, expecting to read a story about Di and how she struggled with a graph until she finally understood it. Well, I'm sorry to say that I've brought you here under false pretenses. This sidebar has nothing to do with graphs and doesn't even mention Di and what she's up to. *Di's graph* just sounded so much more friendly and interesting than what I actually have to tell you about. You see, reading involves sounds called digraphs. I think *Di's graph* is far easier to remember. But no one listens to my great ideas, so digraph it remains.

A *digraph* is a unit of sound made from two letters that join together to make a new sound. So, this chapter is, in fact, a chapter all about digraphs. That's why I mention it. *Ch, sh, ph,* and *th* are digraphs. And many people count *wh* as a digraph, too (though I dispute that — who says *wh* any differently than they say *w?*). The word *digraph* can come up in meetings with teachers (at least those who use jargon). So now you can really wow those teachers and understand what in the world they're talking about by knowing about digraphs.

Table 6-2	Words with the Special Sound at the End	
ch words	**sh words**	**th words**
batch	ash	bath
bench	brush	cloth
blotch	cash	fifth
branch	crash	math
bunch	dash	moth
catch	dish	path
clench	fish	sixth
clutch	flash	tenth
crutch	flesh	width
ditch	flush	with
drench	fresh	
fetch	gash	
flinch	gosh	
hatch	hush	
hitch	mash	
hunch	mush	

ch words	sh words
hutch	slosh
latch	slush
lunch	smash
match	swish
much	wish
munch	
notch	
patch	
pinch	
punch	
ranch	
rich	
sketch	
stench	
stitch	
stretch	
such	
switch	
twitch	
witch	

Looking at the Letters

Because pairs of letters make the *ch, sh, ph,* and *th* sounds, some teachers show those sounds as two letters joined together. Those teachers always write the pairs of letters joined so that children always see them as one unit. You can do the same, or you can make the pairs stand out by coloring them a different color from the other letters in words. Point out that the second letter in every pair is *h*. Your child can remember them a bit more easily with that fact in mind.

Besides joining these pairs of letters together or making them a different color, how can you help your child remember how they look? To get familiar with letters, you can use some of the standard activities, including

- Playing listening games.
- Matching pictures to letters and letters to pictures.
- Having your child write the letters for himself when you say the sound or show a picture. He can have the letters in front of him to refer to, or he can go for the harder option that gives him no letters to sneak a peep at.

If you want to refresh yourself on these activities, flip to Chapter 5. You can find a few tips about making a scrapbook in Chapter 5, too. If you're happy with everything so far but wonder what happened to the *wh* sound I mention in the "Di's graph" sidebar, read the next section in this chapter, "A Word about the *wh* Sound."

A Word about the *wh* Sound

A lot of really important words start with *wh*. Nearly all the questions you ask start with *wh* words: *why, what, when, where, which,* and the odd one out, *who.* You should tell your child that *w* often appears with *h,* and does so in nearly all questioning words. But is this the right time to do it? I don't think so. Some argue that *wh* makes a whole new sound, but to my crass ears, *wh* sounds just like *w.* I don't pronounce *wh* any differently than *w,* and I've never met anyone who does. When I last listened to the Queen of England, I think she may have said a fancy *wh* rather than an ordinary *w.* But because that was only a once-a-year TV broadcast, the Queen doesn't count. You hear a lot about *wh* when I discuss sight words because all the questioning words I list at the beginning of this paragraph are sight words (see Chapter 11 for a discussion of sight words). Don't bother your child with the *wh* words now. She'll easily accept *wh* when she gets started on sight words.

In some books, you find more digraphs than *ch, sh, ph, th,* and *wh.* Sometimes writers include pairs like *ck, kn,* and *wr* in this group. I put these pairs under other categories, like silent letters, because I think those letter combinations make more sense in those other categories. Just remember that these categories are supposed to make helping your child read easier (not more confusing!), so use the letter categories that make sense to you.

Part II
Building Words from Letters and Sounds

The 5th Wave   By Rich Tennant

"I just hope I learn all my short vowels before I grow out of them."

In this part . . .

This part of the book gets right into phonics, or sounding out, starting with the word at. You can show your child how at is made of two sounds joined together and when that penny drops, he grasps the very heart of the whole business of reading. He moves quickly through words like hen, pig, and cot, and then onto meatier words like shelf, kilt, and spill. By the end of this part, he feels that he's accomplished a lot. And, of course, he has!

Chapter 7

Getting Ready for Words and Sentences

"Don't go out without your vest on

Even though you've got the rest on

Don't go out without your vest on

You know what'll happen to you!"

This song, heard in a children's play many years ago, was such sound advice that it stuck in my brain all this time — when other things, like the names of politicians and the dates of historical events, slipped sneakily but definitely away. It's good advice to wear your vest. It's not good to brave the elements unprepared. When you teach your child to read words and sentences, there's preparation you should do for that too.

This chapter is a quick overview of some of the nuggets of wisdom I've gathered in my years of teaching children to read. I tell you how to be a good teacher so your child won't wander off to watch TV instead of listening to you; I tell you how to give your child a sense of control; I show you how to check that your child is ready for the words that are coming later in this book. After all that, I help you to guide your child through sounding out his *first* word: the small but powerful *at*.

General Guidelines Before You Get Started

When you take your child from single letter sounds to sounding out words, you want her to

- ✔ Listen to your instructions.
- ✔ Watch you when you model tasks.
- ✔ Watch you come to grips with combining sounds.

Follow the guidelines in this section, and the time you spend helping your child will be more enjoyable and constructive. This section also gives you specific, practical ways to prepare for the hands-on exercises that you can find throughout this chapter.

Set your child up for the challenge

If you want your child to be really interested in what you do with him, and be motivated to come back for more, spice things up. Playing games and keeping an upbeat, fun attitude help keep your child's attention. Build a challenge into the tasks you set your child so that he wants to rise to meet that challenge. Set tasks that you know your child is capable of, but act as if you're not sure he can do them. "These words may be too tricky for you" can be a great motivator. When your child succeeds in reading the words you're referring to, he feels like a conquering hero with your praise as his spoils.

Keep your hands off your child's work

Years ago, when I was lamentably short of computer know-how, I took a *Computers For Beginners* course. The course gave me a supportive learning environment (where my husband couldn't see me) and had me feeling good about my progress. Then that changed. One evening I asked for help, and the instructor mistook my request. He seemed to think I wanted to be humiliated and reminded of how little I really knew. In answer to my request for help, he moved me away from my keyboard, tapped away furiously and mysteriously and told me he had fixed a problem that was too technical for me to understand (the type of response I could easily have gotten from my husband). I felt stupid. But I figured out, at crushing first hand, one of the best guidelines I know to being a good teacher. Those who know certain things can unwittingly demoralize those who don't. It's especially easy for an adult to crush a child's confidence. I have seen even very good teachers discourage students unintentionally sometimes, so here's a maxim that's worth reciting, writing down, or even tattooing on your palms: "Keep your hands off your child's work." Your job is to guide, assist, and facilitate — but not to take over. Apply this maxim to the exercises coming up in this book. Remember that you *should not*

- Hold the flashcards when your child can hold them.

- Pick up your child's work uninvited.

- Tell her what to do when you can just as easily give her a choice of what to do.

When you give your child control and ownership of her tasks, you send her the message that she's capable and that you have faith in her ability.

Make it fun

All of us want to feel that we achieve something, even if that thing is small. We like to take care of ourselves and manage our own lives. Kids love having their own special jobs to do and showing off their skills or independence. I talked before about spice and challenge, and now I should say a few words about psychological safety. Your child needs a safe place to tackle reading, a place where he can achieve and feel happy. You have to be responsible for preventing (figurative) falls in order to create an environment where your child can be successful.

You may run into a common problem about this time — your child struggles with sounding out a word. The answer? Give quick help. If you let your child struggle with a word for more than a few seconds, he's likely to feel frustrated and embarrassed, and then he certainly can't improve. Even if he doesn't go through those nasty feelings of embarrassment, he still spends longer than he needs trying to work out the problem. He's less intimidated by his task, and therefore a more willing participant, if he gets help quickly. Help him by sounding out the word with him a few times until he gets the hang of it. Finish off on a positive note by having him read some easy words he has already mastered. Perhaps rearrange the words so the task seems new.

What if your child grows tired or fidgety? Change pace, change materials, or move on to a new activity. If you're cheery and upbeat, and you keep your sessions fun and varied, you will keep your child's interest. He sees that reading can be fun and not just a series of drills or exercises. Try these simple tactics:

- Have a quick competition.

  - Can your child read out ten words in less than 30 seconds?

  - When he shows you ten words and has you cover your eyes while he takes one word away, can you remember the missing word?

✔ Switch your materials.

- Change your letter cards for a whiteboard. Give him a bright marker and make him the teacher.

- Give him a tray of sand, sugar, or rice. Tell him which words to write (or have him choose for himself) and see whether you can read the words.

✔ Play a quick celebratory game. (The game doesn't have to be strictly educational because you're playing it for fun, to celebrate your child's effort and success.)

- Have a few swings on the tire.

- Try some shots at the net.

- Have some scooter races around the block!

✔ Move your session to the garden, porch, or floor. (Simple, yes, but a change from the usual.)

If you have a really bad reading session, don't try to plough on; take a break. Now you have time to rethink your strategies, and hopefully you keep your child from thinking that reading sucks!

Have your materials ready

Nothing irritates you more than having to stop, mid flow, to get a marker, pencil, or whiteboard. Also, this type of interruption makes you look (and probably feel) flaky. While you're off rummaging, your child may wander off, too. And if you have an older child, even if she doesn't wander off in body, she'll almost certainly wander off in mind and spirit. Don't be caught unprepared. Have your gear ready within the first three sessions. By that time, you know for sure the materials that are your mainstays.

You definitely need a good marker, a pair of scissors, and index cards (or you can use cut-up pieces of paper if you don't have index cards). A small hold-in-your-hands type of whiteboard proves very useful, too. And your child may find letter tiles or magnetic letters a fun variation from index cards.

After you gather your kit, stick with it. Don't be tempted to keep adding fancy pens, stickers, and other paraphernalia. These unnecessary gadgets only distract your child. Keep a limited set of materials, used only for reading, and your child will regard them as special and important.

Without being fearsome, adopt a serious and efficient attitude

Children figure out how to assess *vibes*. They gauge atmospheres and behave accordingly. When they start school, children know which teachers mean business, and which ones don't, in next to no time. Your child soaks up all your vibes when you set out to get him reading. Be one step ahead of him by having an established time and place for reading and by treating your reading times as special and important. Your child will take his cue from you and get into reading mode. You have a calmer time than if you hadn't set this tone, and you get more done.

Don't let your child get too distracted. He will love telling you a lot of tidbits and anecdotes. Gently but firmly bring him back on task and give him time to chat later. His attention span isn't much longer than ten minutes (neither is your own, come to that), and you want to claim every single one of them.

Forget letter names for now and deal only in letter sounds

One more thing to think about before you start sounding out the first word with your child: It's really important for her to hear the sounds that comprise words. She'll be manipulating letter sounds, especially short vowel sounds, for quite a while, so forget letter names altogether for right now. Don't refer to letters by name at all because switching back and forth between letter names and sounds confuses your child. If your child talks in letter names, tell her that she's right about the letter name, but the important thing about the letter right now is its sound.

When you sound out letters, beware of the *uh* factor. I'm talking about the *uh* that you find yourself voicing on the end of letters, the one that has you confusing your child when you say things like *a-tuh* for *at* and *a-nuh* (like the name Anna) for *an*. You may have difficulty shaking off *uh,* but now that you know about it, you can be on your guard.

Is Your Child Ready for Short a Words?

Before launching in to short *a* words, you want to make sure that your child is ready to handle them. You don't want to overwhelm him, and you certainly don't want to make his first experience of reading words an uncomfortable one. To avoid any potential problems, take stock of where your child has advanced to and what you've achieved already, so you can be sure you've properly prepared the groundwork.

Before you start guiding your child through the following word exercises, ask yourself the following questions:

- ✔ Does he know that the words he speaks can be broken into sounds that can be written down in letters?

- ✔ Can he identify the first sound in spoken words? If, for example, you ask, "What do you hear at the start of the word *kite*?" can he answer "cuh?"

- ✔ Can he say the sounds of individual letters when you show them to him?

- ✔ Can he hear the *ch* and *sh* sounds?

- ✔ Can he recognize the written forms of *ch* and *sh?*

If you answered yes to all the above, proceed. If not, check out Chapters 3 through 5 on sounding out single letters and pairs of letters.

at: Small but Powerful

You are about to launch your child into reading by helping him make small, phonetically regular words that have short vowel sounds. That's quite a mouthful, and here's what it means:

- ✔ **Phonetically regular words** sound out the way you expect them to. Your child starts out with these simplest of words because she doesn't need to know any fancy spelling rules to decode them.

- ✔ **Short vowels** are vowels that mostly appear on their own inside short words. When you read little words like *hat, hen, hit, hot,* and *hut,* you're reading short vowels. If you read words like *ape, eve, ice, oats,* and *huge,* you're reading long vowels. Long vowel words usually have two or more vowels.

Reading words is easier than writing them

Children catch onto reading before they can write, so don't waste valuable time fussing about legible writing if your child's ability to write comes slowly. You can spend time on writing later, but your child is ready to forge ahead with reading now, so get on with it!

Some of you may be asking yourselves, "Why *at*?" You start off with *at* because *at* is small — a two letter word. Reading mostly involves sounding out, and the easiest words to sound out are made of only two letters. A child can hear and sound out *at* easily, and *at* paves the way for quick progress to words like *mat, hat,* and *sat.* If you step out with the word *at* and walk purposefully on with *mat, hat,* and *sat,* you soon leave a *flat, splat,* and *chat* trail behind you, and you should see *attention* and *attitude* up ahead in the distance!

It's time to help your child make that very first word, *at.* The following easy exercise gives you a hands-on way to show that when *a* and *t* join together, they make *at.* Find a quiet time and space to do this exercise with your child, and spend about ten minutes on it. Play again the next day. When your child feels comfortable with *at,* move on to the other exercises in this chapter.

In this exercise, you make flashcards of the letters *a* and *t* and have your child slide them together to make *at.* Explain to your child that you're going to make a word and then help your child sound out and hear the merging letters. Read the following activity for a step-by-step method to introduce your child to *at.*

When you make letter cards, use lowercase letters, and continue using lowercase in all the writing you do. In school, teachers explain to children that you use capitals only for names and starting sentences. You confuse a school-aged child if you mix uppercase and lowercase letters. And if you're helping a preschool child, you start him off on bad habits.

Activity: Making *at.*

Preparation: Take one index card and cut it in half. Write *a* on one half of the card and *t* on the other. (Be consistent, and make sure you always refer to these letters by saying their short sounds, *ah* and *tuh*). Have a clear, slippery table or floor to work on. Your child is going to be sliding the two letters together, so sit where you can watch and help him. For Steps 1 through 5, use the dialogue marked in bold text.

1. **You're going to make a word. To make a word, letters have to join together (a bit like friends holding hands). *Ah* is the first sound of this word.**

2. **Put down the *ah.***

3. **Say *ah.***

4. **Slide the *tuh* next to the *ah.***

5. **Say *tuh.***

6. **Pick up the cards and do it again. Put the *ah* down and keep saying "*ah*" until you add *tuh;* then say "*tuh.*"**

7. Repeat Steps 2 through 5, increasing the speed, and instruct your child to listen to the sounds he makes.

8. **Can you hear the word?**

If your child has trouble hearing the word *at*, do Exercise 1 a few times. Sound out the individual letters with your child and tell him that the word you're saying is *at.* Do a few slow runs and then speed it up, all the while joining the two sounds together.

First things first

In Step 1 of the above exercise, I ask you to describe words to your child as letters joining together. You may be wondering about the single-letter words *a* and *I.* Well, at this point, you really needn't worry about them. The idea of letters joining together is the important thing at this stage, and your child won't have any problem understanding *a* and *I* later. In fact, the word *I* belongs with a bunch of tricky but important words that you introduce after your child has the knack of joining letters together. See Chapter 11 to find out how to guide her through words, like *I, said,* and *are,* that don't sound out in a straightforward way. For now, don't overload your child.

Chapter 8

Reading Short *a* Words

* *

In This Chapter

▷ Discovering short *a* words

▷ Building short *a* words into longer *a* words

▷ Playing cards to work on those reading skills (and have some fun!)

▷ Using big lists of words for a challenge

* *

Until I read it on the walls of every gymnasium I worked out in (granted, a truly modest number), I loved the Confucius saying about every journey beginning with one step. Well, if Confucius were alive today, and if he wanted my advice about teaching a child to read (and why wouldn't he?), I'd tell him that his first step should be sounding out *a* words.

In this chapter, you find out how to walk your child through the process of sounding out words, starting with *at* and progressing to words like *mat, hat,* and *sat.* Then you can tackle words like *an* and *am* with your child and show him how these small words also build into bigger words (like *pan* and *ham).* I give you some bigger *a* words, too, so you can present your child with a challenge when he's ready for it. But before you get to all that, you need to get started on the right track. In my years of teaching children to read, I've gathered a few nuggets of wisdom that I've put into some down-to-earth guidelines to help you out.

Adding Letters to at to Make Words Like mat

After your child becomes well acquainted with *at,* she's ready for word building. Although *word building* simply means adding letters onto an existing word to make a longer word, it's a crucial process because it requires your child to read in chunks of sound rather than in single-letter sounds. Poor readers tend to read in single-letter sounds. You hear them trying laboriously to make words from a long chain of sounds that they can't possibly remember. If, for example, I show a child who reads in single letters the word *remember,* he'd read something like *rr eh mm eh mm buh eh rr.* He's forgotten the first sound by the time he gets to the last sound, and he can't make any sense of this impossible task. He should be reading in chunks of sound, and that's why you introduce your child to *at* early on and show her how to add to *at*. From the very beginning, you show your child how to read chunks of sound so she doesn't fall into the trap of reading words in single letters. Your child will read the word *remember* as *re-mem-ber*.

Making bat, cat, fat, hat, mat, pat, rat, and sat

This exercise introduces eight words: *bat, cat, fat, hat, mat, pat, rat,* and *sat*. The same process applies to joining *a* and *t* together to make *at* (see Chapter 7), and your child naturally progresses into adding letters to *at*.

Preparation: Have *at* written on one whole index card. Cut four other index cards in half and write the single letters *b, c, f, h, m, p, r,* and *s,* one on each of the eight halves of card. Follow these four simple steps, using the dialogue (given in bold text), when guiding your child through this exercise.

1. **Put *at* down in front of you.**

2. **Spread the other letters around the *at* card.**

3. **Choose a letter and slide it over to the front of *at*.**

4. **What word have you made?**

5. Repeat Steps 3 and 4 with the remaining letters.

Making flashcards of words

Your child has had a lot of practice with *at* words, so now he needs a set of flashcards. Write each of the *at* words on a separate index card (*bat, cat, fat, hat, mat, pat, rat,* and *sat*) and encourage your child to read his cards to family members and friends.

If your child likes to write, let him write his own cards. Many children prefer an adult to write the cards for them because adults do a neater job, but if your child makes his own cards, he feels even more proud of them.

Use flashcards for practicing skills, but flashcard games and drills should augment, not replace, your one-on-one instruction.

Buying flashcards

After you've practiced with a few homemade flashcards and your child has the hang of them, move on to commercial flashcards. You can buy whole packs of flashcards in school supply stores and many bookstores. Most of these flashcards have a word on one side and a corresponding picture on the other, so you read *hat,* and turn the card over to see a picture of a hat. You can use these cards easily and effectively, if you know how.

Start with commercial flashcards by selecting from the pack only the words you need, the ones you have already had some practice with. Right now, you'd select from the pack only the short *a* words. Have your child read a word and then turn over the card to check his reading against the picture.

Building at into Words Like flat

To help consolidate your child's understanding of sound chunks, ask him to make bigger *at* words by adding more letters to *at,* including blends like *fl* and partners like *ch.* Flip to Chapters 5 and 6 if you want to review blended letters or special sounds like *ch.* You help your child make the six words *flat, chat, brat, spat, splat,* and *drat* in this exercise. Before beginning, try the strategy of presenting her with a challenge that you know she can accomplish. Tell your child you have a challenge you're not sure she's up to. Would she like to give it a try? It's pretty hard! After she aces this exercise, she'll feel even more confident about her word-building skills.

Making flat, chat, brat, spat, splat, and drat

Preparation: Have *at* written on one whole index card. Cut three other index cards in half. On each of the six halves, write one of these six pairs of letters: *fl, ch, br, sp, spl* and *dr.* In this exercise, your child makes the words *flat, chat, brat, spat, splat,* and *drat.* Use the direct dialogue given in bold text as a guide.

1. **Put *at* down in front of you.**

2. **Spread the other cards around *at*.**

3. **Choose a card and slide it over to the *front* of *at*.**

4. **What word have you made?**

5. Repeat Steps 3 and 4 with the remaining letters.

Using 14 at flashcards

This exercise helps your child increase the speed with which she reads the words she has a grip on so far. Write each of the words *flat, chat, brat, spat, splat,* and *drat* on a separate index card. Add these new flashcards to the eight flashcards you made before (*bat, cat, fat, hat, mat, pat, rat,* and *sat*) so you have a set of fourteen. You can use the dialogue in bold text when following these steps with your child:

1. **Spread the cards face down on the table.**

2. **Turn them over one at a time and read them to me.**

3. **Turn them back over and jumble them up. Can you still read them to me?**

4. **Walk around the room twice and see if you can *still* read them to me!**

In Step 4, your child can do whatever action you like — jump up and down ten times, knock on the front door, have 20 swings on the swing, — your options are open.

Playing with at Words in Card Games

You can use your flashcards in card games as an excellent way to reinforce the concepts and skills you've just worked through with your child.

Spending big on real playing cards

Most of the time, I advise parents not to spend their money on gizmos and extras. However, here's an item that I make an exception for. Real playing cards, with one blank side, cost more than index cards, but feel *so* nice in your hands. And kids think flashcards made from real playing cards are way more cool than those made from index cards, so they're not shy about being seen holding them. The coolness factor is important with older children, and you can keep some cards in your car to use in spare moments.

Preparation: Write each of these seven words on three separate cards: *bat, cat, fat, hat, mat, rat,* and *sat,* making a total of 21 cards. On five more cards, have your child draw a funny face. Now you have a final set of 26 playing cards.

Hide the cards *(Funny face cards not needed)*

Hide all 21 word cards around the house (or garden) and have your child find them and read them out to you. To direct him to the cards, tell him when he's *getting hotter* (getting closer to a card) or *getting colder* (moving farther away from a card). Change roles so you're the finder now. To add something sweet to the game, tape a candy to the back of one of the cards and have your child guess which word the candy is on the back of before you send him hunting.

Read the cards *(Funny face cards not needed)*

In this game, you simply get your child to read words out to you — but you tell him three slightly different methods. Here are the three variations of the same basic task:

✔ Have your child spread the cards out facedown, turn them over one at a time, and sound each word out.

✔ Have him shuffle the cards and then stack them face down in one pile. Ask him to overturn one card at a time, sounding each word out.

✔ This time you hold the cards like a fan, words facing you, and have him take single cards and read out the words.

When you do these three activities, you can include some exaggerated card shuffling and general hooting and hollering to get your child even more excited about the game!

Pick up the cards *(Funny face cards needed)*

Have your child deal all the cards out until you each have an equal-sized pile. Don't look at your cards. Take turns turning over a card from your pile and reading out the word. If a player turns over a funny face, the other player picks up all cards and adds them to her own pile. When one player has no cards left, she wins (except if it's you!).

Noisy at *(Funny face cards needed)*

Have your child deal out all the cards. Don't look at your hand. Turn cards over one at a time, taking turns. When you turn over a funny face, you must make a noise (or run around the table, or run and touch the tree — you have artistic license here). Play until you've used all the cards. To make a longer game, have the funny face mean you shout *and* pick up all the cards. When one player has all the cards, the game ends.

Sore Loser (One funny face card needed)

This game is just like Old Maid. You can play with just the two of you, but you have more fun with three players. Have your child deal out all 22 cards (all the word cards and one funny face card). Look at your hand and put down your families. A *family* is a set of three identical words — like *bat, bat,* and *bat* or *hat, hat,* and *hat.* Now take turns taking a card from the other player's cards as he holds them in a fan for you. (Little children with small hands can spread their fan on the table.) Keep making families and putting them down. The player who gets left with the funny face card has to gather up all the cards and not be a sore loser about it!

I call this game Sore Loser because older kids like having a Sore Loser card rather than a funny face card. Simply write "Sore Loser" on a card for this more grown-up version of the game.

If you use index cards for Sore Loser, don't make the mistake I once made. My students decorated the backs of the cards, and I didn't realize that the different patterns made each card identifiable. Everyone knew which card was the Sore Loser card, and we had to make a new pack of cards with plain backs. Something else I got wise to with Sore Loser — bends or tears in the cards. The Sore Loser card can get pulled around in the excitement, but if it gets torn or bent, you have to replace that card (or even make a new pack), so no one can tell the Sore Loser card from the other cards.

Making your own playing cards: It's worth the effort

Sometimes my children are around when I'm working with other children. They don't usually interfere because they're old enough now to get on with their own quiet activities. And besides, they want the ice cream I've bribed them with. But when I'm playing Sore Loser, they want a piece of the action. They don't care that they're fluent readers and I'm using words like *hat* and *mat.* They just love joining in the game. Card games can be like that. Even though kids love Nintendo, they still enjoy an old fashioned game of cards because personal interaction counts. When you teach your child, remember how powerful human interaction is.

If you show your child how to do things — just you, she, and a lot of interaction — she understands about a hundred times more quickly (and retains a ton more) than if you leave her to work independently. Keep that in mind while you're buying cards, counting them out, and neatly writing words on them. It's worth the time and effort because taking the time to do fun stuff with your child is important, educationally.

Some at Words for a Challenge

By now your child is ready to tackle lists of words. Table 8-1 features a nice long list of *at* words. The list contains a few easy words like *hat,* but it also contains several new and longer *at* words for a challenge. The split-up words on the left help your child see the *at* part of the word and read in chunks, but he doesn't have to use the broken-up words if he prefers going straight to the regular words written on the right. The words don't go from easy to hard — your child may find a simple word right above a really challenging one in Table 8-1. This variety adds a bit of spice once again because, after all, quite a bit of (albeit subtle) repetition goes on here. Tables 8-1, 8-2, and 8-3 later in this chapter have extensive word lists for you to use in the following activities (or your own word games).

Card activities

You can make fun flashcards with your child, using the words you find in word lists I give (and any other good word lists you find). Write each word on an individual card and play with these cards often. Schedule a reading time every night (20 to 40 minutes is good) and play card games until your child masters short *a* words or grows altogether sick of card games!

The Read It, Find It, Write It Routine

This routine gives your child ways to practice new words, each one a little harder than the one before it.

1. Have your child read out the words in Table 8-1 from top to bottom.

2. Have your child read out the words in Table 8-1 from bottom to top.

3. Look at the list together. You call out a word for your child to find, read out, and cross off. Read words until the two of you have gone through the whole list.

4. Have your child write the words as you call them out, one by one, in random order. She can use paper and pen or a whiteboard. If your child has difficulty writing, do only a few words.

5. Celebrate with a round of applause, a high five, or an ice cream cone!

Table 8-1	A Challenging List of *at* Words
Word in Chunks	*Regular Word*
br-at	brat
f-at	fat
fl-at	flat
m-at	mat
p-at	pat
s-at	sat
c-at	cat
sp-at	spat
spr-at	sprat
scr-at-ch	scratch
th-at-ch	thatch
l-at-ch	latch
p-at-ch	patch
b-at-ch	batch
h-at-ch	hatch
ch-at	chat
r-at	rat
spl-at	splat
att-end	attend
att-ic	attic

Reading More a Words

By now your child knows a lot of *at* words. He's grasped the idea that *at* is a chunk of sound that occurs in a lot of words. He understands that reading involves breaking words into chunks of sound. Now you show him new chunks of sound with *a* and how those chunks fit into bigger words. Some of the *a* chunks form real words, like *an,* but others, like *ag* and *ab,* aren't words in themselves, just common chunks of sound. In some of the words you help your child read, you see the *ck* ending and some double letter endings, like *zz* and *nn*. Explain to your child that these pairs of letters occur often, especially at the ends of words, and tell him that these double letters sound out just as he expects them to.

Use the next two lists for the card activities and the "Read It, Find It, Write It Routine" activity earlier in this chapter. Table 8-2 warms your child up for the harder words in Table 8-3.

Table 8-2	A List of Three-Letter *a* Words
Word in Chunks	*Regular Word*
an-t	ant
an-d	and
b-an	ban
v-an	van
t-an	tan
r-an	ran
f-an	fan
c-an	can
A-nn	Ann
p-an	pan
m-an	man
h-am	ham
d-am	dam
S-am	Sam
r-am	ram
t-ab	tab
c-ap	cap
f-ad	fad
c-ab	cab
w-ag	wag
g-ap	gap

(continued)

Table 8-2 *(continued)*

Word in Chunks	Regular Word
l-ag	lag
p-at	pat
p-am	pam
l-ad	lad
m-ap	map
j-am	jam
b-ad	bad
d-ad	dad
add	add
s-ap	sap
j-ab	jab
t-ax	tax
n-ag	nag
l-ap	lap
m-ad	mad
s-ag	sag
y-am	yam
t-ag	tag
n-ap	nap
b-ag	bag
w-ax	wax
h-ad	had
t-ap	tap
s-ad	sad
r-ap	rap
r-ag	rag

Table 8-3	A List of Bigger *a* Words
Word in Chunks	*Regular Word*
j-azz	jazz
m-ass	mass
b-ack	back
St-an	Stan
p-ant	pant
p-ants	pants
ch-ant	chant
sl-ant	slant
dr-ank	drank
bl-ank	blank
h-ack	hack
p-ack	pack
s-ack	sack
c-amp	camp
sc-ab	scab
gl-ad	glad
br-ag	brag
sc-amp	scamp
d-amp	damp
sl-ap	slap
fl-at	flat
fl-ap	flap
st-amp	stamp
l-amp	lamp
t-ask	task
bl-ast	blast

(continued)

Table 8-3 *(continued)*

Word in Chunks	Regular Word
gr-and	grand
str-ap	strap
sl-am	slam
tr-ap	trap
s-and	sand
fr-ank	frank
tr-ack	track
st-ack	stack
sp-at	spat
b-and	band
pl-ant	plant
h-and	hand
cl-ap	clap
cr-am	cram
l-ast	last
p-ass	pass
b-ank	bank
fl-ag	flag
r-amp	ramp
dr-ab	drab
bl-ack	black
sp-ank	spank
st-ab	stab
sc-alp	scalp
gl-and	gland
cr-ack	crack
sn-ap	snap
pl-ank	plank

Word in Chunks	Regular Word
st-and	stand
f-act	fact
tr-amp	tramp
m-ask	mask
f-ast	fast
cl-ass	class
scr-ap	scrap
sn-ack	snack
dr-ag	drag
fl-ab	flab
cr-ab	crab
pl-an	plan
cl-am	clam
cr-amp	cramp
str-and	strand
sl-ab	slab
l-and	land
pr-ank	prank
t-ank	tank
br-at	brat
r-aft	raft
m-ast	mast
p-ast	past

Chapter 9

Reading Short *e, i,* and *o* Words

A few years ago, when I was at a playground with my children, I was nearly knocked over by a cyclist. When I saw him, I had to look twice. Bold, fearless, and very fast, he was no more than 3 years old. Curious, I asked the child's mom how her son had learned to ride a two-wheeler at such a tender age. Calling him over, she yanked off his sweater to give a demonstration.

Holding a sleeve in each hand, the woman twirled the sweater over and over in large circular movements until it was like a thick rope in her hands. Keeping hold of the ends, she threw it over her son's head, around his chest and under his armpits, so the ends met between his shoulder blades. She twisted the ends together to make a firm handle. She was set. With the handle in one hand, she could run alongside the bicycle, pulling to steady her son if she needed to.

Both my kids learned to ride their bikes with this sweater technique, and like the little boy, quickly became a danger to other park users. You can help your child get a grip on short vowel sounds much like I helped mine get a grip on a two-wheeled bicycle. If you run alongside him, giving him free rein but ready with support if he needs it, he can be a speed king in no time.

This chapter gives you a warm-up exercise that uses words like *pen, bit,* and *hot,* and then more exercises with bigger words, like *spent, chip,* and *cost.* You can print out new activities (or complete them right here on these pages) and play with new sentences. To finish off, I talk about how to give thrill-seeking cyclists a few word wheelies and book bumps.

Is Your Child Ready for Short e, i, and o Words?

Before you forge ahead with a whole bunch of new short vowel words, make sure that your child is ready. If you sailed through Chapter 8, you remember starting off with a similar check back then. In this chapter, your check is a quick hear-it, see-it, make-it exercise. I've broken that check into three sections, following this introduction. If your child finds this exercise easy, she's ready for the harder exercises to come. If she has trouble, check out Chapter 7, which introduces the whole fun process of sounding out words.

Step 1: Hearing the e, i, and o sounds

This step shows you whether your child really hears the e, i, and o sounds. Read out words and ask your child to tell you the first sound he hears in each word. Just say the following:

Listen to the words I say. Tell me the sound you hear at the beginning of each word: infant, ostrich, olive, if, odd, everybody, exit, ebony, impossible, evidence, effort, ink.

Say the words in a normal way, unless your child has trouble hearing the sounds. Then you should slow down and enunciate clearly. Although the words are long, the beginning sounds should be easy to hear. If your child can't hear them easily, spend five minutes doing this exercise each night, for a few nights. Use different words starting with short e, i, and o.

Step 2: Sounding out those letters

This step shows you whether your child can sound out the letters e, i, and o when she sees them written down. Show your child the letters and ask her to tell you their sounds.

You may feel that you're spending a lot of time on single vowel sounds. Well, you are. A shaky grasp of vowel sounds can hold your child back later, so it's really important for her to know them well.

Activity: Laying down those vowel cards.

Preparation: Cut 6 index cards in half so that you have 12 small cards. Write single letters, in lowercase, on these small cards. Write the letter *e* on three separate cards. Write *i* and *o* each on three separate cards. Follow these steps and say the dialogue (marked in bold text):

1. Shuffle the 12 cards and give them to your child.

2. Now say these instructions:

   Put a card down and tell me its sound.

   Do the rest of the cards.

If your child struggles with a particular sound, work just on that sound for a while. Have your child draw the letter and say the sound. Get the cards of that sound and one other sound and practice reading them. Add another letter when your child is ready. Work your way up to reading the complete set of letters. If you feel your child needs extra practice, spend five minutes on this activity each night for a few nights.

Step 3: Merging sounds together

This step tells you whether your child has the knack for merging sounds together. Have your child make words from letter cards.

Preparation: Cut five index cards in half so you have ten small cards. Write these nine letters (one letter on each card, leaving one card blank): *b, d, e, g, i, n, o, p,* and *t.* Follow these steps and say the dialogue marked in bold text:

1. Give the nine cards to your child.

2. Tell him to spread out his cards so he sees the letters. Now give these instructions.

   I'll tell you a sound. You make it from two letters. Here's the first sound:

   > **et**
   >
   > **in**
   >
   > **op**
   >
   > **og**

eb

it

ig

ot

ed

od

If your child races smoothly through these sounds, read each one once. If you're taking it at a more leisurely pace, read each sound out twice. Enunciate slowly the first time and then repeat the sound in a normal, clipped way.

Building Short e, i, and o Words

You have your sounding out cyclist (remember him from the beginning of this chapter?) all ready to go, and she can use the next task as a speed builder. If you feel uncertain about your child's progress, take a quick glance back at Chapter 8 to recap on how you helped (or can help) your child read short *a* words. When you're ready to start off, head straight into this exercise where you dictate words for your child to make from letter cards. (You make the letter cards ahead of time.) I've broken it down into easy steps, and give dialogue you can use in bold.

Activity: Putting words together.

Preparation: Cut 6 index cards in half so that you have 12 small cards. Write the following letters on the cards, one letter on each card: *b, e, g, h, i, l, n, o, p, s, t,* and *w.* (If you saved the letter cards from Step 3 in the previous section, you only need four new letter cards: *h, l, s,* and *w.*)

1. Give the 12 cards to your child and say the following:

   Spread out your cards to see the letters.

   I'll tell you a word. You make it from three letters. Here's the first word.

2. Read out each word from Table 9-1, twice. The first time enunciate slowly; then repeat the word in a normal, clipped way.

Table 9-1	Making Three-Letter Words with Letter Cards	
bet	bin	bit
get	got	hen
hit	hot	lip
lot	not	pet
pit	pot	set
sit	ten	tip
top	web	wet
wig		

Reading Short *e* Words

The next few pages give word lists to practice with. Table 9-2 presents short *e* words. For different ways to use the lists, flick back to Chapter 8, which tells you about card activities and the Read It, Find It, Write It Routine.

Table 9-2	Short *e* Words	
beg	bell	Ben
bent	best	bet
deck	den	dent
desk	dress	egg
end	exact	exit
expect	fed	fell
felt	flex	get
hem	hen	jet
Ken	kept	leg
lend	lent	less

(continued)

Table 9-2 *(continued)*

let	Meg	melt
men	mess	met
neck	nest	net
next	peck	peg
pen	pest	pest
pet	press	red
rent	self	sell
sent	set	slept
smell	speck	spell
spend	stem	step
swept	tell	ten
tent	test	vest
weld	well	went
wept	west	wet
yell	yelp	yes
yet		

Reading Short *i* Words

Use Table 9-3 to perform the Read It, Find It, Write It Routine (see Chapter 8) for short *i* words.

Now is a good time to introduce your child to the word *is*. She can easily sound out the *i* part of *is*. She finds a surprise with the *s* sound, though. Explain to your child that the word *is* looks very tiny and simple but that she needs to watch out for *s*. She needs to remember that it's pronounced like *z*. Later, your child will come upon a few other words with an *s* that sounds like a *z*, such as *always, use,* and *easy.*

Table 9-3	Short *i* Words	
bib	big	Bill
bin	bit	blimp
brink	click	did
dig	dim	dip
drift	fill	fin
fit	fix	flick
flip	gift	glint
grill	grin	grit
hid	hill	him
hint	hip	hit
impact	impress	lint
ink	intend	lit
Jill	Jim	kick
kid	Kim	kiss
kit	lid	lift
limp	link	lip
list	lit	mint
mix	nit	pill
pin	pink	rib
rim	rip	script
sit	six	skill
skin	skip	slim
slip	sniff	snip
sprint	stick	still
stink	strip	swim
tilt	Tim	tint
trip	twin	twist
will	wilt	wind
wink	zip	

Reading Short *o* Words

Table 9-4 gives you short *o* words. Keep going with the Read It, Find It, Write It Routine.

What tiny but deceptively tricky word belongs in the short *o* group? *Of.* Tell your child that the *o* part of this word behaves itself and sounds just as you'd expect. But watch out for the *f.* In this little word, *f* sounds out as *v*, like in violin.

Table 9-4	Short *o* Words	
block	blond	bond
boss	box	clock
cod	cop	cot
crop	cross	dock
dog	doll	dot
drop	flock	flop
fog	fox	frog
frost	got	hog
hop	hot	job
jog	lock	log
lost	lot	mop
moss	nod	odd
of	off	on
ox	pod	pond
pop	prod	rob
rock	rod	rot
shock	slop	sob
sock	soft	spot
stop	strong	top
toss	trot	

Reading Simple Sentences

By now your child has read dozens of words but not one sentence! You get to change that absence here, but first your child must know a few more words. Why? Because real sentences can't be made totally from the words you've gone through so far. You have a great relationship with words that sound out easily, but they alone don't make real sentences. Sure, you can scrape together a few sentences, like, "Rat and pig got wet," but better sentences use words like *they, our,* and *were.* So you must prepare your child for those words in advance.

Preparing for first sentences

Many children have bad experiences with reading. They feel they can't read and lose confidence because they've tried to read books that someone told them they could tackle easily, but they couldn't. Just this week, I browsed in a book shop among the beginning readers' books and found these words in the first pages of the books I picked up: *gleams, races, caught, showed, together, mouse, want,* and *pencil.* Who said those words are easy? They're too hard for a beginning reader, so why are they in books for beginners? Well, you just can't write an interesting story with only beginning words. So be prepared to help your child with those kinds of words, the ones he can't sound out.

Before you show your child a book or some writing, scan through it. Find the words he doesn't know and needs to get familiar with. Ideally, the book has a lot of words he can sound out, like *plan, that, pick,* and *test,* and only a few that he can't sound out, like *they, said, you,* and *want.* Go through the new words with him before starting the reading. Write them on cards or a white-board. Practice saying them and remembering how they look. The last thing you want is for your child to start a book without this coaching, find it's too hard, and decide he hates reading.

Introducing the words *the, a,* and *no*

Just like the books I talk about in the previous section, I use some new words in the next exercises. Before continuing on, you need to tell your child that some new words are coming and spend five minutes getting familiar with them. The new words are *the, a,* and *no.* Those words are a part of a bunch of words called sight words or most common words. Your child needs to have instant recognition of these words (that's where the term *sight* comes from) because they occur so often in any text (hence *most common*). You come upon *the* and *a* in any book you look at, and *no* usually makes an appearance in beginners' books.

Here are some good ways to remember *the, a,* and *no:*

- ✔ When you help your child remember *the,* show her that this word is the *th* sound with *e* added on. The *e* is pronounced as long *e,* but your child isn't ready to tackle long *e* yet. So just tell her to say the *name* of *e* every time she sees the word *the.* Say *th* (the sound) then *e* (its name). This exercise is a bit tricky at first, but your child soon gets to know *the* well because it's such a common word. At school, too, teachers show *the* to kids in this way.

- ✔ You can tell your child about *a* in two ways. Either suggest to your child that she pronounce it as people normally do *(uh)* or have her sound out and say *a,* as in apple. Many teachers prefer this last way because it makes introducing *a* easy. It stops the word *a* being confused with the sound *u,* as in *bun.* Later, when she's a better reader, your child can switch to saying the regular *uh.*

- ✔ Sounding out *no* requires your child to have her first glimpse of long vowel sounds. The long sound of every vowel is the same as its name. *O* says its name at the end of the word *no.* If you want to hear much more about long vowels, check out Chapters 11 and 12. For now, explain the word *no* and add *so* and *go,* as well. For fun, try "Ho, ho, ho," too!

One last word list

I have one final word list for you. Table 9-5 mixes all the words you've covered, so far. Instead of having your child read through separate lists of *e* words, *i* words, and *o* words, he now gets to flex his muscles with a list of them all. Zip quickly through it and then head for the Draw It, Read It, Yes-or-No It activities that follow.

Table 9-5	A List of Mixed *e, i,* and *o* Words	
beg	bell	Ben
bent	best	bet
bib	big	bill
bin	bit	blimp
block	blond	bond
boss	box	clock
deck	den	dent
jog	lock	log
lost	lot	men
mess	met	mop

moss	neck	nest
net	next	nod
odd	of	off
on	ox	peck
peg	pen	pest
pest	pet	pin
pink	pod	pond
press	red	rent
rib	self	sell
sent	set	sit
skin	slept	slip
smell	sock	soft
speck	spell	spot
sprint	stink	stop
strong	tilt	top
trip	will	

Draw It, Read It, and Yes-or-No It

The next three exercises give your child new activities that progress in difficulty. Your child needs to read and draw for Exercise 1, he only has to read for Exercise 2, and Exercise 3 asks your child to give a *yes* or *no* response to a few sentences. Grab some markers and paper, and have fun!

Exercise 1: Draw It

For this exercise, simply provide your child with paper or a whiteboard and pens, and ask him to read these sentences and draw a picture for each:

1. A pink pig in a box of dolls

2. A fat black cat on a big soft red bed

3. A rat in a dress with a long thin belt

4. A man sitting in a pond with a big fish

5. A kid sitting in a sand box full of socks

Exercise 2: Read It

This exercise involves simply reading. Show your child the sentences and ask her to read them to you. Some of these sentences include commas, so you can talk about punctuation with your child. Explain that periods and commas tell us where to pause. Help her to read the sentences with the right pauses.

1. Jan got the plant from Ted, the man from the bank.

2. A man sat on a bench, and then a big dog ran up and bit him.

3. A cat sat on a rug on the kitchen shelf.

4. Ann went in the shop and got a dress.

5. The black cats, Jim and Peg, had a nap on the rug in the shed.

6. The dog got a smell of ham and ran to the kitchen.

7. The chimp ran from branch to branch.

8. A strong wind swept the top off the kid's tent.

Exercise 3: Yes-or-No It

Here's a silly exercise. Have your child read the sentences and spot the silly ones. All he has to do is answer the sentences with *yes* or *no*.

1. Can a man drink ham and eggs?

2. Will a frog hop on wet grass?

3. Will an egg sing a sad song?

4. Can a lamp yell at a big cat?

5. Can a man sit on a bench on the grass?

6. Will a full glass of pop slop if a man runs fast with it?

7. Can a sick pig skip and sing?

8. Can a dog bang a clock with a stick?

9. Will a big rock sink in a pond?

10. Can a kid cut up a plank with a bun?

11. Is a glass of pop hot?

12. Is a drink of milk wet?

Chapter 10

Reading Short *u* Words

. . . .

In This Chapter

▶ Making sure your child can handle short *u* words

▶ Putting short *u* words together

▶ Reading short *u* words

▶ Putting your child to the test with fun activities

. . . .

*T*his whole chapter is devoted to just one letter. Why? Because the letter *u* is a vowel with attitude. It's important that your child can sound out all the vowels — after all, there's a vowel in almost every word, but *u* is especially important. It makes the *uh* sound, even though another very conspicuous letter makes that sound, already — the letter *a*. This similarity can unsettle your child, but you can help.

When *a* appears on its own, thousands of times, as in *a bag, a cat,* or *a man,* you say the *a* out on its own as *uh,* just the same as you do when you see *u* in words like *bun, hut,* and *fun.* Confusing, right? Have your child sound out single *a* not as *uh,* which is how you say it in regular conversation, but as *a* as in *apple.* This pronunciation gives you a temporary measure that stops him from confusing *a* and *u.* When he gets better at reading, he starts to pronounce *a* in the normal way (as *uh*), but he has to establish a firm grip on the sound of *u,* in the meantime.

A quick readiness check and some exercises (with words like bun, fun, and hutch) make up the bulk of this chapter, and you should be used to them if you've read through the previous chapters. If you've opened the book to this chapter first, that's no problem — I lead you through the process. Because this chapter completes the journey through short vowel sounds, I finish it with exercises that use every vowel to keep you and your child on your toes.

Is Your Child Ready for Short u Words?

Before going ahead with this chapter, you need to check that your child hears the sound of *u* and knows which letter makes that sound. You want to be sure that your child doesn't confuse the letter *u* with any other vowel. You can test your child's familiarity with *u* by doing the two quick tasks that follow. I've broken them into easy steps with the dialogue you can say to your child in bold.

The listening task

With this activity, your child identifies the sounds she hears in *a* words.

Activity: Listen up!

Preparation: None. Just read the list I give you here.

1. **I'm going to read out a word. You tell me what sound you hear in the middle. We can do the first one together.**

2. **Hot.** Give your child time to answer. Repeat the word if she wants you to.

   If she can't answer, answer for her and repeat the word and some more *o* words *(mop, top, stop, pop, dot)* until she hears the sound. When she's comfortable with this vowel sound, continue on to Step 3 of this activity.

3. **Here are some more words. I'll read one word at a time, and you tell me what sound you hear in the middle of it:**

   1. **Fat**
   2. **Ten**
   3. **Doll**
   4. **Sock**
   5. **Tip**
   6. **Rock**
   7. **Can**
   8. **Bed**
   9. **Cup**
   10. **Bus**

The matching task

You show your child the vowels, and he tells you their sounds.

Activity: Finding a perfect match.

Preparation: Cut 8 index cards in half so that you have 16 small cards. Write *a, e, i,* and *o* on three cards each and write *u* on the remaining four cards.

1. Shuffle the 16 cards and give them to your child.

2. **Put down a card and tell me its sound. Keep going with the other cards.**

If your child whizzes through this readiness check, you're all set to go on with the chapter. If your child confuses any sounds, spend five minutes reviewing. Have him draw the letter he's not sure of and say its sound a few times. Next, he should read the cards with the letter he's focusing on, plus the cards of one other letter. When he feels ready, he can use all 16 cards again.

If your child confuses more than one vowel, focus on one of the troublesome vowels at a time and give your child practice saying it and writing it. Flip back to Chapter 4 to recap on the characters that you can draw into the letters — Allie, Eddie, Inky Pen, Ozzie, and Up Man. Have your child draw the character into his letter and talk about words that begin with that sound. Then do the "Finding a perfect match" activity, using just this one vowel with a mix of consonants that your child knows well. Now add another vowel and do this routine again, this time with the two vowels. Keep adding and practicing until you're using all the vowels.

Building Short u Words

This quick and easy exercise involves building words from letters. You prepare letter cards for this activity and read out words for your child to make. If she's a whiz and likes being timed, set your timer at 5 minutes and get going.

Activity: Putting it all together.

Preparation: Cut four index cards in half so that you have eight small cards. Write these eight letters, one on each card: *b, c, f, n, r, s, t,* and *u.*

Follow these steps. The bold text gives you what to say to your child:

1. Give the eight cards to your child.

2. **You have eight cards. Spread them out to see the letters. I'm going to say a word, and you make it with these letters. Here we go:**

    1. **sub**

    2. **fun**

    3. **but** (you're allowed to snicker)

    4. **nut**

    5. **bun**

    6. **cut**

    7. **tub**

    8. **sun**

    9. **cub**

    10. **rub**

Reading Short *u* Words

Table 10-1 features a list of *u* words, ranging from the really simple to the not so simple. For different ways to use word lists, flick back to Chapter 8, which tells you about card activities and the Read it, Find it, Write it Routine. Notice that plenty of *u* words end in *ch* or *tch*. Point this out to your child and see if he can spot any pattern. When does a word end in *ch* and when in *tch?*

Most children find the pattern that *ch* (not *tch*) always follows an *n*, like in *bunch, punch,* and *lunch.*

Table 10-1	A List of Short *u* Words	
blunt	buck	bud
bug	bump	bun
bunch	bunk	bus
club	cluck	clump
clutch	crust	cup

cut	drug	drum
duck	dug	dull
dump	dusk	dust
fluff	fun	fuss
grub	grunt	gull
gulp	gum	gust
gut	hum	hump
hunch	hunt	hut
hutch	jump	junk
luck	lump	lunch
much	muck	mud
mug	munch	must
nut	pump	punch
pup	rub	rug
run	runt	rust
scrub	skill	skull
stuck	stuff	stump
stunt	such	sum
sun	truck	trunk
trust	tub	tuck
tug	tusk	

Activities for More of a Challenge

By now, your child's ready for reading words from every vowel group and may want to show you how fast and accurately she can read. Lead her through the following activities. You get to see just how far she's come and have some fun, too. (Beware — you find a lot of nonsense in the following sections.)

An every-vowel word list

This list in Table 10-2, the last in this chapter, mixes up all the vowel groups. Use it for the Read it, Find it, Write it Routine, which you can find in Chapter 8.

Table 10-2	A List of Mixed Short Vowel Words	
blank	blunt	brat
buck	bud	bug
bump	bun	bunch
bunk	bus	cat
club	cluck	clump
clutch	crust	cup
dog	doll	dot
drank	drop	end
exact	exit	expect
fat	fed	fell
felt	flat	flex
flock	flop	fog
fox	frog	frost
get	got	hack
hem	hen	hog
hop	hot	jet
job	Ken	kept
leg	limp	link
lip	list	lit
mat	mint	mix
nit	pack	pat
pill	pin	pink
rib	rim	rip
sat	scratch	script
slant	spat	

Crossing off the bad endings

The following activity can give your child the feeling of really reading. In Chapter 9, I talk about preparing your child for real reading by showing him any new words before he starts. For this exercise, the words to show him in advance are *to, she, he, when,* and *which*. He can get the hang of them easily because he only has to handle five words, and only *to* is tricky.

Here are some teaching tips to help you introduce the five new words:

- ✔ **to:** This tricky guy of the group has no rule; just tell your child he needs to remember that this word is *to*. Show him that it's really small so he can just remember that it starts with the *t* sound then, to be tricky, has an *o*. With *to,* and all the five new words, write the word on a card to practice with.

- ✔ **she** and **he:** Here, the *e* says its name, not its usual short sound. Later on, your child can find out more about this kind of long sound.

- ✔ **when** and **which:** No tricky business here. Show your child that *w* often appears with an *h* next to it. When he sees *wh,* your child should just say *w* as usual. Some hard-line sounder-outers maintain that you can hear the *h* sound in words starting with *wh,* but I never have.

In this exercise, your child needs to figure out which word makes the most sense in the sentence. Help him read each sentence and the word choices, and then ask him to circle the right choice. Alternatively, put your feet up for a few minutes. Your child may want to do this activity all by himself, except for asking you the odd question.

> The man went to the **bit bank stank.**
>
> The dog ran to the man in the **shell chop shop.**
>
> The man got the clock from the top **shelf stink stamp.**
>
> She had a black hat and a red **dress drank dentist.**
>
> Ted and Jan went to the shop to get a drink of **pong pop pond.**
>
> A big cat ran to catch a **rug rat rust.**
>
> A man put on a big black **hut hug hat.**
>
> A duck ran to the **shed song sit.**
>
> Sam had a bag of **nuts cluck crust.**
>
> Which drum will he **bud brick bang?**
>
> She went to skip on the grass with **hit hot him.**

The truck went past him **fist fast fan.**

The man shifted the box from the shelf to the **shed bunch crash.**

Dad sang in the hot **strong flash tub.**

Sam shut the pigs in the **shed dog chick.**

Crossing off the nonsense word

Your child can read the title of this exercise if you point out two things. The *e* on the end of *nonsense* is silent. (Explain that a silent *e* often sits on the end of a word and that you may see more of them in Chapters 11 and 18.)

Your child just has to cross off the word that really isn't a word in this activity.

drum	drog
bront	brick
stromig	strap
blish	vest
long	lobik
fluzon	flag
pling	plant
crab	crid
stamp	stalt
tent	tef
trag	trip
pink	pulf
chick	chog
shelf	shigf
fetch	flum

Matching the pairs

You can find some simple compound words in the following minitable. Can your child draw a line to connect the partners? Show her that the best way to do puzzles like this one is to do the ones you're sure of first.

fishing	cloth
hand	net
bus	stop
traffic	dog
hot	hutch
rabbit	pants
dish	jam
track	box
lunch	bag

These two words rhyme: *bag* and *nag.* Can your child find the rhyming pairs in the following minitable?

hat	man
kit	mat
scratch	much
fan	lot
pot	hit
such	latch
witch	peg
lock	ditch
punch	sick
leg	lunch
pick	sock

If your child chooses the wrong word, saying something like *witch* rhymes with *latch,* tell her that those words do sound similar, but another word rhymes even better. This kind of correcting is easier on your child than when you give her a straight, "No, that's wrong."

Filling it in

Have your child read the words in bold and then put each one on the end of the sentence it belongs with.

dog, pond, chips, van, dish, hatch, shelf, jam, kitchen, hot

1. Mom got a shock when the truck hit the . . .

2. At lunch, I had a big bag of crunchy . . .

3. Will the egg crack so that the chick can . . .

4. Sam flung the rock into the . . .

5. She had melons in a big glass . . .

6. The tall man got the bags off the top . . .

7. Ants got in the pot of red . . .

8. I can bring lunch to the . . .

9. His pasta was too . . .

10. The kitten hid from the big black . . .

Fill-it-in activities can frustrate kids. If your child can't do them without getting upset, fill in the first letter for him. Do the same with word searches. Circle the first letter of each answer and your child will want to persevere.

Part III
Advancing to Sight Words and Long Vowel Sounds

The 5th Wave   By Rich Tennant

"Mommy, what does 'XXL' spell?"

In this part . . .

This part shows you how to help your child learn sight words inside-out and back-to-front . . . Okay, maybe not that well, but at least pretty well. You can have fun doing it with the activities I suggest, too. And then things get even better. I show you the brilliant *Bossy e* rule, the wonderful *When Two Vowels Go Walking* rule, and what to do when *y* behaves like a vowel.

Chapter 11

Understanding Sight Words

I'm the type of person who can't figure out what to do if a light blows or a toaster stops working. And I make things worse for myself by taking no notice at all of instructions. Bearing this in mind, you'll appreciate why, for months, I've instructed my kids to cook microwave popcorn by typing in 2 minutes 30 seconds into the microwave and watching. (The watching part is key because we once cooked popcorn at 2 *hours* 30 minutes, and lived with the haunting smell of burnt popcorn for the next six months.)

Well anyway, my kids were used to watching popcorn, until a few weeks ago when my daughter invited friends over. As my daughter stood watching the microwave popcorn (as usual), one of her friends casually pointed out the *Popcorn* button. "You press this," she said, as if it were a small thing. Now how come I'd never noticed that button? Would she tell her mom about my dismal housewifery? Did she know how any of the other buttons worked? My children can now cook popcorn *and* move, and all our lives are better. What a day that was. Now, in case you think you've accidentally stumbled into *Microwave Popcorn For Dummies,* let me explain. When you discover what sight words can do for a beginning reader, it will be like discovering the popcorn button. Really, it will be *that* good.

What Are Sight Words?

Sight words are words that you should be able to read by automatic recognition, or by sight. Why? These words are so common (they often get called the most common or most frequent words) that it's well worth spending time on them until your child has instant recognition of them. When your child instantly recognizes common words like *the* and *what,* he can read more fluently. He doesn't get delayed trying to sound out these words, so he can spend more time figuring out other words. He develops better comprehension, too. He can follow a plot better because he's not stopping and starting so much, so he'll understand or "comprehend" better.

Sight words make up about 70 percent of all words in most text. If your child instantly recognizes these words, he's 70 percent closer to being a fluent reader.

I know you probably think I'm repeating myself here, but I want to make really clear that sight words really do mean *sight* words. If you want your child to make smooth progress, be sure he has instant recognition of these words, not "I'll get it in a minute" recognition. Spend time going over these words until your child responds automatically any time you flash one at him.

A big list of sight words

Sight words are words you see everywhere. Schools and a lot of Web sites have lists of these words. You see the top 100 words, or maybe the top 200 words, but I have a list that beats both of those. Table 11-1 lists 220 words. This list has been around since the 1960s and has served millions of teachers well. And most importantly, it's my favorite. I've used this list with an awful lot of children and have never come across a child who can't get a really good handle on them. Two-hundred twenty words sounds like a lot, doesn't it? But your child can quickly and painlessly add them to his repertoire of words. And you can both have fun along the way.

Table 11-1			220 Sight Words			
a	and	away	black	call	cut	drink
about	any	be	blue	came	did	eat
after	are	because	both	can	do	eight
again	around	been	bring	carry	does	every
all	as	before	brown	clean	done	fall
always	ask	best	but	cold	don't	far
am	at	better	buy	come	down	fast
an	ate	big	by	could	draw	find

first	her	little	only	seven	these	well
five	here	live	open	shall	they	went
fly	him	long	or	she	think	were
for	his	look	our	show	this	what
found	hold	made	out	sing	those	when
four	hot	make	over	sit	three	where
from	how	many	own	six	to	which
full	hurt	may	pick	sleep	today	white
funny	I	me	play	small	together	who
gave	if	much	please	so	too	why
get	in	must	pretty	some	try	will
give	into	my	pull	soon	two	wish
go	is	myself	put	start	under	with
goes	it	never	ran	stop	up	work
going	its	new	read	take	upon	would
good	jump	no	red	tell	us	write
got	just	not	ride	ten	use	yellow
green	keep	now	right	thank	very	yes
grow	kind	of	round	that	walk	you
had	know	off	run	the	want	your
has	laugh	old	said	their	warm	
have	let	on	saw	them	was	
he	light	once	say	then	wash	
help	like	one	see	there	we	

A man named Dolch originally figured out these words (just think of all the words he must have counted to work out this list!). You can find Dolch lists in other books and on some Web sites. If you want to download the list, visit www.readingpains.com (which just happens to be my Web site).

Sight words aren't *look and say* words

Be careful not to confuse sight words with look and say words. The *look and say* theory is that you can flash words in front of your child for her to look and say, and with enough looking and saying, she can remember those words. The look and say technique was once fashionable but isn't popular nowadays. Teachers found this method wasn't very successful (even with a lot of looking and saying). Now, you don't find much looking and saying going on in classrooms.

But sight words are a different matter. Kids get automatic recognition of sight words, using phonetic and visual cues. They sound out the word when they can, and when they can't, they find ways to remember how the word looks. This is pretty much what they do for all words, but they have to recognize sight words with extra speed.

Getting Instant Recognition of Sight Words

When you find groups of words that rhyme and have the same spelling pattern, like *around, found, sound,* and *shout,* you're making *word families.* Families really help your child because he can more easily remember a family than one isolated word. The *around, found, sound* family is easier to remember if you show your child that *ou* makes the sound he'd make if you pinched him!

And here's a family you'll notice! The *could, would, should* family. It uses the *ou* chunk but doesn't use the usual *ou (that hurt!)* sound. Remind your child to watch out for this family and not to get it mixed up with the bigger *ou* family (*around, found, sound, shout, cloud, loud,* and so on).

When you're looking at word families and chunks of sound, you sometimes think to yourself, "Aha, but those letters make another sound, too." I took time to mention the two *ou* families because both families are very common. Usually, you don't need to worry about presenting your child with variations on each family sound. Show your child the most common sound only and leave other sounds for later.

Working with ten sight words at a time

This section shows you how to walk through the 220 words in Table 11-1, five to ten at a time, for about 20 minutes each day. First, find a relaxed time and place to tell your child about the words in Table 11-1. Explain that these words are all over the place, in every piece of writing she can ever read. Explain how knowing these words propels her reading forward. Put the list in front of her and have her read out the first word, *a.* Move down the list, letting her read the words she knows and telling her those she doesn't know. Stop when you come to the tenth word that she doesn't know. Copy the ten words she isn't familiar with onto a clean sheet of paper.

To decide whether your child knows a word, remember that she should quickly recognize sight words. Give your child only a few seconds to get a word before counting that word as one she doesn't know. But if she wants you to include a word she told you after several seconds as a word she knows, give in! You need to keep this activity fun.

Focus on ten words at a time. Your child can't remember any more than ten words easily. If she finds using ten words hard, use less than ten. But even if she's doing really well, don't go above ten. Your child should get a firm grip on a few words rather than a loose grip on many words.

Finding ways to remember words

Look carefully at each individual word in your list of ten. How on earth can your child remember them? How do you sound them out? What if you don't know how they sound out?

You really *do* see sight words everywhere

Your child can discover the importance of sight words by finding some for himself. Copy a page of writing from a book, or find a page of writing that your child can mark, and have him find the words *a* and *and* in the page. Before he starts looking, both of you can take a guess about how many he can find. Tell him to highlight every *a* and *and* he sees. Your guess can be kind of wild, making his guess nearer the mark and giving him that lovely feeling of having done better than you! (I'm assuming that your pride can take it; for now!)

To answer all these questions, you need to get to know the bits inside each word. You can find quite a few different chunks of sound and different ways to remember them. The following list of questions outlines what your child should ask himself when he sees a tricky new word and what he should do to answer his own questions.

Can I sound out the whole word, or parts of the word?

Your child can sound out nearly every word, in part — even if it's just the first letter. Break the word into chunks of sound and get your child familiar with any chunks he hasn't yet seen. Here are some examples:

- *About = a + bout. Ou* is the unfamiliar sound here. Teach that sound by explaining that it sounds like the sound he makes if you pinched him (do a mock pinch)! Show other words with the *ou* sound in them: *around, out, found, round, sound, trout, shout, cloud, our.*

- *after = af + ter.* Explain that *er* crops up all over the place. Make a family of *er* words from words like, *her, stern, fern* and *stronger, fatter, bigger, blacker.*

Can I find a word family?

The previous section gives you examples of word families with *ou* and *er* words, but you can find a lot more. Don't forget to look for *families* (words that rhyme and have the same spelling pattern) in the words your child reads. Here are some other word families you see in the 220 sight words in Table 11-1:

- *all, tall, call, small*
- *be, he, me, we*
- *old, cold, hold*

The words in this list are very common but hard to sound out, so putting them in families helps a lot:

- *where, there*
- *come, some*
- *could, should, would*

What do I do if I can't sound the word out and I can't see its family?

You come across a few words, like *who* and *what,* that don't give you much to go on. Don't be put off by them. Just sound these words out where you can and then highlight the tricky letters. Your child just has to remember the tricky letters by their appearance. To help keep the look of the word in your child's mind, have her outline the shape of the letters, trace over the letters, and write the whole word down several times. Stick words up on walls (the bathroom is a good place) and put five to ten words in an envelope to pull out and read each night.

Can I find a little word inside this big word?

Finding little words inside the big words can really make reading easier on your child with words like <u>an</u>imal, <u>in</u>side, be<u>cause</u>, ab<u>out</u>, and <u>together</u>. Words like *an* and *in* crop up in loads of words, and your child already knows them. Show him that he does.

Does this word have a silent e on the end?

Many words have a silent *e* on their end. Sometimes the word isn't affected by the *e*, but most of the time, that *e* exerts its influence:

- ✔ The *e* has no affect in words like *give, live,* and *little.*

- ✔ The *e* makes the earlier vowel have a long sound in words like *white, those, three, these, five, gave, like, use* (*s* pronounced *s* or *z*), *here, ride, made, make, came,* and *take.*

Does this word have a y on the end?

On the end of a small word, *y* sounds like *eye* (or the long *i*). On the end of a long word, *y* sounds like *eee* (or the long *e*). To read more about short and long sounds, flip to Chapter 12.

Does a bit of everything go on in this word?

Some words do a bit of it all. Look at *before.* Inside *before,* you can find the little words *be* and *or.* And a silent *e* sits on the end of the word. Highlight the *be* and *or* parts to make this word easier to remember, and explain to your child about the silent *e*.

Having Fun with Sight Words

You shouldn't have any trouble persuading your child to play these quick and easy sight word games. (And you should have some fun playing them, too!)

Some basic fun

Here are some easy and fun activities to do to imprint those sight words on your child's mind:

1. Have your child read out all ten words from her list, top to bottom.

2. Have your child read the same list, bottom to top.

3. Call out words, in random order, and have your child point to each word as you say it.

4. Silently point to random words and have your child read each word as you point to it.

Notice that the last two tasks in the list look pretty similar but get your child to do quite different things. When you call out words, she has to remember the words and find the right one, but when you point to a word silently, she has no lead from you. She has to sound out the word from scratch.

The Words Envelope (It's more fun than it sounds)

The following activity includes a lot of repetition and consolidation. Everyone has problems remembering things without a lot of exposure to them. This activity makes sure you give your child the practice he needs. Don't skip it. Be enthusiastic and make it fun for your child.

Activity: Practice makes perfect!

Preparation: Cut up pieces of paper to the size of Post-its or get ten index cards:

1. Either you or your child writes each word on a separate card.

2. Color, highlight, or underline any key letters in each word. Focus on special sounds or letters that your child has problems recalling.

3. Have your child spread the cards out, facedown, and then overturn each one and read out the word.

4. Have him respread the cards (facedown, again), turn them over, and read out each card, again.

5. Have him shuffle the cards and lay the pack facedown. Now he overturns and reads each card.

6. Have him reshuffle and again turn over and read out each card in the pack.

7. Have him give the cards to you. Hold the pack in a fan facing you. He takes the cards one at a time and reads each one out.

8. Have him spread the words out. You close your eyes, and he takes a card away. You must guess which card he took. Have three turns each and see who's best. Be sure he wins — narrowly, of course!

9. When you're all done, grab an envelope. Write *Words* on the envelope, put the ten words in it, and put it away until tomorrow. Pull the words out every night and ask your child to read them to you. Do this activity for a week until he really has a by-sight grasp of them.

On your official testing day, ask your child to read the words to you for the last time. When he reads them quickly and easily, put them into an envelope marked *Done.* Now you're ready to move on to another ten words. Go back to Table 11-1 and continue reading down the list of words until you again find ten words your child doesn't know. Repeat the routine this chapter outlines with these words, using the envelope every day and testing at the end of a week. Add to the *Done* envelope, and throw in some words from that envelope with your ten new words on testing days. Your child will enjoy showing you that he can still remember all those words. If he *really* enjoys doing loads of words, have him read out the whole *Done* envelope.

If your child hesitates with a word after he does a week's practice, put that word back into the *Words* envelope. You need to practice it some more before it goes into the *Done* envelope. Include it along with nine new words for the week and make light of it with your child. Explain that a few words always take a little longer to recognize, and repeating a word is no big deal. Point out how many words he's already finished and how well he's doing.

Because I'm pretty cheap, I always use cut up pieces of paper for the ten words that go in the *Words* envelope. I save myself about five cents a child, so you can see the massive financial benefit. But making the word cards yourself is a teaching trick, too.

Your child gets restless when he's doing a lot of thinking, so a quick task change helps. He can cut or tear the paper, moving to the floor or standing up while he does it. And you two can have a quick chat, too. Small breaks make a big difference, especially if your child is fidgety. (Anyone know a child who *isn't* fidgety?)

You can use the *Words* envelope at any time of day, but be sure to use it. Your child takes about five minutes to read the words to you, and this activity pays back richly. As soon as your child easily recognizes ten new words, you see a difference in the way he reads. When he knows 20, 40, and 100 new words, you'll be really glad you made room in your days for that envelope.

The bottomless envelope

Not long ago, I was teaching a little boy, Adam, his sight words. I saw Adam once each week to work on paired reading, phonics, and sight words. Adam especially liked sight words. He added ten sight words to his *Done* envelope every week, took them home, and could hardly wait to add to his growing cache of *Done* words.

The first few weeks sped by for Adam and me. We read a lot of books, and Adam made quick progress. We kept adding to the *Done* envelope, and every week, without fail, Adam wanted to look at the envelope first thing. By week five, Adam had a very fat *Done* envelope. He had worked on 50 words and had added several word families, too. He had at least 70 words. I looked at his bulging envelope and suggested that we pick a few random words to test. Adam was appalled. What, and miss out on reading all those words?

The highlight of the lesson for Adam was taking every last word from the *Done* envelope and reading them to me. So that's what we did. At every lesson, Adam swelled with pride at the sizeable stack of words he'd mastered. And every lesson, I pronounced him an excellent student. Adam was 5 back then. He's now 7 and a fluent and eager reader. His mom still calls me to ask if I know any new book series. Adam has worked his way through *Nate the Great, Bailey School Kids, Magic Tree House,* and *Amelia Bedelia.* He's starting on *A to Z Mysteries,* and his mom tells me he remains a great hoarder and counter of things — mostly books!

The moral of the story: If your child wants to do something that interests him and only changes your plans a little, go along with his interest.

Don't skip using the *Done* envelope, either. By going back to the words he's already done, you revise and reinforce what your child has already accomplished. And you get a chance to spot any words that slipped through the net, too. Get on top of words your child forgets right away, going over those words with him until they stick.

Trying More Challenging Sight Word Activities

Your child's really doing well with sight words, and you feel she can handle more of a challenge. Here's what to do:

✔ Remember those word families — *out, shout, about,* and so on? Now you get to think up a few more so your child gets a mental workout. Look at your child's envelope of words and find any that belong to a family. If one of his words is *kind,* you can think of *mind* and *find.* Now add *mind* and *find* to his envelope of ten new words. Do the same with any other words that fit into a family. These words provide your child a challenge without being too hard because she already knows all about families. Your fast-moving child understands more than just the word you show her; not just *kind,* but also *find* and *mind;* not just *went,* but also *spent, bent,* and *sent;* not just *carry,* but also *marry, Harry,* and maybe *funny, silly, sloppy,* and *spotty,* too (because they have the same y ending).

Always let your child do as much cutting, writing, and deciding as she can. The more ownership she feels over the activities, the better she'll understand. Always put her in charge of thinking up word families, highlighting words, and so on. And help her only if she wants you to. Put sheets of words in front of her, not you; put paperwork at her fingertips and in her line of vision, not yours; let her choose pens, games, and reading books.

✔ Remember the *Done* envelope? If your child wants a challenge, use it with a timer. Give her a time limit in which she reads the words to you. Act like you doubt she can do it. Pretend you're worried that the challenge may be too much. Then lavish her with praise when she succeeds!

✔ Flashcards give you a great way to consolidate what your child already knows. And you can use them to give your child a challenge, too. Buy a set of flashcards that have a sight word written on one side and a sentence with that word in it on the other side. Frank Schaffer (a product line published by McGraw-Hill) makes a good set of these flashcards, called *Sight Words,* divided into boxes of 100 words. You can find or order them in school supply stores or large bookstores. Have your child read the word on the card and then turn the card over and read the sentence. Use the cards in the car, the doctor's waiting room, or the shopping mall. You can even use them at home!

✔ If your child likes to write, have her write words down. After she reads her ten words to you, read them out for her to write. Read them in random order and add some word families, too. Put the words that she writes all by herself on display for other family members and friends to admire.

What if the sentences on flashcards are too hard?

Flashcards are wonderful teaching tools. But you have to use them wisely. Be sure your child already knows the words on them, or knows how to work the words out. If you taught your child to sound out *dog,* it's fine to give him flashcards of *hog, bog,* and *log;* if you taught him a lot of short vowel words, go ahead and pile him up with *chop, ship, clap, bunch, step,* and so on. But don't give him words like *were* and *their* if he's only a beginner. Always teach the words, or skills, first before giving your child flashcards. And select only the flashcards you know he can cope with from the flashcard box. If you're using flashcards to give your child a challenge, you can let him loose with them and step in when he needs help. Tell him any words he's stuck on or draw his attention to chunks of sound that help him sound them out.

Keeping Track of Progress

Keeping wall charts that show the progress your child makes is fun, and sight words lend themselves ideally to charts. You have to decide on the design of your wall chart, first. Let your child choose a theme (remember to be realistic about what you can draw!). If you're prepared to buy materials, take a trip to your school supply store and indulge. If you're taking the homemade option, decide whether you want a bar chart, pie chart, or maybe a rocket flying to the moon.

After you have a theme, you need units of measurement. Should you give your child one point/star/sticker per word, or should he get a sticker for every group of ten words he masters? Don't put your pen on the poster until you have a plan. But after you have it all figured out, go to town. Make sure your child has a lot of markers and stickers and help him with the decorating, if he wants you to.

After he finishes his poster (with a little help from you, probably), display it prominently and keep up with it. Make sure you work on the sight words regularly so the poster isn't a two minute wonder. Make it a work in progress. Each time your child can read new words, have him draw on the poster, or put stickers on it, to represent the number of words he has a handle on. When your child has completed the entire poster, have a celebration!

Starting to Read Books

If you're diligently reading to your child at bedtime, making sure she sees you read, and doing word activities with her, then you're doing everything right! But you may be wondering when to give her some all-by-herself reading books. As soon as your child can sound out three-letter words, like *hat* and *bun,* and knows a few important sight words, she's all set to read by herself. The sight words that she should see before setting out on reading books for herself are: *a, and, the, this, they, is, are, he, she,* and *said.* If you find others, tell her what those words are and then let her read the book for herself. Jot the words she's unfamiliar with onto individual cards and use them in the "Practice makes perfect!" activity in the section "The Words Envelope (It's more fun than it sounds)" earlier in this chapter. Your child needs to master at least the sight words I've just mentioned in order to read all by herself.

When you first choose reading books for all-by-herself reading, choose simple books. Look for interesting pictures and short, easy to sound out text with just a few sight words. If you haven't yet joined the library, do it now and go there every week. Let your child choose a big armful of books and, if she enjoys having a reading buddy, pore over the books with her. Let her have time alone with the books, too.

As well as regular reading books, grab a few stories on tape for your child. Then she can enjoy more exciting books and look forward to being able to read them. Meanwhile, she feels good when she can master simple reading books all by herself. Here are some of the best books for beginners:

- *Bob Books* (readily available in U.S. and Canadian shops)
- *Real Life Readers* (in U.S. and Canadian libraries and shops)
- *Primary Phonics* (U.S. readers, order from www.epsbooks.com)
- *Fitzroy Readers* (Australian readers, order from www.fitzprog.com.au)
- The *Ladybird* series (in the U.K., Canada, and Australia)

Don't crowd your child. She needs to feel in control so that she's confident with books, forevermore. If you think she may be skipping some words in a book, don't worry too much. Beginners, first and foremost, need to maintain enthusiasm and confidence. If you're itching to make her take home the library book *you* like and put back the book *she's* chosen, back off. If she wants to flop on the floor with a comic, and you want her to sit up with a real book, loosen up. Your child can't feel that reading is *her* special activity, and not something you're pushing on her, unless you inspire and guide her rather than dictate to her. Also, stock up on good books, yourself. If you want your child to be a good reader, you go a long way by simply letting her see you read. Kids copy adult behavior — you can't get away from that fact. If you have a son, be sure that he sees Dad and any other important males in his life pick up a newspaper, at the very least.

And while I'm on the subject of supporting your child, be sure to move away from situations where you feel frustrated. Don't ever shout at your child or humiliate her by saying things like, "You *must* know that word, you learned it only last week!" Remember that your child is trying her best and that she needs all the support and encouragement you can give her.

Cool things about early reading books

What does your child want from a first reading book? To be able to read it. "How obvious," I hear you say. But you'd be surprised how many early reading books feature words like *enough* and *want*. A lot of early reading books aren't very easy at all, and that's why I've just suggested a few book series to make life easier for you (see the section "Starting to Read Books"). Plenty of books feature just a few hard words, which you can point out to your child in advance, and a lot of fun rhymes and pictures that help your child figure out the text. This sort of helping is called giving *contextual cues,* and you should look out for this kind of help because it gets your child truly engaged with a book.

Have you seen the book *The Very Hungry Caterpillar* by Eric Carle? Well it's a story that really hooks kids in because it follows a repetitive pattern (so they can predict a lot of text) and involves moving parts. Your child becomes engaged in books like this one, as well as the books that use predictability and humor, like Dr. Seuss books.

Don't forget pop-up books or those books with tabs (things slide about on the page when you pull a tab), either. Your child may really love interactive stories on CD-ROM, too. One of my kids spent hours listening to titles like *Sheila Rae, the Brave* and *New Kid on the Block* (Living Books: Random House/Broderbund), and she can still sing the Sheila Rae song! With stories on CD-ROM, you get to choose different ways of listening and reading the text. Your child also gets to play an active part in storytelling because when he clicks on the screen, he can make things happen to the characters and surroundings.

What else? Big books. Ask at your library for any *big books,* or giant-sized books that teachers use with groups of kids. The teacher sits in a chair and faces the book towards the children so they can see the big print and pictures when she reads the story out. When you borrow these books, you add some variety to reading with your child, and he may like using these books to play at being teacher.

Chapter 12

Making Big Progress with Little Rules

My daughter's class recently worked on telling the time. One evening, she was figuring out her math homework when I heard her mutter, "The little hand has all the power; it's the one that tells the hour." I was delighted. The teacher was obviously giving her easy ways to remember all the information she needs to know. Rhymes are *mnemonics* — memory joggers that help us recall larger pieces of information. This chapter gives you two mnemonics to help your child sound out hundreds of words. Take half an hour now to teach these mnemonics, and you'll do your child lasting good.

The Brilliant Bossy e Rule: Your First Foray into Long Vowel Sounds

Some people teach children a whole bunch of spelling rules. Maybe the children remember all those rules, maybe they don't. I have no idea how effective teaching a lot of rules can be because I've never done it. The children I teach want to read books, not memorize a lot of rules — and I can relate to that. So I prioritize. I teach the most important rules of all, and that's just two or three rules. Children enjoy learning these rules because the task isn't too big and they can see how the rules work inside real books. They make the connection between understanding the rules and getting better at reading, and they become eager students. The first rule I introduce a child to after he can read regular words like *hat* and *chat* is the *Bossy e* rule. This simple rule introduces children to words that look very grown up, like *chase* and *shake*.

How Bossy e bosses other vowels

The best way to understand something is to do it (or in this case, spot it) for yourself. With that in mind, take a look at Table 12-1 to spot the *Bossy e* pattern.

Table 12-1		Bossy *e* Words		
ace	gate	shape	bike	mile
ape	gave	shave	bite	nice
bake	grade	skate	bride	nine
base	grape	snake	crime	pile
blade	graze	spade	dice	pine
blame	hate	stale	dime	pipe
blaze	lace	state	dive	pride
brave	lake	take	drive	rice
cake	lame	tale	file	ride
came	lane	tame	fine	ripe
cane	late	tape	fire	rise
cape	made	trade	five	shine
case	mane	wade	glide	side
chase	mate	wake	hide	site
crate	name	wave	hike	slice
date	pale	whale	hire	slide
drape	pane	compete	hive	slime
face	plate	complete	ice	smile
fade	rake	Eve	kite	spice
fake	sale	Pete	lice	spike
flake	save	stampede	life	strike
flame	scrape	Steve	like	stripe
frame	shade	theme	line	tide
game	shake	these	mice	tile

time	wise	home	role	tone
tire	bone	hope	rope	woke
twice	broke	hose	rose	cute
vine	chose	joke	slope	flute
while	code	mope	spoke	fume
whine	cone	nose	stole	fuse
white	dome	note	stone	pollute
wide	doze	poke	stove	rule
wife	drove	pole	stroke	salute
wine	froze	pose	swipe	
wipe	hole	rode	those	

Table 12-1 gives a lot of *Bossy e* words — but you can find a bunch more! That's why knowing the *Bossy e* rule can be really handy. When you show this rule to your child, a whole plethora of new, and quite complex, words open up to her. She can make a giant leap from words like *bag* and *hut,* to *tame* and *fume,* feeling that she's making good progress. So what's the deal with *Bossy e? Bossy e* sits on the end of words and makes the earlier vowel say its long sound. The *e* makes no sound itself — it's just a silent bully. Sounds quite ominous, doesn't it!

Explaining long vowel sounds

The *Bossy e* rule takes you into long vowels. So what exactly am I talking about here?

- ✔ A long vowel sound actually sounds long, as compared to short vowel sounds — for example, *mate,* as compared to *mat.* When you say "mate" it feels like a more stretched out sound than "mat" (It does! Try it.)

- ✔ You usually find a long vowel sound in words with more than one vowel — for example, *hail* and *late.*

- ✔ The long sound is the same as the letter's name, so your child can remember it easily.

To help your child hear the difference between short and long sounds, run through the next activity with her.

Activity: The short and the long.

Preparation: None. Just read out the word list I give. Follow the dialogue in bold.

1. **Listen to the word *cat*. Inside *cat*, you hear *a*. You hear *a* in words like *mat* and *hat*, too. But listen to this word: *late*. Now I'm saying *ay* (like the name of the letter). In *date* and *cane*, I'm saying *ay*, too.**

2. **Listen to the words I say and tell me if I'm saying *a* or *ay* inside them: *bat, pat, pale, mane, wade, fat, bat, male, cat, cape, hat, mat, man, fade, made, jam, pan, ran, van, came, fake.***

3. **Here are some new sounds. Some words have the *e* sound in them and some have the *ee* sound (like the name of the letter). Listen. *Hen*. Do you hear *e* or *ee*? *Pen*. Do you hear *e* or *ee*? Let's try some more.** Say the next words to your child and help her hear the short and long sounds. *Pet, wet, weed, seed, feel, bet, set, sell, feed, seen, meet, feet, hen, pen, week.*

4. Repeat Step 3 with the short and long sounds of *i, o,* and *u.* Here are some words to use for each letter:

   • *i* words: pig, pin, lip, dig, bit, hit, pipe, line, wide, fine, hide

   • *o* words: hop, dog, mop, log, chop, hope, joke, bone, home, phone

   • *u* words: cut, bun, fun, hut, sun, cute, flute, rule

Pronounce the short and long vowel sounds clearly and exaggerate them to start if this helps your child distinguish between them. Explain to your child that the long vowel sound is also the vowel's name.

Attacking and decoding words

Every time your child comes across a new word, he has to try to figure it out. If he's a fairly good reader, contextual cues help, and if he's an early reader, he can try to sound out and think of word families. Often, he just has to ask you. When he tries to figure out new words by sounding out and remembering other words, he's using *word attack* skills or *decoding.* You may see these terms in other books or hear them at school. If they sound rather imposing, don't worry. If you're helping your child break words into sounds and recognize common letter clusters (which is a theme through this whole book!), you're already a dab hand at helping him attack and decode.

Special features in Bossy e words

Many words have special features that you should show your child so he can remember the word better (see Chapter 11 for more on sight words). Well, *Bossy e* words come with special features, too. You should explain several of the words in Table 12-1 in a little detail. Here's a rundown of the features you should take note of:

- ✔ **W or wh?** When you come to a word that starts with *w,* that word may have an *h* following the *w.* A lot of words start with *wh,* and your child gets to know those words over time. In Table 12-1, you see *whale, while, white,* and *whine.* (When you talk about these words, explain that the *h* in *wh* stays almost silent. You can just about hear the *h* if you speak really clearly, but you can't hear it most of the time. So let your child know he can just ignore it.

  If you're looking at the *wh* words in Table 12-1, you may see *whine* and then spot *wine.* Take a few minutes to explain how some words sound just the same but have different spellings and different meanings. To show a few examples, try these pairs: *hare* and *hair, whale* and *wail, tale* and *tail, pear* and *pair, stare* and *stair.*

  One *wh* word that's like no other is *who.* Tell your child to take a good look at *who* and get to know it. Write *who* down on a card to help him remember it. Pin it on your wall. *Who* is a tricky word, and your child will come across it often.

- ✔ **S or z?** The letter *s* usually makes its normal *s* sound but can make a *z* sound, too. Just look at *wise, rise, these, fuse, hose,* and *those.* If you see *es* on the end of a word, sound it out as *z,* like with *potatoes, tomatoes, churches,* and *switches.*

- ✔ **C or s?** You can find the *ace* and *ice* words within the *Bossy e* words. In these words, the *c* makes an *s* sound — like in *ace, face, lace, pace, ice, lice, mice,* and *rice.*

- ✔ **Long or short vowel?** Sometimes a word looks as if it has a long vowel in it when you actually pronounce the vowel as a short vowel (like with *give* and *gone*). Try both vowel sounds to figure out the words that don't do what you expect them to. If a long sound doesn't work, try saying a short sound. Sometimes the vowel works both ways, depending on what word you're using, as in *I* **live** *in a house* and *the wire is* **live.**

- ✔ **Long vowel, short vowel, or unexpected vowel?** An important little group of words make neither the long or short vowel sound but a new sound. These words have an *o,* but that *o* sounds like a *u.* Go over these words with your child until he recognizes them. Then those words can't surprise him. Here they are, in families to help your child remember them more easily:

- *come* and *some*

- *other, mother,* and *brother*

- *love* and *dove*

- and all on it's own, *done*

Using Bossy e words

If you've glanced at the previous chapters, you know all about reading a table top to bottom, bottom to top, and then selecting words randomly. You know about making a pack of cards from the words and playing with them each night. Here's a rundown of the activities I'm talking about:

Do the following with Table 12-1:

1. Have your child read out all the words from the list, top to bottom, in each column.

2. Have your child read the same list, bottom to top, in each column.

3. Call out words, in random order, and ask your child to point to each word as you call it.

4. Silently point to random words and have your child read each one as you point to it.

With Table 12-1 and 20 small pieces of paper or index cards:

1. Either you or your child write 20 random words from Table 12-1, each on a separate card.

2. Color, highlight, or underline any key letters in each word. Focus on special sounds or letters that your child has special difficulty recalling.

3. Have your child spread out the cards, facedown, and overturn each one and read it out.

4. Have her respread and again turn over and read each card.

5. Have her shuffle the cards and lay the pack facedown. Now she overturns and reads each card.

6. Have her reshuffle and again turn over and read out each card.

7. Have her give the cards to you. You hold the pack in a fan facing you. She takes cards, one at a time, and reads each one out.

8. Have her spread the words out. You close your eyes, and she takes a card away. You must guess which card she took. Take three turns each and see who's best (it's her, of course)!

The Wonderful "When Two Vowels Go Walking" Rule

I bet you're wondering about the rest of the verse from the heading. Well, it's a short verse that your child can remember easily, which makes it really useful. Here it is, in full:

"When two vowels go walking,

The first one does the talking."

As with the *Bossy e* rule, I give you a table now (Table 12-2) so you can see just what's going on with those two vowels.

Table 12-2	When Two Vowels Go Walking, the First One Does the Talking		
ee	feed	keep	seem
bee	feel	meet	seen
beep	feet	need	sheet
bleed	fleet	peek	sleek
breed	free	peel	sleep
cheer	freed	peep	sleet
creek	glee	queen	speech
creep	greed	reed	speed
deed	green	screen	steel
deep	greet	see	steep
deer	heel	seed	steer
fee	jeep	seek	sweep

sweet	hear	teach	rain
tree	heat	team	sail
weed	lead	tear	snail
week	leak	weak	sprain
ea	lean	wheat	stain
bead	leap	year	tail
beak	least	**yeast**	trail
beam	meal	**ai**	train
bean	mean	bait	wail
beast	meat	braid	**wait**
beat	near	brain	**oa**
bleach	neat	chain	boast
cheap	pea	drain	boat
cheat	peach	fail	cloak
clear	plead	faint	coast
creak	reach	frail	coat
cream	read	gain	croak
deal	real	grain	float
dear	rear	hail	goat
dream	scream	jail	load
each	seal	laid	moat
ear	seat	maid	oat
east	sneak	mail	road
eat	speak	main	roast
fear	spear	nail	soak
feast	squeak	paid	soap
gear	steal	pail	throat
gleam	steam	pain	toad
heal	streak	plain	toast
heap	stream	rail	

Andrew's big pile of books

A few months ago, I had to close the reading clinic I ran in my old hometown because I was moving from the area. I gave everyone a lot of notice that I was leaving, but nine weeks before my move, a mom came to my door. "My son doesn't do anything," she said. "I can't get him to read. He just plays on his computer. I'm not the kind of mom who's confident with helping him read either. To be honest, I'm not great at reading myself, and I'm worried that if I don't do something, my son will end up like me. I know you're leaving soon, but can you help me?" Behind this woman's hips peeked two boys. The biggest was the son she was concerned about, and he'd just listened to his mom's description of things. How could I possibly refuse? So I had nine weeks to work with Andrew.

Andrew came to work with me for 12 hours over those nine weeks. In that time, we went through the 220 sight words and the two best spelling rules _(Bossy e_ and _When two vowels go walking)_ and read plenty of books. Did Andrew do anything for his mom at home? You bet! After he figured out ways to sound out words and knew the sight words, he couldn't be stopped. He looked through my reading books and asked if he could take home not the usual three books that I give to children like him, but ten. His mom was amazed, and I must admit I was more than a little dubious. But sure enough, Andrew read all ten books and continued taking home more than three books each week. He started with titles like _Fat Cat_ and _Big Pig_ and quickly moved to titles like _The Ride Home._ Andrew had been drowning in a sea of words that simply looked arbitrary and tough to him. He didn't have any idea how to work out new words and couldn't skim through sight words like _they_ and _want._ No wonder his mom couldn't get him to do anything. Today, Andrew can read basic books, and his mom tells me he scores ten out of ten most weeks in his school spelling test. She takes both boys to the library every week now so she can keep up with Andrew's continued enthusiasm for reading great stacks of books.

Table 12-2 has just as many words as Table 12-1, so you can see right off how useful your child can find the _Two vowels go walking_ rule. How does the rule work? Four main sets of vowels walk together; _ee, ea, ai,_ and _oa._ These vowels walk together, but only the first letter talks. The second vowel stays silent while the first says its long name.

Tell your child that the first vowel shouts out its name (remember that the long vowel sounds the same as the vowel's name).

Getting used to two-vowel sounds

To get your child used to the sound and appearance of the four most important pairs of vowels — _ee, ea, ai,_ and _oa_ — go through Table 12-2 with him, saying the sounds and highlighting the vowel pairs. Then point to ten random words for him to read to you. To finish off, take a look at the ten groups of words that follow. Have your child highlight the vowel pairs inside each word. Can he read out all the words? Can he figure out the odd word out?

You may want to copy the next activities instead of marking these pages. That way, your child can do the highlighting activity more than once.

1. road, toad, lame, boat
2. coat, snail, pail, rail
3. seal, meal, toast, deal
4. train, pain, tail, feet
5. bleach, reach, squeak, boast
6. speed, sleet, throat, greed
7. main, laid, sail, read
8. week, beer, weep, mail
9. paid, tail, maid, heat
10. sweet, screen, load, bleed

Using two-vowel words

Repeat the activities for Table 12-1 (see the section "Using *Bossy e* words" earlier in this chapter), using Table 12-2. But when you want to consider the special features of the words in Table 12-2, you have a few more features to think about.

Sometimes a two-vowel word has more than one meaning (and more than one way to pronounce it). The word *tear* falls into this category. You can cry a *tear,* and you can *tear* a piece of paper, too. *Read* is the same. You may want to *read* a book now, or perhaps you *read* a book yesterday.

Then you have the words that sound the same but that you spell differently. When you look at two-vowel words, you see plenty of pairs of words like: *meet* and *meat, feet* and *feat, week* and *weak.* Table 12-3 shows you a few more of these same-sounding words.

In case you're wondering, you call a word that sounds like another (meet, meat) a *homonym,* or a *homophone.* A *homograph* is a word spelled the same as another but with a different meaning (going to the *fair* and playing *fair*). To get even more technical, *hom* = same as; *nym* = name; *phone* = sound; and *graph* = visual representation.

Table 12-3	Different Spellings of the Same Sound
hear	here
weak	week
team	teem
steal	steel
seam	seem
meat	meet
reel	real
read	reed
whale	wail
made	maid
pale	pail
sale	sail

Read Table 12-3 with your child and discuss the meanings. When your child has looked at the words carefully and understands which word belongs with which meaning, have a go at the following ten sentences.

If you spent time on the sight words in Chapter 11, these sentences should be easy. If not, you should explain any unfamiliar words to your child. These words may include *want, doesn't, have,* and *very.*

1. The man got a green case at the sale/sail.

2. I want to see a real/reel whale/wail.

3. My pet hamster doesn't eat meet/meat.

4. I am on the soccer teem/team.

5. You can go in a jail sell/cell if you steal/steel.

6. I have a good comic for you to read/reed.

7. The sick man looked very pail/pale.

8. I broke my fishing reel/real last week/weak.

9. I just made/maid a cake.

10. This class isn't as bad as it seams/seems.

Now that your child has seen *Bossy e* and two-vowel words, she has a new spelling skill. When she writes words that have a long vowel sound, she can try out a few different spelling options. She can ask herself, "Is it a *Bossy e* or a two-vowel word?" Give your child some scrap paper on which she can write down the options. Encourage her to do this exercise any time she gets stuck, and she can only get better and better at figuring out new words. She gets better at spotting what looks right — a key strategy for good spellers.

By now, your child probably wants to do some real reading. The exercise that follows is a *true* or *false* task. Your child reads out sentences and decides whether or not they make sense. First have him spot all the two-vowel words, underline them, and sound them out. This exercise primes him for reading all those long words. Now have him read each sentence and circle a *T* for true or an *F* for false.

1. You can get clean in a pail of black mud.   T/F

2. You can eat a box of nails.   T/F

3. Toast is soft and wet.   T/F

4. It's nice to boast all the time.   T/F

5. A speedboat is fast.   T/F

6. You always scream when you see feet.   T/F

7. You need to hide from a peach.   T/F

8. You can sweep a path with a brush.   T/F

9. You can ride a long way on a train.   T/F

10. A hill can be steep.   T/F

11. You can eat a hot meal.   T/F

12. You can read a toad.   T/F

13. I like to eat roast chicken.   T/F

14. When I see my team, I cheer.   T/F

15. My throat is long and green.   T/F

Use this fun and easy quiz to get your child thinking about two-vowel sounds. Read the questions with your child and let her come up with the answers:

1. This thing rhymes with *coat.* You see it on the sea or a lake.

2. This is not a blanket, but it's on your bed. It rhymes with *meet*.

3. One of these has seven days.

4. If you play outside in this, you get wet. It rhymes with *pain.*

5. You have these on the end of your legs, and you put your socks on them.

6. A dog wags this when he's glad.

7. You can hammer this into a plank.

8. This animal can't win a fast race.

9. This cute animal lives in the sea. It rhymes with *meal.*

10. This is a strong metal. It rhymes with *peel.*

Uh oh! What happens when two vowels form a different sound?

A few lines from now, I'm going to casually write a teacher term and assume you know what I'm talking about. The term is *contextual cues,* and teachers use it instead of saying, "Clues from the rest of the text."

Every time your child comes across a word that doesn't do what he expects it to, he must try out these strategies:

✔ Sound out the vowel in both its long and short forms.

✔ Look for a word family.

✔ Look for a little word inside.

✔ Use contextual cues.

When none of these strategies work, your child should simply write the word on a card, highlight any tricky letters, and put that card in an envelope. Label the envelope "Words" and have your child add new tricky words to the envelope as he comes upon them. He should read all the cards from the envelope to you every day for a week so that he really gets on top of them.

Having your child read an envelope of words to you each night sounds a bit dreary. Well, your interest and enthusiasm count in this activity. The envelope routine gives your child your attention in a great way, and you get to show him you're proud of him. Keep your attitude light. Have fun. And if an activity isn't working for you, leave it. Like all things, reading is a matter of finding the best routines and strategies for your child, and you shouldn't force things. You can always come back to this book in a few days' or weeks' time. You can repeat the activities that your child liked best, or you can read a good book, instead. (You can find advice about choosing good books in Chapter 20.)

ACTIVITY

Getting a challenge out of two-vowel words

If your child is really racing and wants you to pile the challenges on her, try having her write out words from Table 12-2. Start by dictating a few words from each column and telling her which column they're from. Next, mix up words from the *ai* and *oa* columns and read those words to your child. Lastly, read words from all the columns and have her figure out the sounds for herself, including the same-sounding *ea* and *ee* words. Make sure she has scrap paper on which to jot down her options.

Table 12-4 has a few words you should take special notice of. I include some examples below to prepare you. You can find whole families to practice with in Table 12-4:

✔ **Bread.** In *bread,* the *ea* doesn't make the long *e* sound you expect. It makes the short *e* sound. But your child doesn't need to remember this word all by itself — it's part of a whole family coming up ahead.

✔ **Moon.** You find this *oo* sound all over the place, so you should help your child get the hang of this family early on.

✔ **Book.** After you shown your child the usual *oo* sound (as in *moon*), show her the word family that takes the same *oo* and pronounces it differently. Tell her that this family is small, so anytime she sees *oo,* she should first try out the more common *oo*-as-in-*moon* sound.

✔ **Cloud.** You have an easy way to show your child the *ou* word family. When she sees *ou,* give her a gentle pinch. Ask, "What would you say if I pinched you?" and explain that *ou* makes that sound.

TIP

Sometimes *ou* makes another sound. Don't worry about it. Teach your child words like *bought* later.

Table 12-4	Two-Vowel Words with Sassy Sounds		
bread	*moon*	*book*	*cloud*
dead	weather	lead	leather
head	thread	instead	heather
feather	read	ahead	wealth
meant	breath	dread	broom

bread	*moon*	*book*	*cloud*
croon	school	soot	couch
doom	tool	good	pouch
fool	swoop	wood	crouch
goose	troop	stood	slouch
loose	root	wool	pout
noon	hood	about	trout
spoon	nook	shout	found
stool	took	loud	sound
snooze	look	proud	ground
tooth	shook	house	amount
cool	cook	mouse	pound
room	hook	mouth	round
mood	foot	south	

Two common words that do their own thing with their two vowels are *great* and *does*. Write these unusual words on separate cards for your child to practice with, explaining that these two words don't fit in a family.

Buying flashcards

After your child understands how the *Bossy e* and *When two vowels go walking* rules work, use flashcards as an easy way to practice those rules. (Check out Chapters 7 and 11 for the lowdown on flashcards.) Here are some sets of flashcards I recommend:

✔ *Easy Vowels* by Frank Schaffer

✔ *Easy Blends and Digraphs* by Frank Schaffer

✔ *Beginning to Read Phonics: Fishing for Silent "e" Words* by Judy/Instructo

✔ *Beginning to Read Phonics: Word Family Fun, Long Vowels* by Judy/Instructo

Frank Schaffer and Judy/Instructo are product lines of McGraw-Hill. You can find or order them in school supply stores from McGraw-Hill.

Chapter 13

y: A Letter Like No Other

*I*f you had spoken to me when I was 15, I would have told you anything you wanted to hear. I agreed with everyone back then and thought nothing of changing my story two or three times in a day, depending on who I was speaking to.

There's a letter with this kind of attitude, too. The letter *y* is to the alphabet what I was to classmates — changeable. It appears predictable and straightforward enough in the word *yam,* for instance, then shows up with a new sound in words like *symbol.* It tags onto the ends of words, too. In words like *cry* and *happy*, *y* makes a completely new sound in each case. Well, I'm a tad older than 15 now, and I'm here to sort *y* out for you. In this chapter, I pin *y* down and show you how to explain its appalling behavior to your impressionable child.

Teaching the Different Sounds of y

The thing to look for with *y* is where *y* comes in a word and what letter's next to it. If *y* starts a word like *yacht* or *yam*, it makes a straightforward sound. But, if *y* comes at the end of a word or somewhere in the middle, you get a different sound. You get the sound of a vowel (either the *e* or the *i*), and you have to figure out which vowel you're dealing with and whether that vowel sound is a short or long one. But, rather than reading a lengthy explanation, you can figure out the *y* sounds much more easily by seeing how they work in real words. So that you can do this, I give you Tables 13-1 through 13-6 later in this chapter.

Because *y* is a pretend vowel, making *e* and *i* sounds all over the place (long or short *i* but only long *e*), teachers often introduce it along with the vowels.

How y can sound like long a

Your child can whiz through the *ay* family because these words are short and quite common. Show him Table 13-1 and maybe make a copy of it so he can highlight the *ay* part of each word. Have him read the table from beginning to end, from end to beginning, and by choosing words in random order. Dictate five words for him to write down and then display his work for a few days.

Table 13-1	−*ay* Words	
bay	day	Fay
hay	Jay	Kay
lay	may	pay
ray	say	way
play	stay	tray
clay		

How y can sound like long e

When *y* comes at the end of a longer word, it adopts the long *e* sound. These words are common, so your child can see and practice them often in books.

Before going over the *y* words in Table 13-2 with your child, check the unusual features (which I italicize in the table) in the following list so that you can explain them to her:

- ✔ The sound *ar* and the same-sounding pairs *ir* and *er* (mention that *ur* is the same, too!).
- ✔ In the word *country*, *ou* makes the short *u* sound.
- ✔ In the word *fancy*, the *c* says its soft sound.
- ✔ The word *ghostly* has a silent *h* and a long *o*.
- ✔ *Naughty* and *pretty* are such strange words — *augh* is pronounced *aw*, and *pretty* should really look like *pritty*!

Table 13-2	*y* on the End of Longer Words	
baby	berry	body
bumpy	bunny	cherry
chilly	cloudy	copy
country	crazy	creepy
dirty	dizzy	empty
enemy	entry	family
fancy	funny	ghostly
granny	happy	holly
hurry	jolly	lady
lanky	lumpy	many
marry	merry	milky
nanny	naughty	party
plenty	pony	pretty
property	silly	skinny
sorry	spotty	sunny
tiny	ugly	very
windy	worry	

Some of the words in Table 13-2 are harder than others. Look at the harder words for ways to remember them. Talk to your child about them and look for special features together. Can you sound out, make word families, or high-light prominent letters with any of the difficult words? Write the difficult words onto cards for your child to read out every day. Make wall posters of the words you're focusing on. Look for them in books that you read together.

The *–try* and *–ly* word families sit among all the *–y* words. These families are so common that you may want to spend a little time showing them to your child. Table 13-3 gives a few words to get going with, but you'll see that this is a pretty challenging bunch of words. Read the words with your child and point out the tricky soft *c*'s and *g*'s. Then see if your child can find words that you call out to him. Show him, too, that *ful* on the end of a word has only one *l*, but *fully* has two. For a challenge, you can dictate a few words for your child to write out.

TIP

The *y* in *–try* and *–ly* words isn't tricky — it still sounds out like a long *e*. Check out the italicized letters in Table 13-3, though. Show these soft letters, silent letters, or unusual sounds to your child. Have her highlight the unusual letters and make sure she pays special attention to those words.

Table 13-3	*–try* and *–ly* Words	
boldly	bravely	breezily
clearly	c*ou*ntry	dangerously
ea*s*ily	entry	generally
gently	gra*c*efully	gravely
helpfully	hotly	hu*g*ely
industry	lamely	mildly
ni*c*ely	pantry	plainly
p*ou*ltry	puppetry	really
shapely	simply	sin*c*erely
stran*g*ely	tapestry	timely
widely	wildly	wintry
wisely		

Hazey or hazy; shiney or shiny?

Words like *hazy, shiny,* and *shaky* deserve a little extra attention. Explain to your child that he has to get rid of the *e* on words like *haze* and *shine* before adding *y*. Show him that even when the *e* is gone, he pronounces the original word as if the *e* still sat there. You pronounce *shiny* shine-y, not shinny. Help your child understand this concept by having him write out some words and add the *y*, using the words in Table 13-4.

Table 13-4	Adding *y* to Words Like *bone*	
bone	flake	grime
haze	nose	shade
shake	shine	snake
stripe	wave	whine

When your child starts writing these words, tell him two tips:

- ✔ When you add a *y* ending to a word that ends with *e* (like *lace*), drop the *e* and you're probably right *(lacy)*.

- ✔ Whenever you're not sure of a spelling, any spelling, try out your options. Write down the possibilities and go for the one that looks best. (Or type the word and use your spell check!)

How y can sound like long i

Show your child all the little words in Table 13-5. Their size makes remembering them very easy. Do a quick read-through, beginning to end, end to beginning, and randomly. Now dictate all the words for your child to write. Have her do her writing on poster paper or a whiteboard so you can display it proudly for a few days.

Table 13-5	The *y* as Long as *i* Family	
by	cry	dry
fry	my	pry
sly	sty	try

What about *cycle?* The *y* makes an *i* sound, too. Words like *cycle* pop up to make you think you've forgotten something. Don't worry about these kinds of words. Every time you teach a family of words, you find a latecomer or gate crasher — words you think you should have mentioned or words that break all the great rules you just taught. When you come face to face with these words, tell your child that you and she need to figure out this word. In the case of *cycle,* sound things out. Explain that *y* makes different sounds, so you need to try out each one. Is it long *e* or *i,* or maybe short *e* or *i*? When you come to the *le* part of *cycle,* explain that *l* sounds out as usual but *e* just tags along silently. (See Chapter 12 to introduce silent *e* to your child.)

Instead of going over masses of words and pointing out all sorts of sounds, give your child just one or two guidelines. The guideline for *y* is that it makes the *e* or *i* sound (long *e,* or long or short *i*). Your child's task is to figure out which sound *y* makes in a word. The job of working out such a puzzle is more appealing to her than memorizing individual words.

How y can sound like short i

The next table of words, Table 13-6, gives your child a real challenge. You may want to skip past it for right now and refer to it later, or you may feel that your child can handle it. Whatever you decide, take a quick look at this table because the words in it demonstrate why your help is so important. If you use this table, you teach your child how to break words up and sound them out (remembering the tricks and twists), and he gets a wide vocabulary, too. Your child wouldn't be able to figure these reading methods out by himself.

Table 13-6	*y* Sounding Like Short *i*	
crypt	cryptic	cymbal
gymnastics	gypsy	mystery
myth	symbol	system

Sampling the Different Sounds of y

Not all the words in this chapter are easy. Small families, like *day, play, stay,* and *by, cry, sly* are easy, but others get challenging. And your child has a lot to remember. Take your time with the harder words so your child gets a solid grip on them. Have her read the words in order and randomly, have her write those words, and then take a breather with the next few lighter activities (you may feel you deserve it by now!).

If you have your child read out the instructions for the exercises coming up next, he should get used to four really common words first: *one, word, saw,* and *find. find* may be the easiest to teach. With *find,* you can simply explain that the *i* makes its long sound. Tell your child about the long *–ind* family: *kind, mind, find, blind, rind,* and *bind.* With *one, word,* and *saw,* you have to be more creative and see if you can think up ingenious ways to help your child. I often show children that *on* is inside *one.* Okay, that method isn't brilliant, but it seems to help.

From the tables in this chapter, find the word that fits:

1. Not wet but . . .

2. Not sad but . . .

3. Not ugly but . . .

4. Not exit but . . .

5. Not nastily but . . .

6. Not a man but a . . .

7. Not clean but . . .

8. Not night but . . .

9. Not rainy but . . .

10 Not fat but . . .

Before your child starts the next activity, help him spot any words he doesn't know. Always do this word spotting before starting any reading, and your child can figure out every word and doesn't get frustrated. In this case, the word you may not have looked at before is *might.* Take time out now to show your child the *–ight* family if he hasn't come upon it yet: *bright, fight, flight, might, night, tight,* and *sight.*

Again, from the tables in this chapter, find the word that fits:

1. Sneaky is the same as . . .

2. Tall is the same as . . .

3. Merry is the same as . . .

4. If you love doing cartwheels and handstands, maybe you go to classes in . . .

5. You can make pots with this.

6. You may do this if you're sad.

7. This is a plant or the name of a girl.

8. When you have a lot, you have . . .

9. At Halloween, you may act like this.

10. This is another name for a babysitter.

Look at the word endings and spot the odd one in each list:

1. Harry, Beth, Mary

2. hot, windy, rainy

3. happy, funny, mad

4. sly, by, hit

5. fussy, smelly, goat

6. carry, bunny, granddad

7. plenty, merry, moon

8. dizzy, stone, sorry

9. ugly, misty, black

10. dime, copy, hurry

Part IV

Scary Stuff Beginning with *S:* Soft Sounds, Suffixes, Syllables, and Silent Letters

The 5th Wave   By Rich Tennant

I was really thinking about a "Dick and Jane" approach to reading lessons.

You...have...the...right to...remain...silent. Every thing...you say... can...and...will...be...

In this part . . .

*I*f the thought of breaking up words (knowing where to put the break, how to sound out the parts, and whether to even bother) holds about as much appeal for you as dental surgery, don't worry. This part of the book gets into it all, but gently. No Novocain necessary.

Chapter 14

Soft Sounds

Whenever I eat potato chips, I want more. Well, your child is going to feel the same way about soft letter sounds. When he first gets a taste of them, he'll want more. He'll start reading soft sounds everywhere. He'll be disappointed when you tell him that a c or g makes just a regular sound this time.

In this chapter, I lead you through soft sounds and how to help your child use them in moderation. You see how to show him that if soft letters were foods, they'd be right there in the largely-to-be-avoided food group, with the candy and potato chips.

Soft g: Giraffes Age Gently

Kids remember, and keep remembering, this sound of soft g, pronounced like a j. That's the problem. Children don't find it hard to accept that g sometimes makes a j sound, but the *sometimes* part can confuse them. They're not sure when to use a soft sound and when not to. You can clear things up by telling them that a g followed by an e, i, or y makes a soft sound. But your child may have problems remembering that rule, too. You just have to get stuck in soft g words — reading, writing, and playing to remember them — and warn your child that she shouldn't overuse this fun group.

Feel the softness. If you have play dough or can think of other soft materials that make shapes, create some truly soft letters. Mold a g and a c so your child remembers that these two letters are the big softies. Draw big letters for your child to stick soft things onto. Cotton wool works well, and you can add glitter and spray paint, if you have some. Write a simple word like *ace, ice,* or *age* next to the letter and display that word so your child can read it often.

Table 14-1 gives you a bunch of soft *g* words to get a grip on, and you can see at a glance that this group isn't chicken feed. You can skip it for the time being, select just a few words to look at, or deal with the whole list now. Decide which choice best suits your child right now. You have a lot of word choices in this table and some really meaty words for your child to sink her teeth into, if she's ready.

If you plan to walk through all the words in Table 14-1 with your child, you may want to make a copy of the table so your child can mark the special features she sees. Here are the special features you encounter:

- ✔ **dge:** Many words end with this particular letter sequence. Highlight the ones you see so your child gets used to them.

- ✔ **er:** If your child doesn't yet know the *er* sound, take time out now to explain it to her. (See Chapter 17 for some tips on how to make this introduction.) After you start thinking of *er* words, you find you have to make three groups of words because three different pairs of letters make this sound: *er, ir* and *ur*.

- ✔ **ou:** *ou* sounds like short *u* in *courage*. If you want to delve into this some more, you can show your child that the same thing happens in *touch, country, young, cousin, couple,* and *trouble*.

- ✔ **al or le:** Explain to your child that these endings sound pretty much the same, but you get to know which ending goes with which word by practicing. The *le* ending is more common than the *al* ending.

Table 14-1	Soft *g*	
age	bridge	budge
bulge	cage	congeal
courage	cringe	danger
digest	dodge	edge
fudge	gem	general
genie	gentle	gentleman
germ	giant	ginger
giraffe	gym	gypsy
hedge	hinge	huge
judge	knowledge	ledger
lodge	lunge	manger

nudge	page	plunge
rage	range	ranger
sage	singe	sledge
sludge	smudge	stage
strange	stranger	tinge
trudge	twinge	wage
wedge		

Here are some quick activities you can use with Table 14-1:

✔ **Highlighting:** Give your child some highlighters and ask her to find words by saying things like "Find the fourth word down in the second column." When she finds the word you mean, let her highlight it and figure it out. Offer help if she gets stuck, but stay in the back seat with this task. This activity keeps her interested, physically engaged, and in working-out mode.

✔ **Sorting:** Ask your child to color the words that end in *ge* in one color and the words that start with *g* in another color. What kinds of words are left? What groups of letters can your child spot?

✔ **Battleships:** You each need a copy of Table 14-1 for this activity. Each of you chooses five ships (five words from the table that you highlight). Take turns reading out a word each. Each of you crosses off every word that's read. If you read your partners ship word, you sink that ship. The person with one or more ships left when the other person has none is the winner.

Soft c: Mice Race Cycles

Your child can get to know soft *c* (pronounced like an *s*) pretty easily. Many words that use soft *c* fit the *ace* or *ice* family, making understanding soft *c* words easier, right from the start. As with soft *g*, you should look at vowels sitting next to *c*. A *c* followed by an *e, i,* or *y* makes a soft sound, but having your child realize this pattern for himself works better than simply telling him to remember it. Check out Table 14-2 for *ace* and *ice* words, and then see what other kinds of words you and your child can spot. Ask your child things like: Are the other words easy? Which word looks the hardest? What's the longest word?

These words are hard, so your child needs to look at them carefully and break them into pieces. Asking him to highlight them, examine them, and answer questions about them gets him actively involved. If he feels a sense of control and is actively doing things with these words, he gets to know them quicker.

Table 14-2	Soft *c*	
ace	advice	announce
bounce	brace	cell
cement	cent	center
chance	city	conceal
dance	decide	device
dice	dunce	embrace
face	fancy	fence
fleece	France	grace
ice	incident	lace
lice	menace	mercy
mice	mince	nice
niece	notice	office
ounce	pace	palace
piece	place	pounce
prance	price	prince
produce	race	rice
since	slice	space
spruce	trace	trance
truce	twice	wince

Because the words in Tables 14-1 and 14-2 range from fairly simple to pretty hard, here are two quizzes. Your child can have fun with both of them, but he may find the first quiz much easier.

Quiz 1: Easing into soft *c* and *g*.

1. I have some pet . . .
2. Chinese food usually comes with some . . .
3. I can run in a . . .
4. This lets you cross over water.
5. I like to sing and . . .
6. You put this up to keep pets in the yard.
7. Her prom dress is very . . .
8. If you look over this part of a cliff, it's a long way down!

Quiz 2: Time for a challenge!

1. The queen lives in a . . .
2. This person lives in the palace with the queen.
3. It takes this to sing in front of a lot of people.
4. I don't know him, he's a . . .
5. At the zoo, I liked this animal the best.
6. The man was very this with the new baby.
7. The rain leaked in at a crack in the . . .
8. The man who holds the door open for another person is a real . . .
9. A secretary works in this room.
10. At the end of the fight, they called a . . .

Now for some slightly different questions. Read them and find the answers together. You can read the questions and let your child find the word, or, if your child is confident with these words, let him do the whole activity himself. If he's searching the words without help from you, you may want to highlight the answers in advance so that he has fewer words to search through.

Activity: Do you know?

1. Not plain
2. How a cat jumps onto a mouse
3. A diamond
4. Hug

5. To tell everyone

6. A place to exercise

7. A kind of cloth for fancy dresses

8. A kind of candy

9. A sheep's coat

10. A portable phone

One last question:

✔ **Q:** Why did Cinderella's soccer team always lose?

✔ **A:** Because the coach was a pumpkin.

Chapter 15

Endings (a.k.a. Suffixes)

In This Chapter

▶ Introducing word endings

▶ Joining endings onto words

▶ Spotting a good fit

*W*hen I was a school girl, believe it or not, I wasn't always very disciplined. Instead, like most girls, I whiled away many hours daydreaming and doodling. My favorite activity was to experiment with last names. Specifically, I'd think of boys I liked and then try out their surnames, in case I ever married them. I haven't doodled with last names for quite some time now, but I still find them interesting. Some, like mine (Wood) you can easily spell. Others, like Erdozaincy, no one can spell. And some surnames you never forget because they match so well with a first name (Peter Pitts, Sandy Sanders, and Joan Jones — all friends of mine).

Word endings are like last names. They're interesting, and you can spell and remember some of them easier than others. This chapter walks you through some word endings and some easy ways to remember them. It will be better than remembering the names of people too because you can forget a word ending and no one gets offended.

A Quick Overview

Suffix is another name for a word ending, like *ed* or *ly*. This chapter shows you the main suffixes, but you run across a lot more out there in the reading world. Table 15-1 gives you a rundown of all the endings you can find in this chapter and shows how they tag onto the ends of words. From these endings, you get an idea of how to explain other endings your child may encounter later.

Table 15-1	A Look at All the Endings	
Ending	**Examples**	**Rules**
s or *es*	hops cats classes foxes brushes	Add only s unless you hear the extra syllable, *ez* (you hear the *ez* sound in words ending with *ss, x, z, ch,* or *sh*). In words ending with *z*, double the *z* (as in *quizzes*).
ed	hopped hoped looked	Can be pronounced *ed, d,* or *t.* In short vowel words that end with one consonant, double the consonant to keep the short sound.
ing	hopping hoping	Drop the *e* when you add *ing.* In short vowel words that end with one consonant, double the consonant to keep the short sound.
y or *ily*	noisy breezy noisily breezily	No need for an end *e* or *y* (because the add-on makes that sound already).
er, est, ly	later thinner latest thinnest lately	Just add on — but no need for two *e*'s together in words like late + er or three *l*'s in words like smell + ly! In short vowel words that end with one consonant, double the consonant to keep the short sound.

Please don't treat this chapter as an endurance test. Use the tables of words and rules that I give you when the time is right. You don't have to get through them all now. Instead, you can look at a few words now and leave the rest for another time. Or you can scan now and then come back to refer to the tables when your child gets stuck on a word like *sloped* or *shaking*. The tables can help you feel comfortable with taking a good look at words and how they're made up. Whatever you do, don't abandon colorful, exciting, funny reading books to slog through these words.

Adding *s* or *es*

When your child reads about groups of things, or *plurals*, he most often sees an ending *s*, as in words like *girls, boys, apples, oranges, friends,* and *schools.* To make plurals, your child can remember this rule: Add only *s* unless you hear an extra *ez* syllable in words like *glasses, boxes, benches,* and *wishes.* Table 15-2 gives you a lot of these words to look at.

Have your child read the words in Table 15-2, and tell him to listen for the *ez* sound. Have him highlight the *es* endings. Read a few out for him to write down.

Table 15-2			*s* and *es* Endings	
ss	**x**	**z**	**ch**	**sh**
dresses	boxes	quizzes	sketches	dishes
messes	foxes	fizzes	blotches	brushes
bosses	fixes	whizzes	benches	dashes
crosses		buzzes	lunches	pushes
classes			punches	sashes
glasses			patches	blushes
kisses			matches	wishes
misses			pinches	gashes
			riches	rashes
			latches	crashes

Adding *ed*

Explain to your child that when you talk about something that happened in the past, you usually add *ed* to the word. Take special notice of the three groups of words in Table 15-3 when you're adding *ed.*

Table 15-3	How to Add *ed*
Word	**What to Watch For**
Short vowel (tip) tipped (hop) hopped (pin) pinned	When words have a short vowel, double the last letter before adding *ed*.
Short vowel, two consonants at the end (jolt) jolted (pant) panted (sulk) sulked	When words have a short vowel but end in two consonants, you don't need to double anything.
***e* ending** (hate) hated (like) liked (hope) hoped	When words already end in *e*, you don't need to add *ed*, only *d*.

Reading *ed* words

Table 15-3 starts with the short vowel group. Your child can have a lot of fun with little short vowel words. She can add *ed* to these words with no trouble and enjoy doing it on a whiteboard or poster paper, or in a tray of sand. Table 15-4 gives you a lot of words to practice with.

Have your child cover the right column of Table 15-4 with a piece of paper or book and ask her to read the words in the left column. Have her write each word, adding an *ed* ending, and then check her answers.

Table 15-4	Adding *ed* to Short Vowel Words
Word	**Word with *ed* Added On**
bat	batted
hop	hopped
chop	chopped
shop	shopped
chat	chatted

Word	Word with ed Added On
clap	clapped
pin	pinned
slap	slapped
nap	napped
jog	jogged

Words that end with *x* don't follow the pattern. *Box* becomes *boxed, fix* becomes *fixed.* As long as the word ends with one vowel and one consonant, no matter what the words starts with, you double the last letter.

The second group of words in Table 15-3 is the group of short vowel words with two consonants at the end. It doesn't matter if a short vowel word starts with a single consonant, like *bolt,* or two consonants, like *clamp* — it's the ending of the word that affects how you add a suffix. If the word ends with two consonants, you don't have to double anything before adding *ed.* Table 15-5 shows several words that fit this group.

Have your child read the words and highlight the two consonants on the end. You may want to copy the table first to keep your book looking nice and make the activity something you and your child can do more than once.

When a short vowel word ends with three consonants, use the same rule that applies to words ending with two consonants — no need to double any letters before adding *ed.*

"Today I betted Jason I'd win the race"

When your child gives you cute snippets of news, like, "Today I writed a story," you probably want to correct his grammar. "Wrote," you say. "I wrote a story." Your child looks at you indignantly and finds it hard to grasp what you're fussing about. Well, I understand where he's coming from. It *is* hard to figure out the ins and outs of grammar and how endings and tenses work.

Your child can best understand these tricky rules by hearing them. He'll really grasp the language if he hears and reads correct usage every day. You may notice when you're going through the words in this book that words with an *e* vowel sound seldom have *ed* added on in their past tense form. Take *bet, fed,* and *led,* for example. You hear little kids say *fedded* and *ledded* for a while before they become aware that those words just sound wrong.

Table 15-5	Adding *ed* to Short Vowel Words That End with Two Consonants
Word	**Word with ed Added On**
hatch	hatched
wish	wished
flash	flashed
clamp	clamped
hand	handed
plant	planted
stamp	stamped
bolt	bolted
flick	flicked
pick	picked

Table 15-3 finishes with the group of words that end in *e* (like *like*) and there-fore have a long vowel sound. Your child can figure out this group easily when he's thinking about it, but can he spot these words, and pronounce them cor-rectly, when he comes upon them in books?

To help your child recognize these words in books, explain this rule to him: When you see words that end with *ed* but don't have a double letter just before the *ed*, those words originally ended with *e*. Take *pine*, for instance. When you see *pined*, do you see a double letter? No. Because the word doesn't have a double letter, you know the *base* or *root* word (the word that the ending attaches to) is *pine*, and you see *pine* if you cover over the *d*. On the other hand, if you see *pinned*, the double letter (which you make to keep the vowel short) tells you that the root word is *pin*.

A base word isn't a vulgar character you'd be best off avoiding but an original word, before you put any endings on it. You hear this word called a root word, too. Get used to spotting base or root words. Reminding your child of the base word can be very handy so that he can pronounce words like *pinned* and *pined* correctly.

Table 15-6 gives you a lot of words ending with *e* to practice with. Have your child cover the right column and read the words in the left column out to you. Then have her write each word, with an *ed* ending added on, and check her answers. Now cover the left column and see if your child can tell you the base word.

Table 15-6	Adding *ed* to Words That End with an *e*
Word	*Word with ed Added On*
joke	joked
skate	skated
trade	traded
shade	shaded
pile	piled
tape	taped
poke	poked
hope	hoped
blaze	blazed
smile	smiled
glide	glided

Tell your child to make sure he doesn't have two *e*'s. A word like *skate,* for example, becomes *skated,* not *skateed.*

Getting on top of ed sounds

You may notice three different pronunciations of words ending with *ed*. Words like *skated* end with a distinct *ed* sound, words like *squeezed* use just a *d* sound at the end, and the end of words like *hopped* sound more like a *t* than a *d.* Don't worry. Just be sure to give your child some practice with each sound. To make your practice sessions incredibly easy, here's (you guessed it!) a nice table, Table 15-7. Remind your child, when she's working with Table 15-7, that anytime she sees a double letter, the base word is a short vowel word.

You often can't tell the difference between the *d* and *t* sound in Table 15-7 — you can't really tell if you're saying *d, t,* or a bit of each. Just point this fact out to your child and tell him that no matter which of the pronunciations he hears, he should write it as *ed.*

Table 15-7	The Three Sounds of *ed*	
An ed Sound	*A d Sound*	*A t Sound*
skated	leaked	poked
fated	gained	jumped
dented	trailed	hopped
painted	liked	shaped
needed	blinked	scraped
heated	planned	shipped
hinted	piled	sneaked
fainted	sliced	peeped
shifted	talked	stripped
graded	screamed	sloped

What about *slept* and *wept?* Yes, some words sound as if they end with a *t,* and they do! That's okay. Your child can get used to these renegade words. But she should remember that this bunch of words is less common than the *ed* bunch.

Adding *ing*

Drop the *e* when you add *ing.* This simple rule works just like adding *ed.* With short vowel words like *hop,* double the last letter before adding *ing;* with short vowel words, like *bolt,* that end in two consonants, you don't need double letters; with words ending in *e,* drop the e when you add *ing.*

To give your child practice at adding *ing,* go to Tables 15-4, 15-5, and 15-6, earlier in this chapter. Have your child cover the right column and write each word with an *ing* ending added on. Now use Table 15-8 to do the same activity, asking your child to cover the right column and add the *ing* ending to the words in the left column. Next, do the opposite, having your child cover the left column and tell you the base words.

Table 15-8	Adding *ing*
Base Word	*Word with ing Ending*
hit	hitting
sing	singing
pray	praying
shake	shaking
ring	ringing
fake	faking
dream	dreaming
think	thinking
run	running
hide	hiding
ride	riding
call	calling

Adding y or ily

I can't give you a helpful rhyme for the *y* or *ily* endings, but they both work in the same way as *ing:* If a word ends with an *e,* drop the *e* before adding *y* or *ily.* Table 15-9 gives you a mixture of words so your child can spot the ones that end with *e* and see how the *e* gets lopped off.

If your child has difficultly remembering the business of *e*'s and endings, you can give him a quick solution. See if the word reads correctly without the y, and, if not, someone has lopped off its *e.*

If your child asks about the differences between words that end with *y* and words that end with *ily,* you can give a simple explanation. Words ending in *y* are words that describe things, like a *tasty* meal, *breezy* day, or *easy* book. Words that end with *ily* are words that describe ways of doing things, like *happily* or *noisily* eating ice cream.

Table 15-9	*y* and *ily* Endings
Base Word	*Word with y or ily Ending*
taste	tasty
spice	spicy
haste	hasty
breeze	breezy
ease	easy
chill	chilly
sun	sunny
run	runny
wind	windy
fat	fatty
skin	skinny
mud	muddy
happy	happily
funny	funnily
noisy	noisily
windy	windily
cheer	cheerily

Adding er, est, and ly

You just stick these endings on — easy! Have your child read through the words in Table 15-10, and then give her a quick dictation of ten words. Let her write those words however she wants (whiteboard, poster paper, glitter pens). And remind her of tricky features, like *s* sounding like *z (wise)* — but only if she wants your help!

Table 15-10	Adding *er, est,* and *ly*
Base Word	*Word with er, est, or ly Ending*
cold	colder, coldest, coldly
big	bigger, biggest
most	mostly
bold	bolder, boldest, boldly
old	older, oldest
blind	blinder, blindest, blindly
steep	steeper, steepest, steeply
small	smaller, smallest
pretty	prettier, prettiest, prettily
live	lively, livelier, liveliest
tame	tamer, tamest, tamely
grumpy	grumpier, grumpiest, grumpily
loud	louder, loudest, loudly
wise	wiser, wisest, wisely
like	likely, likelier, likeliest
brave	braver, bravest, bravely
white	whiter, whitest
fine	finer, finest, finely
quick	quicker, quickest, quickly
lumpy	lumpier, lumpiest
soft	softer, softest, softly
fast	faster, fastest

In words ending with *y:* the *y* turns into an *i* — prettier, prettiest, prettily; grumpier, grumpiest, grumpily.

Look out, it's *y!*

When you add an ending onto a word that already ends with a *y,* you have two rules to follow:

✔ When a word ends with *y* and you add *ing,* you don't have to watch out for anything.

That surprised you, didn't it! Words like *drying* and *crying* fall into this category.

✔ When a word ends with y and you add any other ending, change *y* to *i: babies, ladies, armies, heavier, craziest, happiest.*

Adding *able* or *ible*

Able and *ible* can throw the best of us into a quandary. Here's some information that can help:

✔ *Able* attaches to words more often than *ible.*

✔ *Able* usually appears on the end of complete words, such as *readable* or *fashionable.*

Sadly, this nice little rule about complete words isn't true 100 percent of the time. But Table 15-11 shows you a whole heap of words where the rule *does* work. Table 15-11 probably has the longest, hardest words in this entire book. But don't be alarmed! You can use these words for reference, and they come in really handy when your child comes back to you in a few years time asking for help with words like *commendable.* (Be sure to have a good spell-checker on your word processor by then!)

Full of *ful*

I didn't mention the *ful* ending in this chapter, so here's a rundown on what your child needs to know about *ful* words. *Full* on its own has two *l*'s. But when you add *full* to the front or back of a word, it loses an *l.*

Table 15-11	*able* and *ible* Words
able	*ible*
fashionable	visible
laughable	horrible
suitable	terrible
dependable	possible
comfortable	edible
advisable	incredible
desirable	eligible
valuable	permissible
debatable	compatible
preferable	legible

When a word ends with *e,* you drop the *e* before adding the *able* or *ible* ending, like with *valuable.*

Chapter 16

Chunks of Sound, or Syllables

In This Chapter

▶ Putting words together from syllables

▶ Listening for clear sound bites

▶ Hitting the syllable highlights

*Y*ears ago, when I was teaching in a high school, I went to a quite good professional development presentation. I was given a fancy folder of information, nice cookies at coffee break, and a lot of advice from slick speakers with high-tech props. Now, I'm not saying that I didn't benefit from the whole day, because I did, but it must've cost an awful lot and could've been condensed. In fact, I can put what that presentation told me into one sentence: Take things one step at a time.

You can use the same advice when you teach your child new words. You should take things one step at a time. Those steps are often *syllables,* or chunks of sound. When you come to tricky-looking or big words, syllables become your best friends. Break words up into syllables, start at the beginning, and take it one syllable at a time.

Syllables: The Building Blocks of Words

A syllable is simply a chunk of a word. Getting to know syllables well can be a really handy thing for your child (and you!) because syllables allow you to figure out big words, one syllable at a time. Understanding syllables isn't difficult, but they do start and end at particular places. And you have to know the rules for finding those places. But do you know what's really nice about syllables? You don't *have* to follow the rules. Many kids break words up in places where the split shouldn't really go (according to English teachers across the globe), but it doesn't actually matter. The important thing is that your child breaks words up. If he breaks a word in a place that feels right but doesn't impress the English-usage gurus, just don't tell any of those gurus!

Thinking back to simple three-letter words

In Chapter 7, I introduce you to words like *ant* and *pan*, and then I bring out words like *bun, him,* and *pot,* to show you the importance of teaching your child to reading in chunks, not single letters. You can attack syllables in just the same way — as two- and three-letter chunks of sound. And you just need to string a few small chunks together to read long words. Just to show you what I mean, take a look at these hard-looking words. They're just a few easy-as-can-be chunks put together:

✔ den–tist

✔ yes–ter–day

✔ vol–un–teer

✔ im–por–tant

In this chapter, I tell you all about the syllable rules so that you know them, and then I let you try them out with your child. I expect you to break up words in all the right places most of the time but occasionally do your own creative breaking up.

Hearing Syllables in Words

Shhhh — listen! You can hear syllables. They're definite chunks of sound, and listening to people's names gives you the best way to show those sounds to your child. Start with your own. *Tracey,* for instance, has two syllables. *Tra* and *cey.* Other names with two syllables are:

✔ Ra–chel

✔ Ja–son

✔ Pe–ter

✔ Sal–ly

✔ Ev–an

✔ Jes–sie

✔ Don–na

✔ Jef–frey

✔ Lau–ren

✔ Ka–ty

English-language names rarely have more than three syllables, so Table 16-1, with one-, two-, and three-syllable names, should help you get the hang of syllables.

Table 16-1	Names Broken into Syllables	
One Syllable	*Two Syllables*	*Three Syllables*
John	A–my	Steph–an–ie
Ben	Da–vid	Am–an–da
Ann	A–lex	Dom–in–ic
Beth	Jo–anne	Greg–o–ry
Joe	Ka–thy	Ma–ri–sa
Kate	Co–lin	Me–lis–sa
Jack	Ter–ry	Na–ta–lie
Tim	Deb–ra	Ma–di–son
Tom	Em–ma	Re–bec–ca
Fran	Brit–ney	Ca–mer–on

Activity: Clapping it out.

Now, it's time to clap along with your child. (This clapping isn't the raucous kind you're used to, though. You and your child need to clap rhythmically, one clap per syllable.)

1. First, explain to your child how chunks of sound, which we call syllables, make up words.

2. Clap out a few family names for her and then ask her to do the same on her own. Clap the words in a sequence without stopping, like A–li–son, Je–ni–fer, Ni–cole.

3. Together, think of three names and then clap them out.

4. Write a list of people and then clap that list out together.

5. Now make a list of random words and clap them out.

Schwhat?

The term schwa (pronounced *shwah*) is about as intimidating as any word can be, so I'm here to prepare you for it in case you find it in another book. A *schwa* sound is an unstressed vowel sound. Not unstressed, meaning laid-back, but unstressed as in the unstressed *a* in words like *ago* and *apart*. When you say a vowel sort of weakly or indistinctly compared to the rest of a word, you call that vowel the schwa sound. I think it's all a bit iffy, myself, because a lot depends on which part of the world you come from. Your accent can make the difference between a schwa and a non-schwa, so my advice to you is just to tell your child that you stress many words unevenly. You say one part in a more pronounced way than another part. That's really all your child needs to know, and she's probably already heard this difference for herself, anyway. In case you want to know about schwa sounds, here are a few words that have an easy to spot schwa sound. The bold part of the word is the stressed syllable, and the plain text has the schwa vowel sound:

secret

hazard

certain

a**drift**

market

If you're a browser of dictionaries (some people are, you know!), you've probably spotted the schwa symbol already. It's an upside down, back to front *e*.

If you want to break words up somewhere other than where I have, you can go ahead and do it. If, for example, you want to say Cam–er–on (rather than the Ca–mer–on I gave), say it however you feel comfortable. You don't have to break words up in any particular way, you just need to break them up. If you want to break words into syllables according to English usage rules, though, here are the basic rules for making syllables:

- A syllable has at least one vowel.
- If two consonants come together, divide between them — for example, mat–tress.
- Can't see two consonants next to each other? Break the syllable after the vowel. You usually pronounce that vowel in its long form — for example, *ba–ker; o–pen; di–rect*.

Two syllables are ea–sy

After you get the hang of breaking two-syllable words up, it will seem like second nature to you. Table 16-2 gives you some words to look at so that you can see where to break each word. The rules for breaking words into two syllables tell you to put a break

✔ Between double consonants (*let–ter*).

✔ Between each whole word in a compound word *(sun–set).*

✔ Between two consonants, if those two consonants follow the first vowel (*nap–kin*).

✔ After the first vowel, if that vowel isn't followed by two consonants together (*be–hind*).

When words like *table* and *program* seem to break the last rule, it's because you must keep blends (*st, str, bl*), digraphs *(ch, sh, th, ph, wh)*, prefixes (*dis, pro, un*), and suffixes together (*ly, tion, ing*).

✔ In words with an *x*, join the *x* to the vowel in front of it — for example, *ex–it, ex–plain,* and *ex–am–ple.*

Don't worry too much about the rules, though. Syllables are supposed to help you, so if these rules seem hard, you can do without them. You can break some of your words in unofficial ways, no problem. In the rest of this chapter, I take a few liberties with syllables. I break some words up where it sounds right, rather than into strictly correct syllables so you see a few unofficial chunks, as well as the strictly correct syllables.

Table 16-2	Where to Put Breaks in Words
Break between Two Consonants	*Break after a Vowel*
cor–rect	ta–ble
nap–kin	be–hind
sis–ter	de–light
let–ter	di–rect
sup–per	la–zy
un–der	ma–gic
ex–plain	pro–gram
hap–py	re–ply
rib–bon	be–lieve
af–ter	o–ver

Three syllables are ter–rif–ic

Three-syllable words are a treat for your child. He may not initially realize it, though. At first sight, big words just look scary. Show your child how to break them up, and soon he won't be scared at all. He'll feel proud that he can read such immense words — and you should show him that you're proud of him, too. Table 16-3 gives you and your child a lot of impressive-looking words to read together by breaking them up into syllables.

Table 16-3	Breaking Up Three-Syllable Words	
di–no–saur	di–rec–tion	dis–cus–sion
ex–cel–lent	ex–ci–ting	in–spec–tion
in–spec–tor	mi–cro–phone	op–po–site
su–per–man	te–le–phone	tri–an–gle

Table 16-3 has a great example of how putting a break where it seems to naturally come can be better than fussing about rules. The official way to break *telephone* into syllables is to say *te–le–phone,* but your child may be more comfortable with *tel–e–phone.*

Great big words are in–ter–es–ting

Sounding out syllables isn't just about rules — you have to hear the chunks inside words and read and write them in the way that feels right. Table 16–4 has words that I've broken up in a way that makes sense to me. Don't have your child read this list. Just read the words to her and see if she can count the chunks. Before you start, you can write the answers on a piece of paper and hide it. Have your child write her answers down and then give her hints until she finds yours. Direct her by saying "You're getting hotter" when she's getting closer and "You're getting colder" when she's moving farther away. The table has ten four-syllable words and two five-syllable words (I've put the number of syllables beside the word in parentheses).

Open vowels (not closed in by a letter on their right) usually make a long vowel sound, like *a*–corn, *o*–pen, di–rec–tion, and dic–*ta*–tion.

Table 16-4	Breaking Up Great Big Words	
au–to–ma–tic (4)	bib–li–og–ra–phy (5)	di–am–e–ter (4)
ed–u–ca–tion (4)	es–ti–ma–tion (4)	ex–pe–ri–ment (4)
ex–plan–a–tion (4)	im–pos–si–ble (4)	for–tu–nate–ly (4)
per–im–e–ter (4)	te–le–vi–sion (4)	u–ni–ver–si–ty (5)

Listen and choose a number

You want your child to be able to hear and say words in syllables for two good reasons. One, so he's primed to read in syllables. Two, so that when he writes, he hears the chunks of sound he's after in his mind. When children hear the parts of a word in their minds, they find writing easier. So, here's a quick and easy game to sharpen your child's hearing.

Give your child a whiteboard or large piece of paper and have a piece of paper, yourself. Both of you should draw three columns marked 1, 2, and 3. Read out words and have your child mark on his board whether he hears one, two, or three syllables. You mark your paper too so that you can compare scores. I've included some words (and an answer key) here:

fat	cottage	deliver
happen	shame	silly
hospital	carpet	hat
ball	travel	electric
shop	milk	bread
open	cabbage	disappear
fun	bag	reading
sulk	pink	nice

Answer key:

How many one-syllable words are there?	How many two-syllable words are there?	How many three-syllable words are there?
Answer: 12	Answer: 8	Answer: 4

Some Syllables and Sounds Worth Knowing

You may find that the next few simple pointers come in really handy. Like the rules in Chapters 12 and 13, you can remember these tips easily, and they help your child an awful lot. They're all about *tion,* words ending with *a,* and *c* versus *ck.*

tion: What's all the commo–*tion?*

tion is my favorite syllable. *tion* really impresses children, it's not hard to get to know, and a child who knows it can spell some really grown-up-looking words. Table 16-5 gives you some words to start with. Tell your child that these words are whoppers but he just needs to break them up. Build the drama and get ready to whoopee when he reads them all to you.

Table 16-5	*tion* Words	
in–spec–tion	pro–mo–tion	in–fec–tion
ac–tion	dis–trac–tion	op–er–a–tion
dic–ta–tion	pre–ven–tion	men–tion
nav–i–ga–tion	re–la–tion	sta–tion
tran–spor–ta–tion	re–flec–tion	di–rec–tion

If he's still eager for more, try dictating the words for him to write. If he can write some, or maybe *all* these words, he's a real champion!

Inside a long word, when you hear long *a* (sounding like *ay*), don't write *ay,* write *a.*

If you're wondering about words that end in *sion* and not *tion,* here's an interesting bit of data. Words end in *tion* much more often than they end in *sion.* In fact, about 95 percent of the time, you deal with *tion,* not *sion.* So you can leave *sion* words alone for now. If you come across a *sion* word, explain it to your child, but don't confuse him by introducing the two endings at the same time.

Words ending with a

Okay, just in case you're drowsing off, here's a puzzle. What have the next words got in common? *America, extra, banana, sofa.* They all end in *a,* but you pronounce the *a* as *uh.* When the last syllable on your word ends in *a,* you probably pronounce it *uh.* And a heck of a lot of names of people and countries end with *a.* Just take a browse through Table 16-6.

Table 16-6	Words Ending with *a*	
camera	idea	delta
insomnia	bacteria	Emma
Natasha	Paula	Anna
Donna	Canada	America
Australia	Indonesia	China
India	Alaska	Venezuela
Nigeria	Siberia	Tasmania

When a word begins with *a,* you often hear the *uh* sound, too. A few important words that begin with *a* are *about, again, above,* and *away.* When your child first sees these words, have her pronounce the short *a* sound (the one we don't really use in normal speech). It doesn't matter that the word sounds a bit funny because after your child takes off with reading, she's soon pronouncing the word like everyone else does.

c versus ck

This chapter is the best place to talk about *c* and *ck* because these letters are firmly tied up with syllables. One of the main ways of deciding whether to use *c* or *ck* when you hear the "kuh" sound is to look at the syllables. Words of one syllable nearly always end with *ck.* Words of more than one syllable usually end in *c.* You don't have to worry too much about explaining these endings to your child because, as you see in Tables 16-7 and 16-8, you can spot which ending the word needs very easily.

Table 16-7	One Syllable Words Ending with *ck*	
back	black	block
buck	deck	Dick
dock	duck	fleck
flick	flock	Jack
kick	knack	knock
lick	lock	Mick
mock	muck	neck
Nick	pack	peck
pick	quack	quick
rack	Rick	sack
sick	stack	stick
suck	tack	tick
tuck	wrack	wreck

Table 16-8	Words Ending with *c*	
comic	elastic	electric
fabric	frantic	magic
mimic	music	panic
picnic	plastic	public
terrific	topic	traffic

When you add *ing* onto words that end with *c*, you must add a *k*, too — like *panicking*. (If you don't, the *c* makes an *s* sound.)

oi and *oy:* Don't be coy

In Chapter 13, you can see the *ay* word family, with words like *say, bay,* and *play.* The *oy* and *oi* families look very like the *ay* family. You can whiz through these two nice families in no time (especially if you've already gone through the *ay* family with your child). Show your child words like *boy* and *toy* to start with. Then show him the *oi* family, explaining that this family sounds just the same as the *oy* family, even though it looks pretty imposing at first sight. Table 16-9 gives you the little *oy* words to warm up with, and Table 16-10 digs into words like *oil* and *boil.*

Table 16-9	*oy* Words	
annoy	boy	coy
destroy	enjoy	joy
loyal	ploy	Roy
royal	toy	Troy

Table 16-10	*oi* Words	
avoid	boil	broil
coin	foil	hoist
join	moist	noise
oil	point	poison
soil	spoil	voice

You can lead a rich and fulfilling life without ever hearing the word I'm about to mention. In fact, this word is plain intimidating. And to make things worse, English speakers use it in a way that can confuse the most logically minded amongst us. And because that's not me, I usually don't get into this scary subject. But if you sign up to train as a reading teacher after reading this book, join a dictionary lovers' club, or end up at a party and get cornered by a Professor of Tedious Things, you shouldn't miss this word: Diphthong. You pronounce it *dif-thong,* and here's my interpretation, such as it is. A diphthong is similar to a digraph (see Chapter 6 to find out about digraphs) except that a diphthong only applies to vowels. A *diphthong* consists of two vowels making a new sound that you can describe as sort of lilting, like in *oi.* You sort of move from one letter to the other in a, well, lilt. But I have read a lot of books about diphthongs (right now, I can't think why), and although I understand how *oi* is a diphthong, I don't understand why *oy* is always included in this group too. *oy* only has one vowel, and *ow* (which I show you in the following section) only has one vowel, too. So I think you can better describe a diphthong as two vowels making a nice lilting sound like *oi* and *ou,* or a vowel and a consonant that can sometimes make a vowel sound (like *oy* and *ow*).

ou and ow: How now brown couch?

All the threatened pinching that comes with introducing *ou* really keeps children listening to you. They're never quite sure whether you plan to pinch or not, even though you've been perfectly nice with them before. Good for them, I say. It's a wise person who expects the unexpected, I expect. Anyway, knowing *ou* (and its partner *ow*) can prove useful. I mentioned *ou* in Chapter 12, but I'm unashamedly coming back to it now because it's a common sound that your child encounters again and again.

In Table 16-11, I give you *ou* to start off with. And Table 16-12 introduces you to *ow*. Have your child focus on one table at a time, reading the words first to last, last to first, and then randomly. Dictate a few words for her to write by herself. And you can copy the tables and ask her to highlight the *ou* and *ow* parts of each word for extra practice.

Table 16-11	*ou* Words	
about	aloud	amount
bounce	cloud	couch
count	flour	ground
house	loud	mouse
mouth	pound	proud
round	scout	sound

Before you ask your child to read the words in Table 16-12, check that you have shown her the *er* sound (see Chapter 17 for good activities to make this introduction) because she comes across it in *flower* and *shower*.

Table 16-12	*ow* Words	
ow	brow	brown
clown	cow	crown
down	flower	frown
gown	growl	how
owl	power	shower
tower	town	vow

au and *aw:* I saw you being naughty

Tables 16-13 and 16-14 present examples of *au* and *aw* words. The *au* words are a challenging group. You may want to use them just for your own reference for now, or you can read them with your child, if you think he's ready for them. Point out these things to your child: the *er* sound in *daughter;* the silent *gh* in *caught, daughter, naughty,* and *taught;* the *s* pronounced *z* in *cause* and *pause;* and the *ce* ending in *sauce.*

Table 16-13	*au* Words	
astronaut	auction	author
auto	caught	cause
daughter	exhaust	fraud
haunt	laundry	naughty
pause	sauce	taught

Table 16-14	*aw* Words	
awe	bawl	brawl
claw	crawl	dawn
draw	fawn	hawk
jaw	law	paw
raw	saw	straw

oo and *ew:* The goose flew the coop

This sound is cute. Your child will like the feel of saying "oo" because it's a sound that goes with statements like "Oooh, this cake's yummy" or "Oooh, that's a huge ice cream cone!" The *oo* sound has a familiar feel, so your child can quickly hear it in the words in Table 16-15. Spend time getting comfortable with the words in Table 16-15 and then introduce your child to the words in Table 16-16. They make the same sound but with a new letter combination — *ew.*

Tired of tables?

If you've been working through this chapter from start to finish, you may be getting heartily sick of tables by now; but I feel obliged to give you just a few more so that you have absolutely all the most common and important word families at your fingertips. I know I'm piling you up with things, but you may thank me later. You may want to leave this book and go watch television right now, but when your child is cruising through his books and comes to a halt at words like *proud* and *power,* you'll be glad that you have every angle covered. So please feel free to take a break or skip this section for now, but I'm going to sneak in just a few more tables. Think kindly of me later.

If you're conscientiously working your way through all these tables, you need to take stock at this point. These tables are here to help your child read, so are you reading with your child regularly? Be sure to keep reading good books with and to your child so these word tables have a purpose and come as a useful supplement to reading (and aren't the main menu).

Table 16-15	*oo* Words	
boom	boot	brood
broom	choose	cool
doom	drool	food
fool	goose	groom
groove	loose	mood
moon	noon	pool
roof	room	root
school	smooth	soon
spoon	stool	tool
tooth	zoo	zoom

Table 16-16	*ew* Words	
blew	brew	chew
crew	dew	drew
few	flew	grew
knew	new	screw
stew	threw	

Now you get to delve into the other *oo* word family, with words like *book, look, took,* and *shook.* This *oo* family is a smaller group, but your child comes across these words all the time. You may want to take a quick detour into these words now to prepare her, so Table 16-17 gives you a few to show your child.

Table 16-17	Words like *book, took,* and *shook*	
book	brook	cook
foot	good	hood
hook	look	nook
rook	shook	soot
stood	took	wood
wool		

Chapter 17

Time to Growl: *ar, or, er, ir,* and *ur*

In This Chapter

▶ Introducing a vowel with special guest, *r*

▶ Sorting out your *ar*'s and *or*'s

▶ Looking out for *er, ir,* and *ur*

▶ Getting some *air*

*W*hen your child first comes across a word like *for,* he mispronounces it. He may say a strange-sounding word and will do the same with words like *her* and *car.* He does this weird pronunciation because he doesn't yet know that when *r* follows a vowel, something unexpected happens. Anytime *r* follows a vowel (as in *ar, or, er, ir,* and *ur*), the combination makes a unique sound, and it's not the one you'd expect (if you're a kid who hasn't dealt with vowel+r before). So, unless you want to hear all sorts of weird pronunciations and feel like an elocution teacher, you need to teach this rule about vowels and *r*'s. This chapter should help you do that.

Knowing Your *ar* from Your *r*

You can run through *ar* words easily with your child. This family has quite a few words, and your child can read those words easily after she knows the sound of *ar.* You may come across some confusion in writing words with the *ar* sound. Why? Because *ar* is also the name of the letter *r.* Practice makes perfect, though, and when your child has seen and heard a lot of *ar* words, she should get comfortable with them.

Activity: Rolling out a few *r*'s.

Table 17-1 gives you a lot of words to practice with. Have your child

1. Read all the words to you, first to last.

2. Read all the words to you, last to first.

3. Find a few random words that you call out to her.

4. Read a few random words that you point to.

Table 17-1	*ar* **Words**	
arch	are	ark
arm	art	bar
bark	barn	car
card	carpenter	carpet
cart	charm	dark
darn	dart	depart
far	farm	hard
harm	harp	jar
lark	march	mark
park	part	partner
party	shark	sharp
snarl	sparkle	star
start	tar	tart
yard	yarn	

Playing "Talk about it"

The *ar* words feature so many cute words, so this group lends itself perfectly to the game "Talk about it," a simple talking game. To play, just take turns talking about a word. *Talking* means telling something (anything at all) about the word or putting it into a short story or anecdote. It doesn't take much for your child to think you're a comic genius in this game, so have a blast with silly tales.

To get your game underway, look at Table 17-1 and choose words that you think you and your child can easily talk about. Write each word onto a separate slip of paper. Put all the words in a hat, grab some popcorn, and settle in for some of the quality time you've been meaning to get around to. If the whole family plays, you can add more fun with props, costumes, and a stopwatch. Here are a few examples of talk a younger child may give:

- ✔ *Sharks* live in the sea. Sharks come in all different kinds. You can have a hammerhead shark or a great white shark. Sometimes sharks bite people swimming in the sea.

- ✔ *Stars* are in the sky. You see them at night. They make patterns like the Big Dipper. You can look at stars through a telescope.

- ✔ You have a *party* on your birthday. You get presents and cake and your friends come. You may play games. You get cards.

Playing barrier games

To finish the *ar* words, play some barrier games. In barrier games, you each have a copy of the same picture or piece of writing, but you have a barrier between you so you each can't see the other person's paper. You can use a book as the barrier, or you can just turn your back to the other person. To play the game, you have to follow the other person's spoken instructions and write or draw exactly what he's writing or drawing on his sheet, in exactly the right place on the sheet. At the end of the activity, compare sheets and see how close you and your child came to having the same sheets. This game really helps your child listen, follow instructions, and read. You need to prepare first by making two copies of Table 17-1 and grabbing some colored pens.

Everything old is new again

If, like me, you're a little slow to think up hilarious stories and anecdotes for the "Talk about it" activity, borrow from traditional tales. To make your child laugh, you just have to change everything in a traditional story into its complete opposite. My daughter recently told me a great yarn she'd made up about Rapunzel. (Remember her? She had all that long hair that she let a prince climb up, dirty boots and all.) My daughter's Rapunzel was a modern-day teenager with short hair, attitude, and a rented apartment in a nice witch's castle. Moody Rapunzel treated the sweet misunderstood witch horribly and divided her time between treating the witch badly and trying to get away from a big nuisance prince. For inspiration with this kind of story, check out *The Stinky Cheese Man* by Jon Scieszka and Lane Smith (Viking Childrens Books, 2002).

To play, make sure neither of you can see the other player's paper, and then give directions. Here are some directions to get you going:

- Color the second word in the second column red.
- Cross out the last word in column three.
- Cross off the first word in column two.
- Circle the word *arm*.
- Circle the word that means the opposite of blunt.
- Draw a line joining *card* to *hard*.
- Put a red spot on the longest word.
- Draw a jar next to the word *jar*.
- Draw an apple next to the word *tart* (because apple tarts are yummy).
- Add two letters to the front of *art* to make *smart*.

After your child has the hang of barrier games, you can take turns giving the directions. But remember that no matter who gives the directions, you both have to write the answers on your own sheets so the sheets look the same at the end of the game.

More About *or*

Your child sees *or* on its own and as part of other words, too. She needs to get to know *or* well, so Table 17-2 paves the way. Have your child whiz all the way through the words, reading them to you and then writing a few of them, too. Tell her to watch out for the silent *w* in *sword*.

That *ar* word that begins with *f* and ends with *t*

Well, it's practically inevitable. At some point, your child's going to catch on to that *ar* word. So you may want to beat her to it. A new children's book about just this topic is selling fast. Children adore laughing about bodily functions, and the authors of this book are apparently making a fortune from their bright idea. What's the book the kids are raving about? *Walter the Farting* *Dog* by William Kotzwinkle and Glenn Murray (North Atlantic Books, 2001). You should be able to find this book in your local library. If you do take a look at it, check out the great illustrations and see if you can spot the little spider on every page. Or you can pretend I never mentioned any of this fart business and try not to think too badly of me.

The trouble with *a*'s

I have friends in all parts of the world. When I get together with them, we often tell stories about our accents and how hard it can be to make yourself understood in new places. My favorite story concerns an Irish friend, Sean. Sean, new to Australia from Ireland, stayed in my house for a few days. The first thing he wanted to do, after he got over his jet lag, was buy a phone card. Now the phrase "phone card" has a nice assortment of vowels, and the Irish pronunciation of *a* can mystify the sharpest ear. Anyway, Sean went off to a nearby shop to buy his phone card, and a local woman served him. "Can I have a phone card, please?" he said. But the woman heard something like "foornkeyart." Sean repeated his request several times but couldn't make himself understood. He was embarrassingly aware of the line building up behind him. In the end, he nodded at whatever the woman was equally insistent on saying (which he couldn't understand, either) and had a bag thrust into his hand. Mortified by now, he quickly handed over five dollars, got change, and scurried home to my house. My husband and I thought this episode highly amusing and wondered delightedly what she had sold him. We opened the bag and found that Sean had bought himself four carrots.

Table 17-2		*or* Words
afford	airport	born
chore	cord	cork
corn	corner	for
fork	form	fort
horn	horse	lord
more	morning	normal
or	orchard	order
ordinary	porch	pork
port	short	sore
sort	storm	sword
torch	torn	transport
worn		

er, ir, and ur

You can sound out the straightforward *er, ir,* and *ur* family because one sound fits all. Your child just has to get used to the appearance of the three letter combinations. He needs to read a lot of words to do it, and you can help by offering dictation (another useful way for him to become familiar with the family). You have to provide a lot of words, so feel free to use the ones that appear in Table 17-3.

Table 17-3	*er, ir,* and *ur* Words	
er	*ir*	*ur*
brother	bird	burglar
clever	dirt	burn
computer	fir	curl
farmer	firm	curse
faster	girl	fur
father	shirt	hurl
fern	sir	hurt
germ	stir	nurse
her	third	purr
mother	thirsty	purse
never	whirl	suburb
perch		surf
sister		turf
stern		turtle
teacher		urn
term		
birch		

Activity: The opposite quiz.

For the answers to this quiz, your child needs to look at Tables 17-1 and 17-2. If he likes to write, have him find the answers and then write them down. If he's not keen on writing, have him simply find the right word. If you've made a copy of the tables, he can color, circle, or cross off the answers. This quiz is all about opposites, so you may want to refresh your child on opposites before you start. Tell him about up and down, big and small, and hot and cold. Then launch into the ten questions in the following list of opposites (and almost opposites):

1. Not tall but . . .
2. Not mother but . . .
3. Not blunt but . . .
4. Not knife but . . .
5. Not less but . . .
6. Not beef but . . .
7. Not near but . . .
8. Not stop but . . .
9. Not leg but . . .
10. Not evening but . . .

The next activity calls for some careful looking. Your child needs to find the right word and then the exact letters that make up that word. For this activity, your child can work best on a whiteboard. Print out the words I give you in the following list, including the blank spaces, and have your child fill in the missing letters. You and your child can find the answers in Tables 17-1, 17-2, and 17-3.

Fill in the missing letters:

1. You can play games on it: comput – – .
2. You get out of bed at this time of the day: morn – – g.
3. This person grows crops: f – – mer.
4. You eat this: c – – n.
5. You can ride on this animal: h – – se.
6. This person looks after you in the hospital: n – – se.
7. This is the opposite of him: h – – .

8. You get wet and cold if you're out in a st – – m.

9. A witch can put this on you: c – – se.

10. Apples grow here: orch – – d.

Taking Care with air

I haven't yet mentioned one important sound — the *air* sound that you shouldn't confuse with all the vowel+r words. The *air* sound is a distinctive and common sound. It always sounds the same, but it changes its look from *air* to *are* and occasionally to *ear* (like in *bear*). Table 17-4 gives you a lot of cool words to read through with your child. Don't forget to let your child lead the way because she should find this particular bunch of words *fairly* easy.

Table 17-4	*air* and *are* Words
air	bare
chair	care
Claire	dare
fair	fare
pair	hare
hair	stare
stairs	flare
flair	mare
	share
	rare
	scare
	blare

Here are some nice questions to ask your child about Table 17-5. Put the table in front of her and see if she can tell you the answers:

1. A thing you sit on.

2. A place that has fun pony rides and cotton candy.

3. What you breathe.

4. A girl's name.

5. You walk up and down these.

6. You brush this.

7. When you look hard, you do this.

8. This means two.

9. This animal looks like a rabbit.

10. If you have no clothes on, you're this.

After you've cruised through the ten questions, ask your child to find the pairs of words, the ones that you spell different but sound exactly the same. What does each word mean? The pairs are *fair, fare; flair, flare; hair, hare;* and *stairs, stare.*

Great rhymes for great children

I have a new word coming up in this sidebar, so if you haven't already done it, show it to your child now. The word is *bear.*

I started off sensibly enough with these rhymes. I thought I should include a rhyme that features the *or* sound to help you and your child. Then I got carried away. So now I have four rhymes that I can't fit in to one of the sections in this chapter at all but are really cute (and which you can teach to your child to help him recognize and remember *or, ar,* and *air* words). See if he can find the vowel+r words in these rhymes:

Where's that boy?

✔ Little boy blue, come blow your horn,

The sheep's in the meadow, the cow's in the corn.

And where is the boy who looks after the sheep?

I don't know, but he's in big trouble!

Look out Jack!

✔ Jack be nimble, Jack be quick,

Jack jump over the candlestick.

Jack! Your pants are on fire!

Modest Mary

✔ Mary had a little lamb,

Its fleece was white as snow,

And everywhere that Mary went,

She stepped in lamb poop.

✔ Mary had a little lamb,

She also had a bear,

I often saw her little lamb,

But I never saw her bear. (As my kids would say now, "Get it? Do you get it? *Bear,* you know, *bare!*")

Chapter 18

Silent (But Not Deadly) Letters

Silent letters are strange things. Who knows why you use them in the first place? But because you find them all over the place, this chapter confronts them head on.

Here you help your child get the knack of *knee* and *kneel,* you take care with *comb* and *crumb,* and you may *bristle* over *castle* and *rustle.* You can find all sorts of unlikely combinations of letters in this chapter, and some really handy tips for helping your child sound them out, or not!

A Smorgasbord of Silent Letters

Before going any further, let me give you a table. It gives you a good look at the words I talk about in this chapter. Table 18-1 is long, but (believe it or not) it gives you only a selection from the whole smorgasbord. I've included some tricky words, not so you panic over them now, but so this book is a resource that you can come back to time and time again. If your child's a real high flyer, you may want to go over some of these words now. If not, you can mentally set this table aside for later. Don't think your child has to miss out on this list, though. Table 18-2 features the easiest words from Table 18-1, so you have something to start on right away.

Table 18-1			A Reference List of Silent Letters			
_k_	_b_	_l_	_gh_	_w_	_t_	_g_
knack	bomb	balm	blight	wrap	bristle	align
knead	climb	calm	bought	wreath	bustle	campaign
knee	comb	could	bright	wreck	castle	champagne
kneel	crumb	embalm	brought	wren	gristle	design
knew	debt	folk	delight	wrench	hustle	diaphragm
knick	doubt	palm	fight	wrestle	rustle	resign
knife	lamb	should	flight	wretch	thistle	sign
knight	limb	would	fought	wriggle	whistle	
knit	plumber	yolk	fright	wring		
knob	thumb		high	wrinkle		
knock	tomb		light	wrist		
knoll	womb		might	write		
knot			night	writhe		
know			ought	wrong		
knowledge			plight			
knuckle			right			
			sight			
			slight			
			sought			
			thigh			
			thought			
			tight			

Starting Off Easy

You can find some real whoppers among the weirder silent-letter words. Consider some of the silent _p_ words: _psychology, psychotic, pneumatic,_ and _pneumonia._ You can chew on these words for hours, if you want to! Then you have the words that end in *ue*. Try them out for size: *fatigue, morgue,* and *colleague*. They just get more and more weird, don't they?

Thankfully, beginning readers don't need to get bogged down in all these words — and neither do you. You can come back to the words in Table 18-1 farther down the line. For now, you need only show your child some of the more straightforward words. To make this introduction really easy, Table 18-2 lists the easiest words from Table 18-1.

Use Table 18-2 to show your child how silent letters unexpectedly appear. Then those sneaky silent letters can't catch him unawares when he finds them in the books he's reading. Go slowly and share the quirkiness of silent letters. Have your child mark the silent letters with a pencil circle or a highlighter mark. Spot the other word groups that these words belong to, too. You can see some double vowels and some words that belong in word families. Your child can remember *knew* more easily, for example, if you jot it down with its other family members: *few, new, chew,* and *stew.*

Table 18-2			An Easy List of Silent Letters		
k	*b*	*l*	*gh*	*w*	*t*
knack	bomb	calm	blight	wrap	castle
knead	climb	could	bright	wreath	whistle
knee	comb	folk	delight	wreck	
kneel	crumb	palm	fight	wren	
knew	lamb	should	flight	wrench	
knick	limb	would	fright	wriggle	
knife	plumber	yolk	high	wring	
knight	thumb		light	wrinkle	
knit			might	wrist	
knob			night	write	
knock			plight	wrong	
knoll			right		
knot			sight		
know			slight		
			thigh		
			tight		

Hunting and Highlighting

You know what you may find very useful in your reading activities? Highlighter pens. When you're drawing your child's attention to parts of words, writing the parts out gets tedious. If you have your child find and color different letters, she has much more fun. Table 18-2 has a lot of potential when it comes to highlighter pens, so invest in some groovy colors and venture forth. To keep this book nice, you may want to copy Table 18-2 before letting your child loose with her highlighters. Give her the copy and then tell her things to hunt for, using these examples as ideas:

- ✔ The *ight* family is a big group. Count how many *ight* words are in the table. Write the number on the back of your sheet. Choose your favorite highlighter and highlight the *ight* part in each word so that you can see it really well.

- ✔ You can find four "When two vowels go walking, the first one does the talking" words here. Find them and highlight them in a good color so that you separate them from the rest.

- ✔ In the silent *l* group, you can find three families of words that rhyme and have the same spelling pattern. Choose three more colors and highlight each family in a different color.

- ✔ The *le* ending is very common. I see three of these endings — can you spot them? Highlight them.

- ✔ Put your finger on column three. Look at the words and figure out which one you'd find inside an egg. When you find it, cross it out.

- ✔ Go to column four. A word there means the opposite of low. See if you can find it and put a circle around it.

- ✔ See if you can find the word for what I'm doing. (Now whistle.) It's not at the beginning of the table.

- ✔ Column two has something that you use on your hair. Put a box around it.

- ✔ You can cut with something in column one. Count how many letters are in that word and write the number next to it.

- ✔ You can build one of these from sand. It appears in the last column. Cross it off.

- ✔ What do you switch on at night? It's in the fourth column. Put a circle around it.

- ✔ In the second column, you can find the name of the person who fixes the water pipes in your house. Cross this person off.

- If I'm not right, then what am I? Find this word in column five. Cross it off.
- Column one has a word that's a part of a leg. Put a line through this word.
- Column four also has a word that's part of a leg. Put a line through that word, too.
- In column two, you can find a word that's part of a hand. Put a line through that word.

Knock, knock

How can I pass through *kn* words without being reminded of "Knock, knock" jokes? Knock, knock jokes keep the word *knock* stuck in your child's mind forever. Read my pick of the bunch and see if you can add some of your own. If you feel creative, make a joke book. When you're at the library, grab a handful of joke books. You and your child can have a lot of fun reading, and because you've been concentrating on tables of words for a while now, you both need to reward yourselves!

Knock, knock jokes help your child with the word *who,* as well as the word *knock.* Your child probably finds *who* a really slippery word to get a grip on for two reasons:

- It doesn't belong to a word family (all the words that rhyme with it have different spelling patterns, for instance *zoo* and *too; knew* and *few;* and *true* and *glue*).

- It doesn't sound out properly (why isn't it *wo,* as in *wok?*).

The following "Knock, knock" jokes can help your child get the hang of this stuff:

- Knock, knock
  Who's there?

Justin
Justin who?
Justin the neighborhood and thought I'd drop in!

- Knock, knock
  Who's there?
  Egbert
  Egbert who?
  Egbert no bacon please

- Knock, knock
  Who's there?
  Granny
  Granny who?

  Knock, knock
  Who's there?
  Granny
  Granny who?

  Knock, knock
  Who's there?
  Aunt
  Aunt who?
  Aunt you glad all those grannies have gone!

Your child's paper looks pretty colorful, doesn't it? Now you can use the space at the bottom of the page, or on the other side, for a few dictated words. Dictate these words for her to write. If she can't write the words from memory, let her find them in Table 18-2 to see how they look.

1. light

2. night

3. sight

4. know

5. knew

Your child may not understand what the word "dictate" means. Just tell her that *dictate* means to read or say something out loud for someone else to write down.

Show and Tell

This section focuses on talking, not writing. This activity is a bit like classroom show-and-tell, only you don't get to see any lizards or the novelty soap that little Johnny's dad thinks he has safely hidden away; just some words.

To start, read through the next questions with your child. The questions ask you things about the words in Table 18-2, and you get to decide together how you want to answer. Let your child beat you to the answers, and show him that you're interested in his responses. He likes your attention and doesn't notice that he's having his visual discrimination and reading skills sharpened, in the bargain. (*Visual discrimination* is a fancy way of describing how you start to look carefully at words so that you can see the different letters and word parts.) Ask your child these questions:

✔ What's your favorite word in the list?

✔ What's the easiest word in the list?

✔ What's the hardest word in the list? (This word isn't necessarily the longest.)

✔ Which word do you think you'd see most often in books?

✔ Which word is the longest? The shortest?

✔ How many words do you think are in this table, all together?

✔ Which column is longest? Which is shortest?

✔ Which two words each have a double letter in them?

Be quiet, Quentin, or I quit!

I haven't mentioned one silent letter — the *u* that tags along with *q*. You can teach this letter very easily because you just have to tell your child that while *u* can go out on its own, *u* always has to babysit *q* when it goes out. But also tell her that she should completely ignore that *u*. See how this rule works in these words:

✔ quick

✔ quack

✔ queen

✔ quest

✔ quiet

✔ quite

Pay special attention to *quiet* and *quite* because they look so darned similar. Point out the endings. Write each word in big letters and have your child trace over the end letters in a color and sound them out.

Alphabet of Silent Letters

I have a piece of very trivial trivia about silent letters to share with you: Every — well, nearly every — letter of the alphabet gets into silent mode at some time. Take a look:

✔ **a:** *head, bread,* and *dead.*

✔ **b:** *debt, lamb,* and *bomb.*

✔ **c:** *muscle, yacht,* and *indict.*

✔ **d:** *Wednesday* and (depending how you pronounce them) *handkerchief* and *handbag,* too.

✔ **e:** *live, give,* and all the *bossy e* words that you can read about in Chapter 12 (*tale, Pete, mine, bone,* and *cute*).

✔ **f:** I had a tough time finding a word with a silent f, but *halfpenny* qualifies, at least when pronounced by British people.

✔ **g:** *gnome, fight,* and all the other *ight* words.

✔ **h:** *honor, heir,* and *ghost.*

✔ **i:** *business.*

✔ **k:** *know, knee,* and *knock.*

✔ **l:** *talk, yolk,* and *salmon.*

✔ **m:** *mnemonic.*

✔ **n:** *hymn.*

✔ **o:** *leopard* and *jeopardy.*

✔ **p:** *psalm, cupboard,* and *receipt.*

✔ **q(u):** *lacquer.*

✔ **r:** *myrrh.* (Did I mention that some of these words are a little obscure?)

✔ **s:** *isle* and *aisle.*

✔ **t:** *bristle, fasten,* and *mortgage.*

✔ **u:** *build, guild,* and *plague.*

✔ **w:** *whole, write,* and *sword.*

✔ **y:** sort of silent in *prayer* and *mayor.*

✔ **z:** *rendezvous.*

You're just about to finish with your sheet of paper. You've certainly had your money's worth from your copy by now! Have your child count the words on his paper that have no markings at all. Create a goal first, though. Count the words yourself and write the number in a hidden place. Your child has to find your hidden number (give him hints when he's "hot" or "cold") and check his number against yours.

Chapter 19

Getting Beyond Sounds and Rules

In This Chapter

▶ Looking at reading from a wider perspective

▶ Playing games to build your child's skills

*T*eachers tell you to read to your child as much as possible, not only because they know that your child loves it, but so that your child gets to know text well — how you put words together and how you make stories out of plots and sequences. Why does your child need to know text? When he reads, he can cross the reading landscape better if he's familiar with it.

Say that you have the choice of reading a thesis on vasculogenesis (a quaint scientific term I happened to have up my sleeve) or the parable of the Good Samaritan. Which would you choose? Unless you're bent on broadening your mind, you'd probably go for the Good Samaritan story. You'd be able to read the thesis okay (sounding out the terms you'd never heard before), but you'd find it hard and dull. By contrast, you've heard a lot of stories. You can make good predictions about plot, sequencing, and grammar, so the story would be easy for you to read. The same is true for your child. If he's had a lot of stories and text read to him, he's familiar with plot, sequencing, and grammar. And that helps him read when he starts all on his own.

Reading Well: It's More Than Just Sounding Out Words

Reading isn't just a matter of putting sounds together. Sure, your child starts off relying heavily on phonics and word rules, but she learns to read between and around the lines. She learns to predict and skim, too. In school, her teacher helps her develop these skills by having her talk about text and make predictions about plot. As she gets better at reading, she uses these skills more and relies less on phonics. If you were reading that vasculogenesis thesis I mention in the introduction to this chapter, you'd rely heavily on phonics to sound out unfamiliar terms. If you were reading the Good Samaritan story, you'd assess, predict, and confidently skim your way through.

Looking at the good things teachers do

When teachers read a book to kids, they often spend time doing follow-up activities. They make story webs, maps, and graphs of the stories they read. They make models of the characters. They ask kids to bring things to school that have something to do with the stories. They get kids immersed in stories so that they understand sequencing, plot, and the structure of sentences. Teachers spend time getting kids to evaluate and predict so that they have a reader's eye view of things. This perspective helps the children with their own reading.

Reading around and between the lines

Evaluation is a fancy word for reading around and between the lines. When your child gets an idea of what motivates the characters in a story, what it's like to live where the characters live, and how the story makes him feel, he's evaluating the text. To help your child engage with the text and absorb implicit writing conventions and style, read great stories to and with him. Discuss them. Answer his questions about them. Act out the scenes. Impersonate the characters. Find out more about the setting.

Reading ahead of the lines

When your child guesses about what will happen next in a story, she's *predicting,* or reading ahead of the lines. We all naturally predict when we read, but you can train your child to do it by asking questions. "What do you think will happen next?" "Do you think the good brother will win in the end?" "How do you think the little girl will escape?" These questions help your child get a mental sketch. With this sketch, she can narrow down the choices of plot and vocabulary in a text. If she's reading an adventure fantasy, she expects to read words like *dragon, prison,* and *wizard,* rather than words like *make-up, girlfriend,* and *mall.* She expects twists and turns in plot, maybe some deception and trickery. She cuts herself a rough reading path. She starts reading a book on more solid footing than a child who doesn't read and discuss books.

Finishing sentences before guessing at words

To help your child figure out a hard word, let him read past it until he's read the whole sentence or paragraph. Then, when he knows the meaning of the text, he can make better guesses at how to say the hard word. The sound of the first letter in the word helps, too. To help him get into the habit of relying on meaning, ask him what kind of words would be sensible options for the one he's trying to figure out. Then sound out parts of the hard word with him.

Giving your child control

You can't overlook the important aspect of having your child assess text by giving her control. When she gives her opinions about a story and does activities based on a story, she's in charge. She learns to trust her own judgment and feels she has know-how.

Building your child's confidence is every bit as important as teaching her reading skills. Confident kids do more things. They practice more and progress more quickly.

Don't *ever* let your child hear you say crushing things like, "She doesn't even know the simple words." Even if your child presents a tough front, your comments go deep. Thoughtless or inadvertent remarks hurt her and set her back in the learning process.

Grammar without the grind

The more reading around a text and discussing that you do, the better your child gets at knowing how text flows. He gets a better vocabulary and understanding of the conventions used in written text. He knows about grammar and punctuation without having the faintest idea of what the word *preposition* means. He picks it up by doing it. That's what teachers mean when they say that there's more to reading than phonics. Your child needs to get a grip on phonics, sight words, and reading skills, but he also needs to get immersed in real reading, too. When he chats about text, thinks about the characters, and feels that the story came alive for him, he's moving beyond the basic skills.

Helping your child self-correct

When your child gets to know text well, he's primed for self-correcting. When he writes stories of his own, he has a good inner voice to guide him. He says the story to himself and hears whether it flows smoothly. In later years, he needs to do a lot of self-correcting to write good school reports and projects. Reading a lot of good books and chatting about them in these early years lays a solid foundation.

Using key words and making outlines

Later on in her school years, your child will have to take notes. You can prepare her for note taking by helping her focus on key words now. When you talk about text with your child, ask her to identify the important words or sentences. Rewrite stories to get into the habit of condensing text. Ask your child to retell stories. If she enjoys giving performances, help her act out a story or tell it with puppets. An overturned card table works fine as a puppet theatre.

Using Activities to Improve Skills

You can help your child better understand text by doing activities with him that home in on different aspects of text. Check out some or all of the easy reading and writing activities that I recommend in the following sections.

Book logs

Have your child keep a simple book log. In the log, he records the name of each book he reads, the author, and what he thought of the book. If he doesn't like to write, have him find the title and author for you to write. Have him color or check off a book rating like *bad, OK,* or *good.* When he's read ten or twenty books, give him a reading prize.

Sequencing

For this activity, you read a story to your child and talk it over with her. Then you write or type a short and simple version. Cut your story into segments. Have your child put the segments together again and read the story back to you. Have her do the same in front of other family members and friends (to wild applause, naturally).

Beginnings and endings

You do this activity like you do sequencing. But instead of piecing a story back together, your child has to piece together the beginnings and endings of single sentences. Start by talking about a story and writing some simple sentences about it (Cinderella lived with her stepmother and two stepsisters). Cut the sentences in half. Put the beginnings in one pile (Cinderella lived with) and the endings in another (her stepmother and two stepsisters). Ask your child to fit the pairs together. Then he can put the sentences in sequence to rebuild the story, too.

Cloze it

Teachers do a lot of "cloze" exercises. They get children to fill in blank words in a sentence. To do this activity yourself, find or write a simple piece of text and cover or erase key words. If, for example, you use the story of Little Red Riding Hood, rewrite or copy the text and do something like this to it:

Little *** Riding Hood was going to visit her *******. Her Grandma was sick, so Little Red Riding Hood was taking her a basket of ****. Grandma lived on the other side of a ****. Little Red Riding Hood had to walk through the woods with her basket. Her mommy told her not to stop and not to talk to any *********.

Have your child read the text and guess the missing key words (usually nouns). Your child can fill in the blanks in a few different ways:

- Cover the key words with tape. When your child guesses correctly, have her pull the tape off the word.

- White out or cover over key words and write them on individual pieces of paper. Have your child put the words in place.

- White out or cover over key words and write them on individual pieces of paper. Have your child put the words in place and then take the words away and have her write them in the empty spaces from memory.

- White out or cover over key words and have your child write the missing words in the empty spaces, copying from a missing words list you give her.

- White out or cover over key words and have your child write them in the empty spaces from scratch.

The last two choices in the list are the hardest. Tell your child that you're not sure whether the task is a bit too hard for her, but would she like to try it? When she rises to the challenge, she enjoys showing you how you've underestimated her!

To make this activity more fun, think up silly responses, like "a basket of *wet towels/slime/pencils.*"

"Wanted" or "Missing" posters

Oh no! Little Red Riding Hood's gone missing and your child must make a "Missing" poster. On the poster, he should include a picture of Little Red Riding Hood and headings like *Hair Color, Eye Color, Height, Body Type, Special Features, Clothes,* and *Where This Person Was Last Seen.* He should prominently feature the reward, too. You can use this activity for any character in a book, and you can make it as silly as you want to.

School Report Card

Kids love to give out grades. Choose a favorite book character and have your child write a report card for him. Help your child decide on the school subjects she grades and what kind of grades the character earns. Did the character behave in any exceptional or terrible ways? Can he come back to school next year, or does your child have to expel him? Should the character be working harder at certain things? Subjects don't have to be realistic. In the case of Little Red Riding Hood, you may choose subjects like

- ✔ Packing picnic baskets
- ✔ Basket carrying
- ✔ Grooming (or dress sense)
- ✔ Remembering the path home
- ✔ Hiking
- ✔ Taking care of others
- ✔ Coping with an emergency

Making books

Because children love familiar stories and talking about themselves, your child loves creating homemade books. Make short and simple adaptations of favorite stories and books that tell about your child's life. Put one or two sentences on each page and fill the book with illustrations or photos. Your child loves reading them because they're familiar to him. If he has younger siblings, he feels grown up reading his books to them. And if you make pages from sturdy art paper and laminate the covers, books last longer.

Letters from book characters

Getting a letter from a friend is always nice. Capitalize on this pleasure, and on the power of humor, by writing your child some funny letters. Pretend to be a character from your child's book and write to another character in the book or your child. Adopt an opposite position to the one taken in the book. For example, if you were the wolf in the story of Little Red Riding Hood, you'd present yourself as the mistreated and misunderstood party, like this letter:

> Dear Grandma,
>
> I am so sorry that I gave you a fright last week. But the strangest thing happened to me. I was walking along in the summer breeze when a very rude girl almost knocked me over. She was wearing a red cape and wanted to tell me how much it cost. I tried to be polite, but she just kept bothering me . . .
>
> Your dear friend,
>
> The Wolf

Make your child laugh and show her how you can write stories from different perspectives. If you want to spend a few days doing this activity, make your child a special mailbox (from a cereal box) and send her several letters about the books you're reading together. You can pretend to know nothing about the letters (although your child really knows you write them). Your child may think that you're a comic genius (and you can have some fun).

Lunch bag puppets

Puppets made out of lunch bags are cool! You can have fun making them and using them to act out stories you've read. To make a puppet, you need

- ✔ A lunch bag
- ✔ Markers, crayons, or paint
- ✔ Scissors
- ✔ Glue

Optional extras:

- ✔ Construction paper (for arms, legs, and clothes)
- ✔ Yarn or cotton wool (for hair)
- ✔ Scrap material (for clothes)

You need to remember, with paper bag puppets, to draw the puppet's face on the bottom flap of the bag — the part that would normally sit on the table.

1. Start by laying your bag flat on the table in front of you with the bottom flap facing you.

2. Draw the puppets face on the bottom flap.

   To make a sticking-out tongue, draw only eyes and a nose on the bottom flap. Draw the mouth below the flap and glue a tongue inside the flap, poking out.

3. Draw the body.

4. Add arms and legs by sticking them into the sides of the bag.

5. Decorate and add features as you like.

To see examples and to print templates, visit these Web sites:

✔ www.storyplace.org/preschool/activities/takehomeprint.asp

✔ www.funroom.com/paperbagpuppet.html

The miserable missions

When my family moved to California from Australia, we all had a lot of new things to learn. My kids had to learn particularly fast. Their classmates talked about topics and history that they'd never heard of.

One topic I remember all too well is the missions of California. My eldest child, in grade 4, had to do a report on the missions. That report was loathsome. It seemed like every night she brought home a new wad of badly copied text that was as dull as anything I'd ever been stuck with before. Long columns of dates. Dozens of hard-to-pronounce names. Dreary, 'who really cares?' details. I hated that report and had the hardest time making my child plough through it.

But my story doesn't end there. Next to my child's class was another grade 4 class. The child of a friend of mine was in that class. When I went for a coffee and to complain with my friend, she had a whole different perspective on the onerous missions. "We're just loving this report," she gushed. "Natalie's made the coolest model of a mission, and we've been visiting missions every weekend. The history is fascinating. She's doing theatre performances in class and has done all sorts of role-playing stuff." Out of curiosity (and masochism), I visited Natalie's classroom. Sure enough, the missions were alive. Models and posters adorned the whole place, and the kids were enthused. My daughter was sounding out and decoding long dreary pieces of text while these kids were breathing life into a great story. And that's why reading is just as much about exploring text and bringing it to life as it is about phonics. Who do you think got the most from that report, my daughter or ('you lucked out') Natalie?

Part V
Reading, Reading, and More Reading

"It had an interesting emotional arc and some nice plot twists, but the heroine and subsidiary characters were unconvincing within the historical context."

In this part . . .

When you leave your child to read alone, does he read or daydream? How can you tell? Is his book too hard or perhaps too easy for him? This part helps you guide your child to the book that's just right for him. It takes a look at selecting and using workbooks, too. And after looking at what this part tells you about reading out loud, you may want to squeeze it into your schedule, no matter how busy. The end of this part gives you no-frills, practical information about reading difficulties. Knowing what to expect from your child can be a comfort, so this part shows you how to spot any reading problems and what to do if you find any.

Chapter 20

Choosing Just-Right Reading Books

My children are fluent readers, but the other night, they were entranced with a pop-up book they'd enjoyed as toddlers. I was making my usual ill-fated attempt to get rid of surplus toys and books when *The Lift-the-Flap Animal Book* stymied me. My kids spotted the cover, and there was no going back. For the whole evening, they pored through books they'd last looked at when they were in diapers. When at last they were done, all the books were lovingly replaced on already over-crowded bookshelves. And that's the thing about books. Anything can catch your children's attention, even the things you'd least expect. Should you ban "lesser" reading? No.

You can choose from so many wonderful books these days that it can be hard to know where to start. Should you go for the most attractive illustrations, the coolest theme (ghosts, bugs, Barbie), or the best text? How do you decide the best text, and should you even be doing the selecting at all? Is it best to let your child have free rein? This chapter answers all these questions and more. To start with, though, you need to do some judicious selecting of books for your child to read all by himself and give him the run of the local library, too.

One man's meat is another man's poison

Your child needs to feel, see, and hear good literature. But good literature can mean all sorts of things. It can be *Huckleberry Finn* or a *Tin Tin* comic. Within safe limits, if it appeals to your child, it's good literature for him. Make time to enjoy books, comics, and games with your child, make sure he gets time to browse books by himself, and plan for his success with all-by-himself reading, too. Gather books he can easily sound out, and plenty of them.

Guidelines for Finding the Book That's Just Right

When you're trying to direct your child to themes that may interest her, you probably have a good idea of what you're looking for. Leave her at the bookshelves with books about things that interest her and prepare to thin down the wheelbarrow of books that she wants! It's usually not hard for kids to gather books they want to look at or have you read to them. The harder choice comes with books for kids to read by themselves. Are some beginners' books better than others? Should you keep an eye out for certain book series? What kind of text is just right? Here are a few answers:

✔ Some beginners' books are known favorites. They've been around for years and that's because people go on liking them year after year. The king in this category is probably Dr. Seuss.

✔ Besides the Dr. Seuss books, keep an eye open for beginners' books that limit the number and difficulty of words. Your child may struggle with dozens of new words in one go, so choose books with just a few new words. I really like *Real Kids Readers* (Millbrook Press), but you can find dozens of series out there. The best thing to do is make regular trips to the library. You can get to know the titles that work best for your child.

✔ When you look at the text in a book, look from the point of view of your child. Gauge the text according to how many words she knows and how many she doesn't know. Pick books that don't present a giant leap but give a gentle progression from the last book. Read the book to your child before she reads it and focus on new words so that she gets extra practice on them. Show her the new words and write each new word on a small piece of paper or an index card. Put the new words into an envelope and read them together every night for a week.

What to remember about remembering things

It's a fairly sure bet that if I have something on my mind when I'm at the top of my staircase, and I walk down the staircase, by the time I've reached the bottom, I've forgotten it. My memory is probably worse than most, but all of us need to have several exposures to new information before we remember it. We can only remember a few things at one time, and need a lot of repetition. So, when your child comes upon new words in a book, give her practice with those words so she can remember them for next time. Put words, no more than ten at a time, into an envelope to practice with your child every night for a week. Make it fun, though, and keep the mood light.

If your child is having trouble reading books for herself, make sure you read each book to her first, before she has a go. Have her read one book two or three times so she gets better at it each time and feels more confident. Have her read the book to friends and family if she likes doing it. Tell the audience to be suitably impressed.

The one-hand rule for choosing a book

When your child has made a start on reading books all by himself, he may think he's a little more capable than he really is. After his first burst of success, he may think he's ready for the big, fat books that the bigger kids read. He may gather an armful of books that make your heart sink. Should you tell him to return them to the shelves? Should you let him find out the natural consequences of trying to read these books? Should you pretend nothing's wrong? Here are some tips:

- ✔ When your child chooses an obviously too-hard book, don't panic. Let him have the book to browse.
- ✔ When your child chooses an obviously too-easy book, fine. Let him have some relaxed enjoyment.

When you choose a book for your child to read on his own, choose one with not too many new words. Show him the new words before tackling the whole book so he can read fluently without having to stop and start at unknown words.

If he's choosing a book for himself, show him the *one-hand rule*. The one-hand rule says that if he finds more than five words he doesn't know on any one page of text, the book's too hard. Get your child to put up one finger for every unknown word on the page. When he has all five fingers up (or one hand), he can't allow anymore unknown words.

The one-hand rule is made on this assumption: For text to be within your child's comfort zone, it shouldn't be too hard — only slightly challenging. If it's 95 percent work-outable (or decodable), it's good. Five percent should be unknown words, and that equals 5 words in any 100 words. To make the one-hand rule work, your child should be using it on a page with about 100 words. If he's reading a much shorter page, he should figure on having less than five new words per page.

Size, space, text, and pictures

When it comes to choosing first books for your child to read all by himself, small is definitely beautiful. Beginners want to read a whole book, and they have a hard task ahead of them if the book has a lot of pages and writing. It's better to give your child a lot of short books than one big book, unless your child is very good at pacing himself and getting big tasks done.

Choose short books and look for good spacing. If you want your child to read some of the classics you loved as a child, ask at your library for modern versions. These days, a lot of classics have been reorganized into a collection of shorter and friendlier-looking books. Illustrations are important these days, too. Most books have great illustrations, and some of them include search-for-it features. Let your child pore over the illustrations before and during the reading because, besides being fun, the illustrations give him contextual cues to help with figuring out the words. *Contextual cues* are things in the cover, text, and illustrations of a book that give useful hints about what the main text says. If your child sees pictures of dragons and words like *big, green,* and *hot,* he has the contextual cues to tell him that a long word starting with *dr* is probably *dragon.*

If your child is having trouble with letters and pictures in books, have his eyes examined. Also browse the Internet for advice from other parents. One parent I know found advice about using color filters to help her son read. Her child hasn't been diagnosed as having a vision problem, but putting a colored plastic sheet over the pages in his books helps him.

Series Make Great Sense

When your child starts reading, she's like a fire. She needs a lot of fuel, and you need to keep her supplied. Make sure your child always has plenty of books by becoming a regular library user. Make a routine of going to the library to get an armful of books, stories on tape, CDs, and videos.

Give your child free rein at the bookshelves. Let her choose any books she likes the look of because even if she can't read them for herself, you can read them to her, or you can read together (which I give you some pointers on in Chapter 22). You should also look for books that she can read by herself. Go to the beginner's section and scan through the books. Choose books with just a few words and good illustrations to start with. Look for phonetically controlled books and ask the librarian about good book series.

Some of the best book series for kids to read all by themselves are listed in the next tables, Tables 20-1 to 20-5.

Table 20-1	Level 1: Books for Absolute Beginners	
Title	*Author*	*Publisher*
Bob Books	Bobby Lynn Maslen	Scholastic
Fitzroy Readers	Faye Berryman	Fitzroy Programs www.fitzprog.com.au
Primary Phonics	Barbara W. Makar	Educators Publishing Service, Inc. www.epsbooks.com
Read with Ladybird Key Words to Reading	various	Penguin Books, Ltd.

Table 20-1 gives books that are *phonetically controlled,* meaning the words in these books are limited and easy to sound out. The books warn you of new words so you can go over them with your child before she starts to read the book. Then, when she comes to the new word, she can recognize it and doesn't get halted in her reading. (For more on phonetically controlled books, see the sidebar "Phonetically controlled books.")

I've provided an Internet address for two of the series because you can't get them from bookstores. All these books are great for the absolute beginner or the child who's struggling.

Table 20-2	Level 2: Books for Warming Up Beginners	
Title	*Author*	*Publisher*
Dr. Seuss books	Dr. Seuss	Random House
Real Kids Readers	various	Millbrook Press

Phonetically controlled books

The title of this sidebar is a real mouthful isn't it? I have to put it this way because otherwise the title would be too long — something like: "Books with words that mostly sound out in a regular way." Books that are *phonetically controlled* are books that move steadily forward in terms of word difficulty, starting with titles like *Fat Cat*. They give all phonetically regular words (words that can be sounded out) to start off with, and move forward slowly. You may get *Big Pig* as your second book, *Bug on a Rug* as book number three, *The Hot Pot* as book number four, and so on. You only get about four or five new words in each book, and usually they write these words on the cover so you know they're coming.

Phonetically controlled books are great for a thorough and slow progression. Use them if your child prefers them to the books that move forward quicker because they can work wonders for building your child's confidence and getting him really reading. Many children love these books because they feel like *real* reading. Sounding out feels like something they have control over, so even if you think titles like *Fat Cat* sound tame, your child probably loves being able to read an entire book independently. Ask the local library for advice. When you get a few books, have your child read and reread as often as he likes.

Table 20-3 Level 3: Books for Racing Forward Beginners

Title	Author	Publisher
Reading Rainbow Readers	various	SeaStar Books
Water — All Aboard Science Reader (Station Stop 1)	Emily Neye	Grosset and Dunlap

Table 20-4 Level 4: Books for Seasoned Readers

Title	Author	Publisher
A to Z Mysteries	Ron Roy	Random House
Amelia Bedelia	Peggy Parish	HarperCollins
Arthur	Marc Brown	Little, Brown and Company
The Bailey School Kids	Debbie Dadey	Scholastic
Cam Jansen	David A. Adler	Puffin
Captain Underpants	Dav Pilkey	Blue Sky Press

Title	Author	Publisher
More Clue Mysteries	Vicki Cameron	Running Press
Encyclopedia Brown	Donald J. Sobol	Skylark
Junie B. Jones	Barbara Parker	Random House
The Littles	John Peterson	Scholastic
The Magic School Bus	various	Scholastic
Magic Tree House	Mary Pope Osborne	Random House
Nate The Great	Marjorie Sharmat	Yearling Books
The Secrets of Droon	Tony Abbott	Scholastic
Stories (including *Noddy*)	Enid Blyton	Dean and Son, Ltd.

Table 20-5	Level 5: Books for Fluent Readers	
Title	*Author*	*Publisher*
The American Girl's Collection (including *Kirsten: An American Girl: 1854*)	various	Pleasant Company Publications
Animorphs	Katherine A. Applegate	Apple
Chronicles of Narnia	C.S. Lewis	HarperCollins
Deltora Quest	Emily Rodda	Apple
Goosebumps	R.L. Stine	HarperCollins
Hardy Boys	Franklin Dixon	Price Stern and Sloane Publishing
Harry Potter	J.K. Rowling	Scholastic
Little House on the Prairie stories	Laura Ingalls Wilder	HarperCollins
Nancy Drew Mystery Stories	Carolyn Keene	Price Stern and Sloane Publishing
A Series of Unfortunate Events	Lemony Snicket	HarperCollins
Sports books	Matt Christopher	Little, Brown and Company

A lot of book series have Web sites. You may like to check out:

- **Arthur:** www.pbs.org/arthur/index.html
- **Goosebumps:** www.scholastic.com/Goosebumps
- **The Magic School Bus:** www.scholastic.com/MagicSchoolBus

Your library has lists of award-winning books for different ages and interests. Check out the American Library Association at www.ala.org/alsc (click the Resources link for information about award-winning books).

For interactive storybooks on CD-ROM, check out the *Living Books* series with titles like *Sheila Rae, the Brave* (HarperTrophy, 1996) and *New Kid on the Block* (Greenwillow, 1984).

A Word about Age and Gender

If you're helping an older child, you want to avoid books with babyish pictures and themes. If you're helping a boy, some themes have more appeal for him than others. And if you're helping a girl, you may find that *Animorphs* gross her out. Table 20-6 has a few helpful hints for all these issues. But remember that all kids are different! These books have wide appeal, and your child may surprise you with his or her preferences. I know plenty of boys who adore *Junie B. Jones* and have two daughters who read *Goosebumps* avidly, though I'd never have pegged them as fear-loving types.

Table 20-6	Books Geared Toward Your Child's Age and Gender
Who You're Helping	*What to Take a Look At*
Older children	*Fitzroy Readers:* School teachers in an alternative school for older children write these books.
Boys	Science books published by Dorling Kindersley: Titles include *Facts about Dinosaurs, Facts about Insects,* and *Facts about Planet Earth*
	Nate The Great
	Goosebumps
	Deltora Quest
	Animorphs
	Hardy Boys
	Sports books by Matt Christopher

Who You're Helping	What to Take a Look At
Girls	Amelia Bedelia
	Junie B. Jones
	Nancy Drew Mystery Stories
	Little House on the Prairie stories
	The American Girl's Collection

My guess is that the all-time nonfiction favorite for kids is the *Guinness Book of Records.* This annual publication is filled with short bits of interesting information about who or what is currently biggest, smallest, fastest, or unique in all manner of other ways. A close second may be *Ripley's Believe it Or Not.* This book grabs your attention with the weird-out factor by telling you things like how long a three-headed sheep in Arizona lived. Another phenomenon you may want to look into is the *Where's Waldo?* series. This collection of intricately drawn picture books hides a lot of characters in each picture. You have to read a description of who (or what) you're to find in the pictures, and get searching. Sounds simple, doesn't it? But after you start searching, you may find yourself getting hooked.

Making Room for Comics and 'Zines

If you look carefully at the things you expect of your child, you probably find that you sometimes expect him to do things you never do. Sometimes, you expect him to read books when he just doesn't feel like it. Forcing things on your child is no good because as he gets older, he gets better at saying, "No." It's better to give him a wide choice of reading materials. He may like reading things on the Web, and he may like comics and magazines. You can find some great comics and magazines aimed at children today, and at the risk of repeating myself for the umpteenth time, your library should stock them. Table 20-7 gives a few titles.

Monitor the sites that your child visits to read things online. In Chapter 23, I talk more about how to keep watch on what your child has access to on the Internet without always hovering over his shoulder.

Table 20-7	Comics and 'Zines for Young Readers
Under 7's	*Over 7's*
Ladybug	Cricket
Preschool Playroom	The Adventures of Tin Tin
Zoobooks	Appleseeds
Children's Magic Window	Ask
	Dig
	Muse
	Spider
	National Geographic Kids

When your child has control and ownership of what he reads, he gets more from it.

A Summary of Easy Reading Hints

This heading sums up the whole of this book. Can I put the whole of this book into one little section? No. But here's the next best thing. You can find the essential points I've been making about sounding out, sight words, and all the other great ways to help kids read by themselves in the following sections.

Whenever you listen to your child read out loud to you, be extra sensitive. Try to put yourself in his place and feel how humiliating or deflating the slightest hint of criticism can be!

Spotting new words before reading

Before your child reads a book, skim it for unfamiliar words. Show the words to your child and help her sound them out and notice their appearance. Then she can read them in context, and her reading becomes more fluent. (When your child has to take a lot of figuring-out breaks in her reading, she finds it hard to remember the plot and sense of the text.) See "Guidelines for Finding the Book That's Just Right" earlier in the chapter for more on helping your child with unfamiliar words.

Reading around the book

Before your child starts to read a book, have him look at the title and pictures to get a feel of what's coming up. He gets an idea of the kind of vocabulary and plot to expect.

Sounding out (phonics)

Teach your child to sound out words, or parts of words, whenever she can. (See Chapter 8 for an introduction to sounding out words.) But if your child can't easily sound out a word, maybe a word like *who* or *what,* simply tell her what the word says. And tell her to watch out for it. Break it up and color the tricky letters. For example, you may want to show your child to break *what* into two parts — *wh* and *at.* You can explain that *wh* sounds out but *at* makes an unexpected *ot* sound.

Making word families

Show your child how to put new words into word families (see Chapter 12 to find out about word families). If he comes upon *found,* for example, show him the *ou* family: *bound, pound, loud, cloud, out,* and *shout.*

Spotting visual features

With tricky words like *who,* that don't sound out or belong to a family, your child must remember *visual features* (the shape of the word, the rough length of the word, double letters, or other distinguishing features). Stick words like *who* on the wall so your child sees them often. Put them on index cards (no more than ten) to read every night for a week.

Remembering sight words

Guide your child steadily through the list of 220 sight words in Chapter 11. Play with ten every week until she recognizes them as soon as she sees them.

Regular guided reading

Beginners should read every day. Organize a time, maybe bedtime, for your child to read with you. Have him read out loud to you and guide his reading by correcting his mistakes quickly and kindly.

Regular paired reading

Paired reading is when you read together. You can do it in three ways: by reading out loud together at the same time (often called *choral reading*), by taking turns reading out loud *(alternated reading),* or by having a parent-reads-to-child time followed by a child-reads-a-bit-more-for-himself time *(incomplete reading).*

Chapter 21

Writing and Workbooks

In This Chapter

▶ Taking a look at reading and writing

▶ Introducing your child to writing

▶ Writing letters, journals, poems, and more

▶ Creating books with your child

▶ Wising up with workbooks

Didn't you read somewhere that writing goes hand in hand with reading? Isn't it true that kids write from their first day in the classroom? Shouldn't your child be getting his writing hand limbered up? In this chapter, you find out how writing ties in with reading and what you can do to help your child be a great writer. You get ideas, tips, and pointers on what to do when your child writes something like "*todaiwlgwtosemigrnmr.*" You also hear what to do with those workbooks you've hoarded in your "school things" closet. You get the lowdown on best ways to select, use, and even recycle those workbooks.

Chicken or Egg?

Which comes first, reading or writing? Can a child be good at one but not at the other? Should you pay both the same attention, or do you want to get one well established before concentrating on the other? These questions are all good ones to ask, and some people spend years discussing them. You don't have to do that, though. For your purposes, I have some simple answers. Your child starts practicing prereading skills as soon as he starts to talk. By putting words and sentences together, he's getting the idea that language is sort of like different arrangements of sound blocks. As soon as he fingerpaints and holds a crayon, he's getting warmed up for letters. And all this preparation for reading and writing happens at pretty much the same time.

In these early years, when your child is racing ahead with his spoken vocabulary and likes to write squiggles and circles, keep in mind these tools and activities that can help him most:

- Conversation
- Song and music
- Books and toys
- Blocks, beads, and games and puzzles that require him to get his little fingers moving better
- Crayons, paintbrushes, pencils, chalk, and pens
- Paper, blackboard, and whiteboard
- Sandboxes, tubs of rice, foam, *gloop* (an ooey gooey mixture of soap flakes and other stuff — see the nearby sidebar for the recipe), and anything else he can run his fingers through
- Clay and play dough
- Outdoor adventures and playground equipment

If you're wondering about the outdoor adventures bullet, let me explain. The better your child gets at motor skills, fine and gross, the better he can handle books and pencils. Some studies find that reading improves when kids do things like jumping on a trampoline. If that's true, it's all the reason you need to grab the bicycle, ball, and dog and head outdoors.

Gross motor skills may make you think of all sorts of icky things that have nothing to do with reading and writing. It's a funny word for something that's not icky at all. *Gross* means big. When your child kicks a ball, runs around a field, or jumps off the playground slide, he's doing big physical actions, or *gross motor* stuff. When he does small things with his fingers, like threading beads or sorting buttons, he's doing *fine motor* stuff.

The gloop recipe

Kids love to play with gloop. Here's how to make it:

   1 cup white glue (Elmer's works best)

   1 cup water

   Powder paint or food coloring

1½ teaspoons of borax (from your grocery stores laundry soap shelves)

Mix the glue, water, and coloring together. In a separate cup, dissolve the borax in 1 cup of warm water. Add the dissolved borax to the other ingredients and stir rapidly for about 2 minutes.

First Steps in Writing

Your child does a lot of squiggles and drawings, and you're wondering what kind of activities to put her onto next. First of all, don't lapse with puzzles, blocks, and bead threading. The more fine motor activities your child does, the better she becomes at holding books, turning pages, and getting her pencil to go in the direction she wants.

Play dough recipe

If you're like me and have recipes jotted on bits of paper all over the house, and good intentions of one day gathering them all together, here's a must-have recipe you can't lose:

Easy (and edible) play dough:

2½ cups flour

½ cup salt

3 tablespoons cooking oil

¼ teaspoon food coloring

2 cups boiling water

Mix flour, salt, oil, and food coloring in a bowl. Add boiling water. Mix well and then knead until smooth. (Use the kneading hook on your food mixer, if you have one.) This dough keeps for several months in a plastic bag — but don't freeze it.

Tip: No food coloring? Try mixing Jell-O or Kool-Aid powder into the boiling water, instead.

Fun ways to use this stuff:

Roll

Squeeze

Pinch

Press

Knead

Cut with scissors, table knives, and cookie cutters

Make forms and shapes

Paint with food coloring

Make permanent shapes by drying

Dough for permanent models (like letters of the alphabet):

My daughter's Girl Scout "White Owl" gave me the recipe for this durable dough. She says the mix is a bit messy, but it washes off easily. And you don't have to bake the finished models because they dry at room temperature.

2 cups baking soda

1 cup cornstarch

1½ cups water

Mix all the ingredients together over medium heat until the mix has the consistency of mashed potatoes. Scrape it into a bowl and cover the bowl with a damp cloth while the mix cools. Knead the cold mix on a surface brushed with cornstarch until it's smooth. Now you can use it or store it in a sealed container to use later. When you make figures or letters, just let them dry, and then you can paint them with bright acrylic paints if you want to.

Next, warm up the play dough. Make a batch of dough, throw in a few colors, and sit down with your child for a creative blast. Start with models of all the things she knows — worms, hamburgers, and all that kind of stuff — and then move on to, ta da, the first letter of her name!

From there, you can go through all the letters of the alphabet. Don't go in order, though, because you should start with letters about things and people your child knows. Maybe the letter she wants to look at after the first letter of her name is *m* for *mom*. You can make a nice big fat *m* and chat about things like *mugs, milk, men, mud,* and *melon.* Help your child shape the letters by giving her a template. Draw a nice big clear letter on a piece of paper and then laminate that paper. She can shape her dough on top of the letter, she doesn't make any mess, and you can use the laminate many times.

Later, when you've moved from play dough to crayons, pencils, paints, and pens, use the laminate. Get some erasable markers and have her write on the laminate. Her pen wipes off easily, and she can erase and begin again if she's not happy with her first efforts.

You should have a special set of pens for writing time. Then your child sees this time as special and grown-up.

Sticking with a single-letter theme

When you're showing your child a letter, stick with it for a few days. Make a book of things that start with that letter, adding rhymes and the words of songs, too. Read books that feature your letter. If, for example, you're exploring *b,* you can:

- ✔ Sing and say these nursery rhymes and put their words in the *b* page of your homemade alphabet book: *My Bonnie Lies Over the Ocean, Little Boy Blue, Baa Baa Black Sheep.* Have your child highlight all the *b*'s and write her own capital and lowercase *b*'s.

- ✔ Read *Brown Bear, Brown Bear, What Do You See?* by Bill Martin, Jr. (Henry Holt and Company, 1996) and any of *The Berenstain Bear* books by Stan and Jan Berenstain (Random House).

- ✔ Read nonfiction books about *bears, boats, baboons,* and *the brain.*

When your child can write a few letters, play at writing them, with your fingers, on each other's back. The one getting written on has to figure out the letter.

Is it writing or hieroglyphics?

When your child first writes his name, you'll both be thrilled. From here on, plan to find his name written all over the place, often where it shouldn't be. After this mammoth achievement comes the next writing step. This step certainly happens when your child starts school, but it may happen sooner. You get notes, stories, and cards from your child. They may say things like, "IsndumilovefrumLachlan." He doesn't put any gaps between words, and you have the devil of a time working out the messages and convincing your child you can read them. Then you probably treasure those notes forevermore. Your child's first pieces of writing show what teachers call *emergent,* or experimental, literacy. They're your child's first experiments with words, when he can't make much sense to most other readers. But he's developing his ideas and skills that he can refine later.

You have to handle your emergent writer with care because he believes he's writing, more or less, accurately. Here are a few tips about responding supportively to your child's emergent writing:

- ✔ Your child is taking risks and experimenting, so don't criticize or make spelling suggestions.

- ✔ Do your best at deciphering, but if you're truly stumped by the squash of letters your child gives you, ask him to read it to you.

- ✔ Encourage him to do more writing and share some writing tasks with you. As long as he can read his own writing, he can write shopping lists, notes, and cards.

- ✔ Allow your child several weeks to get the hang of putting spaces between words.

- ✔ After your child is writing real words and sentences, you can gently correct his errors — but not every single one!

- ✔ When you do correct errors in your child's writing, limit yourself to two or three corrections. Take time to demonstrate and practice what you're telling him, too, so he remembers it for next time. If, for example, your child consistently writes *thay,* gently point out that he's perfectly right to think of *thay* because that's how it sounds, but *they* actually has an *e* in it. Have your child write down *they* on a large piece of paper and stick it on the wall. If he sticks it in the bathroom, he can see it often!

Kids refine their writing, in time. Your child's first efforts look like an endless (and vowel deficient) muddle of letters. Although the resemblance between real writing and what your child does is slim, don't make this deficiency obvious. You can damage your child's confidence with an offhand remark or joke.

When the two *r*'s are out of step

Reading and writing do begin at roughly the same time, but as your child moves forward with both, reading generally takes the lead. Your child understands how to read a little quicker than he figures out how to write, and you will notice this fact in the early years of school (and particularly with boys).

Not that you should expect your son to be slow with writing, but if he is, it's fairly typical. Boys tend to develop fine motor skills a little later than girls, so in a typical kindergarten classroom you'd expect to find that the boys are noticeably weaker at steering their pencils and cutting out paper. But writing catches up with reading in the end (and boys get better at steering their pencils). Both boys and girls get very good on word processors, too. By around second grade, your child should be a fluent writer who can sound out and recognize correct spellings a lot of the time.

Journals, Scrapbooks, and Letters: The Early Work of Your Young Writer

Some kids love writing. They compose pages and pages of just about anything. Here are a few categories their writing may fit into:

- ✔ Personal essays
- ✔ Stories
- ✔ Descriptions and directions
- ✔ Poems
- ✔ Lists
- ✔ Contracts and agreements
- ✔ Jokes
- ✔ Cartoons
- ✔ Posters
- ✔ Letters and notes

If your child is a writer, you'll get used to having notes left on your pillow, contracts thrust under your nose for you to agree to and sign immediately, and *privat* or *kep out* posters multiplying on bedroom doors. Read your child's pieces and encourage her. If you can't resist correcting her errors, be selective. Pick words that seem the most important for her to know and give your advice gently.

Silly letters

Teachers usually give children silly letters at some time. *Silly letters* are prewritten letters (the "Dear Mom" kind, not the *a, b, c* kind) with missing key words. Your child fills in the missing words by himself or from a choice of words, and the result is a very silly letter. If you have a rainy day and a willing child, have a go at this silly letter. In this version, all your child does is circle the word he likes best out of the options.

Dear *Friend, Banana, Cutie,*

Today I went to the *mall, bathroom, pig farm.*

I saw a *turtle, pickle, $20 dollar bill* and put it in my *pants, backpack, mouth.*

It felt *wet, cold, lumpy,* but I didn't *throw up, die, faint.*

I hope to *squeeze, kick, kiss,* you soon!

Lots of *love, potatoes, kisses,*

Your *buddy, grandma, sweetheart.*

The last thing you want to do is turn a writer off (you know how temperamental these artists can be). Any guidance you give should be genuine guidance, not nagging, criticism, or exasperation. And never, ever turn your comments into an excuse to harp back to previous errors. If, for example, you're correcting *thay* for the umpteenth time, simply write down the correct spelling and hand it to your child or point to the incorrect letter. Don't get into the "I've told you a million times" put-down.

Supply your writer with nice equipment and some ideas. Buy a scrapbook and help her put things in it. Help her keep a journal. If you have a loving Aunt or Grandpa, get a letter-writing routine established. Kids get excited about getting letters through the mail and may stick with letter writing for months. To make any sort of writing easier for your child, write some of the text for her (if she wants you to).

Poems: A Special Way to Encourage Writing

Poems give you a lovely way to get your child's creativity running wild. Children love reading funny and rhythmic poems and may be enthusiastic little poets, themselves. Your child probably finds writing complete poems all by himself hard, but he can easily write fill-in-the-blanks poems. Repetitive poems start him off in a good place, so the following sections have some examples to give you inspiration.

Poems about people

Pick a person, real or imagined, and write about the kind of person he is:

Ben is big.

Ben is happy.

Ben is my friend.

Ben likes school.

Ben hates onions.

Ben goes to soccer training.

Ben thinks girls are yuk.

Ben has to clean his room.

Ben doesn't mind feeding the cat.

I am Ben!

Other ideas:

I never told anyone that . . .

I am me because . . .

Recipe poems

Modeling your recipe poem on a food recipe, think of a theme (love, happiness, friendship) and the ingredients and measures that could go with it.

Recipe for good times:

A cup of friends

A tablespoon of playground

A dash of softball

A pinch of pop

A slice of cake

A shake of laughter

Mix it all together on a sunny day, and, in a few minutes, you have a grrreat time!

Poems about opposites

Think of two easy opposites (big, small; good, bad; hot, cold) and then think up some stuff that fits with them.

Hello, Mom; goodbye, homework.

Hello, pop; goodbye, milk.

Hello, summer; goodbye, winter.

Hello, friends; goodbye, enemies.

Hello, chocolate; goodbye, vegetables.

Hello, messy; goodbye, tidy.

Hello, noise; goodbye, quiet.

Hello, hello, it's me!

"Love is" type poems

"Love is" is a popular theme with girls. You don't have to stick with love, though. Other feelings or things work fine, too (family is, teddy is, my dad is, friends are).

Love is warmth.

Love is laughter.

Love is puppies.

Love is stories.

Love is cookies.

Love is a warm kitchen.

Love is when you tuck me in.

Love is me and you!

Color poems

With one color or a few colors, you can come up with a good poem.

Green is soft grass

Red is my ball

Blue is a big, clear sky

Black is at night

Brown is my skin

And yellow is my favorite!

Homemade Books

When your child writes, grab the finished product. Put it somewhere safe for a rainy day. When that rainy day comes, get out your glue, scissors, and craft paper and get book-making. If you buy a book of *craft paper* (which is like thin cardboard), you can easily glue pieces of writing onto the pages. You can keep the pages in the craft book or take them out and staple them together. Help your child make a cover for the book and put a strip of sticky tape over the stapled edge so that the staples don't catch on your child's fingers. Now you have a great book for your child to read and to keep as a memento forever. If you were organized enough to record the date of each piece, you can order and label the book chronologically.

If your child likes books that look more like the commercial ones, offer to type her writing for her. Type in big, bold print and have her illustrate the pages. Make journals that record the things your child does, nonfiction books that describe things she's interested in (like dinosaurs), and make-believe books based on stories you read together. Help your child to whatever extent she likes, but make sure *she* directs *you*.

Give your child tips and pointers, and do the typing and cutting that she can't do — but don't take control. Like anyone else, your child has the most interest in things she creates all by herself (or almost all by herself).

Workbooks: They're Fun, Not Work

Workbooks can be useful. The trouble comes when you tend to buy dozens of them and leave your child to use them without any guidance. Sometimes, this approach works fine, but often your child writes on one page in the first book, draws on one page in another, and before long has a pile of used books that he loses interest in because they're no longer untouched and inviting.

When you choose workbooks, ask yourself what your child can do with them. Can he really do all the pages by himself? If so, make sure you encourage him to work all the way through the book. If a book clearly has pages your child needs help with, are you prepared to give that help? Buy just a few workbooks and give them to your child one at a time, when you're close at hand with encouragement. Some kids love it when you give them a mark or comment for every page they do. Others want you to be there the whole time to comment on every pen mark. Grab a cup of coffee and psyche yourself up for being the one who sees, and admires, all!

Deciding what to choose

Here are some tips for picking out workbooks:

- ✔ For a little child, choose books that ask her to do easy tasks like tracing over the top of letters, finding hidden things, matching identical letters, and spotting the differences between drawings.

- ✔ For a child starting out on letters, look for letter-to-letter matching and matching letters to things that begin with that letter. Things like *spot the difference* and *finish the drawing* work well, too.

- ✔ For children who can read simple words, look for *find the word, match the word to the object,* and *spot the mistake* type activities.

- ✔ Unless your child already understands the difference between long and short sounds, he may find tasks that ask him to identify those different sounds hard and boring.

- ✔ Children who can read fairly well like word searches and puzzles. They like funny or quirky tasks and activities where they face a challenge.

Kids dislike reading short stories and answering questions about them. They much prefer being put into the role of detective and answering questions that ask things like, "Do you think a person with a missing finger can really be a good detective? Tell why," rather than something like, "Describe, in detail, (already boring!) which person in the story had a missing finger."

Reusing workbooks

When your child has finished all the activities in a workbook, you may feel cheated. You thought she'd be occupied for endless hours, but she's done in just a few. Not to worry. You can reuse workbooks in a lot of ways, and the next sections run you through them.

Matching letters or words with pictures

Workbooks for little kids are filled with activities for matching letters or words to pictures. Take your scissors to the pages of these books. Cut out letters, words, and pictures that match up (the letter *r* and a picture of a rabbit) and use them like a puzzle. Sit quietly with your child and have him match them all over again. He can paste the pictures into a page of a scrapbook or just put them together in piles. If you use a scrapbook, have him write the letter and then glue all the matching pictures around the letter. If you use words and pictures, have your child look at the words and find the pictures of those words and then look at the pictures and find the words. Last of all, on a new page, have your child write the words and draw the pictures for himself.

Listening games

Play listening games with your child to get her used to listening carefully. Your child needs to know how to listen carefully to be a good reader because she needs to hear distinct chunks of sound inside words so that she can recognize and sound them out in print. In these listening games, you ask your child to find things, too. This activity helps her look for small details, so she'll be better at spotting the differences between letters and words when she reads. For listening games, you can use workbooks your child has finished or books you find in garage sales, secondhand shops, and used bookshops. You just need some text your child can mark.

Give your child some colored markers and tell her that you're playing a listening game. She has to listen to your instructions and see if she can find what you want her to find. Now give her instructions to find words and pictures and do things to them, like crossing out, circling, coloring, underlining, and adding onto. Here are some example questions to get you started:

- Find the dog and write *dog* on it.
- Find the white rabbit and draw a hat on it.
- Find the ball and draw a hole in it.
- Find the word *balloon* and put a green circle around it.
- Find the word *cat* and underline it in red.
- Find five words that have only two letters in them.
- Find the word that is a boy's name.
- Count the number of times you see the word *a*. Write the number on the back of your paper.
- If you add the letter *y* onto the end of *the*, what word do you make? Write this word on the bottom of your page.
- Find the word *small* and put a blue *x* over it.
- Find the words that have more than five letters in them. Put a brown dot on them and count how many dots you have. Write the number at the top of your paper.
- Find the word *it* and make it into *sit*.

If you want to make this game into more of a reading activity, write some simple instructions on a piece of paper and have your child read the questions for herself. You can read through the questions with her first before leaving her to reread and find the answers. Written instructions can be things like

- Find the dog and put a red *x* on it.

- Find *because* and cross it out with a black pen.

- Find ten words that have only two letters in them.

- Count how many times you see *a.* How many is it?

- How many periods do you see?

- How many times do you see *the?*

When the answer to your question is a number, make it more interesting for your child by having worked the answers out for yourself already. Write the answers on a piece of paper and have her check her numbers against yours. For fun, write her a note saying where you have hidden the sheet with the answers on it.

Chapter 22

Having Your Child Read Out Loud

Sometimes, you want to feel youthful. You toy with the idea of drinking coffee *after* 8:30 at night (when you know it'll mean a trek to the bathroom in the small hours), you think about going grocery shopping *without* your list, and you fantasize about switching away from the oldies station on your radio. All these things seem attractive in the heat of the moment. Deep down, though, you know that you have to make less risky choices. You do have one safe option (that still makes you feel young at heart) — listen to kids' books. You can have fun listening to your child read — and it may be just the thing you need to tame your wild impulses.

Listening to your child read helps him become more fluent. Studies prove it, teachers do it as often as they can, and reading programs make sure they include it. You may also find that it's one of the easiest things you can do with your child. So, if you're serious about helping your child make progress

 ✔ Collect a pile of attractive books with simple text.

 ✔ Set aside a regular time of at least 20 minutes each day for reading.

 ✔ Get familiar with the instructions in this chapter.

Setting a Relaxed and Happy Reading Tone

Because you want reading out loud to be a pleasant and frequent thing, plan for it. Know before you start

✔ Where you can do the reading

✔ What small rewards you may give to your child

✔ What intrinsic rewards your child gets

Where do you do the reading?

You can do the reading in bed, if you want. You can plan things around bedtime much more easily than most other times because you get dinner, chores, and homework out of the way first. And you can combine reading out loud time with a bedtime story so your child knows that when he's done his reading out loud, you read a story to him.

You may also want to read at the kitchen table. After your child gets into the habit of reading to you, you may find that reading at the kitchen table suits your schedule. While you prepare meals, he can read to you. This option may suit you well if your child is an early riser and you have a spare 20 minutes before school.

You may find that the sofa becomes a favorite reading place. Perhaps one parent can take the reading duty while the other gets dinner ready. If you're a single-parent family, maybe an older sibling can oblige (especially if his allowance depends on it!).

Should you give your child small rewards?

Like all of us, kids like to have their efforts acknowledged. Because they don't get paychecks or promotions, you just have to give them something else. Think about the things your child likes and try to make sure that she gets some of them when she shows up for her reading and does a good job.

Keep a count of how many books or pages she reads, or how many days of reading she does, and decide on small rewards. Kids usually like to keep their own progress charts by crossing off days, sticking on stickers, or coloring in squares. And you may want to use rewards like comics, books, certificates that go on the wall, small cuddly toys that can be reading buddies, miniature toys (like cars and dolls), pens, play dates, sleepovers, and trips to the playground.

What intrinsic rewards does your child get?

You've decided to buy your child a comic each week for a reading reward. He's going to color his reading chart so he can see that he's read every day of the week and you're planning to get his reading books from the library on Saturdays. Think that's enough? Not quite. You need to make a mental note of your important role as teacher. You're responsible for making your child feel good about reading and for making it all seem worthwhile to him. That's no small task, so here are a few tips:

✔ Be sure to let your child choose his own reading books. To be sure that he doesn't pick books that he may find way too hard, give him a selection to choose from. This way, he doesn't get absolute free rein but still gets the final say.

✔ Make your trip to the library a special event. Be enthusiastic about it and perhaps couple it with an ice cream or hot chocolate stop.

✔ Display his certificates and progress chart so that he gets a kick from seeing them (and from friends and family seeing them, too!).

✔ Remember that your child has been competing with siblings, work, and household obligations for your time for as long as he can remember. He loves to get your special attention. Keep that attention warm and stress-free. If you feel yourself getting short tempered, leave the reading. Resume it at another time or get an easier book.

"Ladies and gentlemen"

You've probably seen your child copy and mimic nearly all your behavior and a lot of other people's, too. Kids are natural copycats. They adore making believe they're other people or animals. You can use their mimicry to inject a lot of fun into reading out loud by helping your child be a narrator or actor.

When you have a few kids gathered together, especially a mix of older and younger kids, get a play going. Have older children write a play for narration (they can base it on a favorite nursery rhyme or story) and direct the cast. Middle-sized children read the narration in big voices and little kids (and anyone without a job) act it out. An enthusiastic and even-tempered teenager is a real asset to home productions, but aunts, uncles, and grandparents may let you bully them into the role of production manager, too. Anyone can serve as an audience. If you're short of audience members, recruit dolls and teddy bears. Your child will have just as good a time as he would if you'd invited the President.

Oh, don't forget to provide a few good snacks and drinks, too. Any good host (or theatre manager) knows the importance of tasty light refreshments (use a pompous voice to get the best ring out of "light refreshments.")

Correcting Reading Mistakes

Kids don't like to read out loud to parents or teachers when they don't feel good at it. How does that come about? It happens when, somewhere along the line, her parent or teacher unintentionally uses a heavy hand to correct her reading errors.

When your child reads out loud to you, she's vulnerable. She's showing you all that she can do and needs you to tread lightly when you spot her mistakes. Imagine yourself in her position. You show your boss your best work and (because you're human) you want praise. Instead, your boss only spots errors. Your child experiences that if you don't temper your corrections. Tread gently around her ego.

Helping sound out

Your child gets stuck with a word like *about*. Easy. This word sounds out in a regular way: *a-bout*. You just have to show your child the *ou* sound. Take time out to talk about *out, shout, cloud, round, sound,* and *pound*. Then look back at the word *about*. Your child finds it easy to sound out now that he knows *ou*. You may notice that, with *about,* you can also break it into *ab-out*. You can break the word up this way if your child already knows *out*.

Any time you come to a word that belongs to a word family, like the *ou* family you just saw, take time to show your child the word family. He can remember whole families of words (words that have a common pattern) much more easily than he can remember isolated words.

If your child gets stuck with a word that he can only sound out half of, like *word* (the *or* part sounds out as *er,* not *or*), what then? With words that only sound out a bit (and you encounter a lot of them), sound out where you can and then say something like this to your child: "The word *word* takes a bit of thinking about. It starts with *w* and ends with *d,* but the middle bit is hard. It sounds like *er,* but you write it as *or*. Highlight *or* so that you know where to find the tricky bit. Write *word* down three times and try to remember how it looks. Write it on a card and stick it on the wall so that you see it a lot. Then you can know it the next time that you see it."

When you break up words whose first syllable ends with a vowel, like *di-rect, re-ply,* and *be-lieve,* the vowel on the end of the first syllable is (usually) long.

If you feel yourself getting impatient or critical with your child, leave the situation. You can harm your child if you say things like, "But we just had that word, you *must* know it!" or "You need to try harder, you can do better than this!" If you feel that your child's not giving his best, ask yourself why. Do you need to take a break or change the activity? Perhaps you should be using an easier book. Remember that it's your job to make things better. It's not your child's job to prove himself or appease you.

Giving answers to avoid frustration

When you come to a word like *who,* you can't go down the sounding out track. Some words just aren't worth the effort of trying to sound out. You can more easily just tell your child some words. Get her to write *who* down and try to remember the look of it. Write it on an index card and read the card for the next few nights.

The following list gives you a few very common words that fit into this not-worth-sounding-out group:

- *because* (just sound out *be*)
- *who*
- *want*
- *what*
- *you*

If you feel like you're telling your child an awful lot of words when she reads out loud to you, flip to Chapter 11 to make sure that she knows her sight words. But don't worry that you're telling her far too much because when you tell her the words that she's stuck on (instead of asking her to figure them out herself), she reads more fluently. She doesn't have to suffer the awful stop-and-start reading that makes children lose the sense of text, which can make them hate reading. Your help keeps your child enjoying reading so that she sticks with it. As she does more reading, she gets better and you correct her less.

Finding words within words

When you look at the word *about* (which you can do in the earlier section "Helping sound out"), you can help your child remember *about* by breaking it into *ab* and *out.* Whenever you come to a word that has a helpful little word inside it, show that little word to your child. You may find yourself doing this word search a lot because plenty of words are made of small words joined together *(in-to, up-on, on-to, book-mark, be-side, ham-burger),* and plenty more words have a little word inside them *(sh-out, p-itch, fl-oat, m-eat, hand-le, p-each, thin-k, c-old).*

Using contextual cues

Using contextual cues overlaps with all other ways of figuring out new words (you can find these other methods in the earlier sections in this chapter). Whenever your child reads, he uses contextual cues to figure out new words. He remembers the plot or details that he's read so far, he looks at the pictures and illustrations, and he makes a reasoned guess at unknown words based on what he knows from all that.

Encourage your child to figure out words by reminding him of the story so far, the illustrations, and what words would make sense. For the sentence "It was *exactly* the right size," ask your child, "What word would make sense there?" He should get into the habit of using contextual cues because all good readers skip and skim through text like this. They predict and figure out words from the cues that they get from the wider story and don't need to sound out every single word.

The word *cues* is a teacher's term meaning clues. What's the difference between *clues* and *cues?* Not much. The dictionary defines a *cue* as a "hint" or "guiding suggestion." Why don't educators say *clues* and not *cues?* I've no idea.

Tracking: You Don't Have to Be a Ranger

Tracking has nothing to do with following footprints and dung. In this case, the word describes keeping your place on a page. When you follow print from left to right, one line at a time, heading down a page, you're tracking. Kids typically have trouble tracking. If your child loses her place on a page and you wonder whether you should tell her to point with her finger or use a ruler to hold under the line she's reading, here's what to do:

✔ Remember that all kids have to learn to keep track on a page. If your child needs help, that's typical.

✔ Show your child how to point to words with her finger as she reads them.

✔ Let your child use fancy pointers if she wants to.

✔ Move to using a ruler when she's ready. Now she sees the whole line at once and moves the ruler down line by line.

✔ Let your child keep using her finger, a pencil, or a ruler to mark her place for as long as she wants to.

✔ If she seems unable to stop marking her place when she's in school, ask her teacher for helpful tips.

✔ If your child's habits with tracking keep worrying you, mention it to the optometrist when your child gets her regular eye examination.

The issue of *aloud* and *out loud*

When I was writing this chapter, I started off with the word *aloud.* I was going to talk about having your child read *aloud,* and then I stopped short. "Uh oh," I thought. "I can just see what's going to happen here. A teacher who's been reading aloud to her kindergarten kids all year will take issue with me." So I stopped myself in the nick of time. Let me fill you in on why.

Aloud and *out loud* don't really have any difference in meaning, but many teachers distinguish between the two for practical purposes. They need to be able to distinguish between the many different types of reading that they're doing. So, for many teachers, reading *out loud* is the stuff that kids do for parents, peers, or teachers. Reading *aloud,* on the other hand, is what teachers do in front of a sea of cute little faces that gather around the mat for story time. Anyway, I'm not going to distinguish between the two in this book because I'm sure to tie myself in knots with all those "alouds" and "out louds." I talk about reading "out loud," no matter who's doing it. Right now, I'm going to give you a few useful pointers about reading out loud to your child and what to keep in mind when you do it:

✔ Read out loud to your child often.

✔ Keep reading out loud to your child, even when she can read by herself.

✔ For little children, choose books with pictures that include some rhyming text.

✔ Put some oomph into your reading and try to read in character (your lion, for example, should sound a tad ferocious).

✔ For a change, use big books. Teachers use these huge books so that kids get to see the text and pictures much better. You should be able to borrow big books from your local library, and after you've read them a few times to your child, she can have fun holding them up and reading them to her toys. Then she gets a chance to be just like a teacher.

✔ If you have more than one child, have an older child read to a younger one. Give the older child a lot of easy books and see if you can make her feel so responsible and clever that she happily reads to her sibling. You may get half an hour's quiet (unless, of course, they can't agree on who holds the book!).

✔ Read all kinds of books to your child and make a point of including chapter books. When you read chapter books to your child, you give her a taste of the exciting stuff she can read for herself when she gets better at reading.

One last thing: You may hear a couple of other terms — *shared reading* and *oral reading.* Just like "aloud" and "out loud," you can't find much difference between the two. They both mean that a book gets read out loud to kids (hence oral), so the story is shared.

Reading Out Loud Together

Besides hearing your child read out loud and reading out loud to him, you have another in-between option. You can read out loud *with* your child. This kind of reading is called *paired reading,* and you can do it in three ways:

- Choral reading
- Alternated reading
- Incomplete reading

Choral reading

Choral reading is reading out loud at the same time. You may want to use this reading approach for three good reasons:

- Your child can feel special because she gets to do her reading right along with you.

- If your child isn't a confident or fluent reader, she may feel better when she hears your voice alongside her own.

- When your child's not sure of a word, she can follow your lead, and the reading stays fluent.

You can even make small changes in choral reading. By reading a hair's breadth ahead of your child, you give her more of a chance to copy you when she gets stuck with a word. Conversely, when she gets better at choral reading, you can read slightly behind her. You can hear her reading better and can fill in the gaps as she comes to them.

A lot of parents find this type of reading the easiest way of all to get their kids to read regularly. You really only have to think about selecting good books with this kind of reading. Choose books that aren't too hard. Don't be too quick to move to harder text. It's good to give your child a lot of practice with books that she can easily manage before moving to harder text.

For confident kids, you may want to use the *tap or nudge* adaptation of choral reading. Your child reads a book with you but has you stop and start reading with her as she indicates. When she wants you to stop reading, or join in with her, she taps the table (or your knee, or whatever you like) or gives you a nudge. This technique provides you with especially good fun when you're first starting it. Getting your taps and nudges coordinated is quite a feat.

Alternated reading

With *alternated reading,* you take turns reading out loud. You can have equal turns of reading, say, one page each, or (more typically) you get to do the lion's share! Your child likes this reading technique because he feels like he has the upper hand. And all the while, he's still reading and getting more practice. If you're just starting out with alternated reading, have your child read just a few words. Increase the amount he reads gradually, but don't force him to read a lot. If he's really reluctant, make deals. For example, you can say that you'll read the whole of the first page if he reads one sentence of his own choosing in the next page. You may want to read the whole piece to your child first. If your child isn't very confident, you need to be patient and give him all the help and encouragement that you can. Doing prereadings and letting him choose just one or two words or sentences to read to start with helps him feel good about reading.

Incomplete reading

This method is a bit sneaky. With *incomplete reading,* you choose an exciting book that you think your child can read. You read it to her, get to a particularly exciting part, and then close the pages. Aargh! "But what happens next?" your child asks. "Ah ha," you reply, "I wish I could tell you, but I'm plum out of time. I have 60 trillion things to do. But because I'm so nice, I'll give you 20 minutes to browse through the book some more, if you want to." Then make a very quick getaway (avoiding any missiles she hurls at you). Many parents have had great success with this method, and their children weren't emotionally scarred (at least, in any way people could trace back to this benign abuse!).

Bounteous babysitters

This book tells you to do a lot of things: Read to (and with) your child, play with new words, and get a handle on sight words. On paper, it looks straightforward and manageable, but in real life you have just a few other things on your plate, like work, other kids, grocery shopping, laundry, walking the dog, and so on. I'm not so engrossed in my good advice that I don't appreciate this fact, so I cut you a bit of slack here.

If you use a babysitter, she's probably young, eager, and far more energetic than you. Reading to your child is easy for her. Grandparents also often find reading to your child easy and fun. An older child may be able to do this reading more easily than you. Recruit help. Delegate your tasks whenever you can. If your child goes to school and you want to be wise to the holiday drop-off in reading skills that the media warn you about, delegate. If you drop into your library regularly, your delegates don't have any excuses. "Here," you can say, "I just picked up a few dozen books to make things easier for the two of you. Bye now, book worms. Have fun!"

Repeat Readings

A reading method that has spawned whole reading programs is the *repeat readings method.* For this method, you just have your child read the same text several times. At first, you may read the complete text to him so that he's familiar with it. After that, he reads the text by himself, getting more confident and fluent with each reading. A lot of teachers I know love this method, and it's very easy to do.

To make repeat readings really count, you need to make sure that your child sees the progress he makes. Praise his readings and point out that his errors or delays get fewer. Have him time himself. Record a time for three consecutive readings spread over a few hours or days. Chart or graph his results so that he sees how his reading got quicker.

In another kind of repeat reading, you read the same story out loud to your child a lot of times. Kids love hearing favorite stories again and again . . . and again. They know when you change details, too, and they correct your omissions. If your child has some favorite books, read them to him often and have him retell the story. This activity gives him good practice in sequencing events and building vocabulary (something I talk more about in Chapter 19).

Make a *storyboard,* a big pictorial representation of a story. Draw a few pictures depicting the story and write words or sentences to go with them. You can explain to your child that you've made a summary and have him read it. If your child likes storyboards, make a great big book of all your storyboards stapled together.

Let your child chat about the stories and encourage him to not only describe what happened, but suggest alternative endings. Ask him to tell what kinds of people the characters in the book were and if the author could've written more or less about some things. This kind of exploration of text gives your child a heap of language, deductive, and analytical skills.

Using a Bit of Everything

I hope you've gotten some good ideas from this chapter. Go forth boldly with them. Don't limit yourself to just one thing. This chapter is a smorgasbord, and you're supposed to try the lot. Read books in all the ways described in this chapter and see if you like one more than the others. Stick with the method that you like and establish a routine. If you do 20 or more minutes of reading with your child every night, she can make great progress.

When you're listening to your child read out loud, correct her mistakes in all the ways that you read about in the previous section. And remember, you know your child better than anyone else (and probably get to see her more than anyone else). It's pretty certain that you'll influence her success with reading more than anyone or anything else in her life.

To make your system watertight, be sure to read a lot of books of roughly the same difficulty before moving to harder books. Start out with very simple books and keep writing the tricky words that you come across on index cards. Read the index cards together regularly. For games to play with the cards you collect, flip back to Chapter 9.

If your child doesn't much like reading out loud, don't pressure her. First, check that you're not using a book that your child finds too difficult because she gets much more from successfully reading a few easy books than she can by struggling with one hard book. Lead her into reading out loud by herself, gently. Begin by reading a book to her and then reading the same book with her. After these two readings, finish up by asking her to read the book to you all by herself.

Straight from the horse's mouth

In this chapter, I thought I'd get some expert opinions. I wasn't sure whether the people I asked would be able to spare the time for my inquiries, but I got lucky. So here it is: sage advise from the little people who often get asked to read out loud and have listened to stories from many an orator:

✔ *If your parents ask you to read out loud to them, you wonder if they think you're dumb.* May I refer you to the section "Correcting Reading Mistakes," earlier in this chapter, where I talk about treading lightly around your child's ego when you correct his reading errors. You should use the same care, even from the very beginning, when you ask your child to read out loud to you.

✔ *Some teachers read stories better than others. I have one teacher who's great at it. She makes you believe she really is the character in the book.* This comment's all about the oomph I refer to in the sidebar "The issue of *aloud* and *out loud*" earlier in this chapter. You make stories much more fun when you read them in character.

✔ *It's awful when kids interrupt a story. I hate it when the teacher lets kids ask questions because then it's hard to remember where you are in the story.* If you read stories to more than one child at a time, establish the ground rules first. Do you allow any interruptions, and if so, what kinds of interruptions are permissible?

Chapter 23

Keeping Your Child on the Reading Track

I hear statements like this one time and time again: "My child *can* read, but he's not interested in reading." If you think your child isn't doing enough reading, you worry. He may fail all his tests. He may start hanging out with the wrong crowd. Maybe he won't be able to get a job later in life. In this chapter, I show you first of all how to be sure that your child can read. Then I show you how to motivate him and keep him motivated.

First Things First

Children who really can't read very well simply say that they don't want to read. Children (and grown-ups, for that matter) hide their limitations and show their strengths. So if your child says that she doesn't like reading, check her skills to be sure that she's not hiding her difficulties:

▶ Does she have instant recognition of the 220 sight words?

▶ Can she sound out phonetically regular words, like *instant?*

▶ Does she sound out whenever she can?

▶ If she can't figure out a word, does she make reasonable guesses based on contextual cues?

If you need to review these skills, take a quick detour through this book. I explain sight words in Chapter 11, sounding out gets under way in Chapters 12 and 13, and you can read more about contextual cues in Chapter 20.

Visiting the Library Often

To keep your child reading, you need the right equipment. You need books, cassette tapes, CD-ROMs, comics, and magazines. In other words, you need your local library! If you do nothing else after reading this book, join your local library and get into the routine of taking your child there every week. You improve his chances of being successful in school (and beyond) so much that you'd be crazy not to go.

Making Reading a Family Event

Okay, you've joined the library — now what? Next, you want to show your child that reading really is fun by doing some of it with him. Go to the library with him. Pick a few videos for the whole family. Choose some stories on tape for your child. Then follow along with him to help him make his own choices. Leave the library with a gratifying collection that can last you through the week and then shop for some popcorn and chocolate milk to complete the total package. Plan times during the week when you can read to and with your child. Schedule a family video night and make sure that your child has a robust cassette player in his bedroom so that he can listen to stories on cassette while he's doing other things, like playing with toys.

Two things at once — surely not!

A few months ago, I got into a homework battle with my child that I thought would never end. Each of us was mad at the other and thought ourselves completely right. For months, my daughter had been balking at homework. She hated doing it, got bad marks, and couldn't see the point. It was tedious busy-work, and she'd rather be reading a book. I maintained that all that may be true, but she still had to do the homework. The experience brought out tears (often mine), threats, bribes, and ultimatums. But nothing made much difference.

Then something happened. My daughter told me that she'd do a better job on the homework if only I'd let her listen to a tape story at the same time. Her rationale was that the homework wasn't hard, it was just so boring. So, now

I had a tough decision! Should I stick to my guns (and could I stand any more stress?), or should I let her have her way and possibly dig myself into a hole I'd never get out of again? I opted for the hole. I was drained and had no more ideas left.

My daughter has been listening to tapes and doing her homework for about three months now. She's heard some terrific books. She's not a model student, but she completes all her homework, and my life is more peaceful. I'm not saying that I necessarily recommend my method, but I meet fewer and fewer kids these days who like to work quietly and on one thing at a time. Most kids like noise, movement, and buzz. Stories on tape can be a great way (and a better way than the latest pop music) to provide it.

Reading Together

Kids like to do things with you rather than by themselves. That's why they follow you to the kitchen, bedroom, and laundry and wait outside the bathroom for you. Don't fight it. You may as well go with it. Here are a few pointers that can help:

- On Friday nights, everyone's finished the week. Have a family evening to start the weekend off on a good footing. Make it a video or reading night. Get a good family video or a story on tape, rustle up some popcorn, and enjoy the time together.

- If you go into your bedroom for a quiet read and have small kids, pretty soon, they come looking for you. Have some of their books conveniently stashed by your bed. Snuggle up together and enjoy the quiet interlude.

- Have bookshelves. Put them where you and your child use them and keep them stocked with books (rather than rocks, feathers, and those McDonald's plastic toys that your child never plays with but insists on keeping).

- Get into the habit of taking a book with you pretty much wherever you go. Your child copies you. The times between errands and appointments become productive, and you reduce those "I'm bored" or "You're a nuisance" times!

- Make equipment, like cassette players, easy for your child to get to. Show her how to work them and how to return CDs and tapes to their boxes so that you're not inviting a broken or juice-covered calamity.

- If you read newspapers and enjoy the sports page, let your child sit on your lap and look, too. If you do crossword puzzles and have (on the really odd occasion!) to look up a word, let your child see how you do it.

- If you read recipes, shopping lists, or checklists, let your child help. Give her the list and ask her to read bits of it. Ask her, for example, to cross off *bananas* after you have them in your shopping cart or check to see if you've written *milk*.

- Leave notes for your child to read. You don't even have to be there for this sharing activity! Children especially appreciate notes on pillows and in lunch boxes.

You may think that your child does exactly the opposite of what you say. But however much she seems to ignore or even defy you, she's a miniature version of you in all the important respects. She absorbs the things you do, down to your smallest mannerisms. She does what you do, and sometimes those actions may conflict with what you say (or think you do). So you'd better watch what you do! You're a role model for your child, and if you tell her that she should read but don't read yourself, you shouldn't expect miracles.

Looking for a good read for yourself?

In the "Reading Together" section of this chapter, I tell you to be a role model for your child. "Just read a few books yourself," I've said. Well, I'm not so insensitive that I don't realize you may not have had a chance (maybe for years) to get a few quiet minutes to yourself. You just happen to have been raising children. And when you go to the library, you still don't have time to browse the shelves for yourself — you're busy browsing for your child. Well, here's a book list that you may want to consider. I'm not saying you'll like all, or even some, of these books because I don't know your taste in books. But you may like some, and if you do, you've saved yourself hours of searching. I've read all these books and loved them (and Oprah's enjoyed many of them, too). When you go to the library, grab two or three of these titles and see if you find one you like. Be warned, some of them are a bit gritty. If you come across colorful language and object, move on down the list:

About A Boy by Nick Hornby (Riverhead Books)

The Book of Ruth by Jane Hamilton (Anchor)

Cloudstreet by Tim Winton (Scribner)

Ellen Foster by Kaye Gibbons (Vintage Books)

A Fortunate Life by A. B. Facey (Penguin)

The God of Small Things by Arundhati Roy (Perennial)

Here on Earth by Alice Hoffman (Berkley Publishing Group)

House of Sand and Fog by Andre Dubus III (Vintage Books)

I Know This Much Is True by Wally Lamb (Regan Books)

A Lesson Before Dying by Ernest J. Gaines (Vintage Books)

Memoirs of a Geisha by Arthur S. Golden (Vintage Books)

My Place by Sally Morgan (Little, Brown & Company)

The Nanny Diaries by Emma McLaughlin and Nicola Kraus (Griffin Trade Paperback)

No Great Mischief by Alistair MacLeod (Vintage Books)

Oscar and Lucinda by Peter Carey (Vintage Books)

Paddy Clarke Ha Ha Ha by Roddy Doyle (Penguin)

The Rapture of Canaan by Sheri Reynolds (Putnam Publishing Group)

The Shipping News by E. Annie Proulx (Scribner)

Smoking Poppy by Graham Joyce (Washington Square Press)

Snow Falling On Cedars by David Guterson (Vintage Books)

The Stone Diaries by Carol Shields (Penguin)

Stones from the River by Ursula Hegi (Touchstone Books)

Unreliable Memoirs by Clive James (Chatto & Windus)

A Virtuous Woman by Kaye Gibbons (Vintage Books)

A Walk in the Woods by Bill Bryson (Broadway)

Where The Heart Is by Billie Letts (Warner Books)

Making Reading Necessary

You can get your child to read by setting up situations where he has to. This trick sounds more brutal than it really is, but you can make it more or less brutal to suit your needs! Things like notes, shopping lists, and telephone messages compel your child to read. Leave notes about simple chores you want your child to do or reminders about the plans you have for the day. Write as many encouraging and nice-surprise notes as you can so that he always reads your notes to see if they're about something nice.

You may, for example, tape two dollars to a note, saying, "You can use this money for chocolate milk at school today." Other possibilities include things like, "Think about what you want for dinner tonight," "You can have a play date on Saturday, who do you want to invite?" and "Thank you for keeping your room clean."

You can engineer a really good read-or-miss-out situation with incomplete reading (which I talk about in Chapter 22). One parent told me this technique worked perfectly for her when she read her disinterested son *The Chronicles of Narnia.* Another found that *The Guinness Book of Records* worked similar magic. The *Captain Underpants* series has appealed to nearly every kid I've ever met. Look for easy versions of classics. You can now find many of the stories that you enjoyed as a child in sets of easier books. Watch for Newbery Award winners, too.

You can find lists at the American Library Association, www.ala.org/alsc (click on the <u>resources</u> link) or at your local library. Check out the book club pamphlets that come home in your child's school bag. If you see award-winning books in it but don't want to buy them, jot the titles down and ask for them at your library.

Reading for Social Reasons

As soon as kids see other kids reading, they're motivated. They want to try to read, too. They want to fit in, share, and generally be in the groove. Children up to about age 7 don't need much persuading at all. Show them that cool, older kids read and give them interesting and fun books, and they try hard. With older kids and kids who find the going a little rocky, you may have to do more.

Is there a budding chef in your house?

A lot of kids like to cook. You can build some extra reading into your weekends by reading recipes, but many recipe books ask for ingredients that you've never heard of or ask you to do elaborate things that you don't have time for (whisk this, separate that, steam the other). I include a recipe that's easy, great to eat, and made from simple ingredients in this sidebar. I got it from the dad who used to cook meals in my kids' childcare center. He was a great cook and made huge slabs of this cake for the kids to gobble up and the parents to help out with. (I had the hardest time convincing my kids that they really couldn't eat *all* their cake.)

Ken's Yummy Chocolate Cake

1. Get a big cooking pot.

2. Ask a grownup to turn your oven to 350°F (or 180°C).

3. Look at this list of ingredients and put them all on your table before you begin. Have a grownup help you find ingredients and be careful with hot things:

    2 eggs

    1¾ cups of sugar

    4 tablespoons of cocoa

    2 teaspoons of vanilla

    2 teaspoons of sodium bicarbonate

    3 cups of self-rising flour

    8 oz (or two sticks) of margarine

    1 cup of milk

    1 cup of boiling water

4. Put the margarine into your big cooking pot.

5. Melt the margarine on the stove.

6. Take the pot off the stove.

7. Measure all the ingredients and plop them all into the pot.

8. With a big wooden spoon, stir the mix.

9. Stir and stir until you stir away all the lumps. (If your arm starts to hurt, get some help from a grownup.)

10. Get a cake tin (9-inch round tin or similar).

11. Spray some cooking oil into the tin so that the cake doesn't stick to the tin.

12. Ask a grownup to help you pour the mix into the tin.

13. Get a grownup to help you put the tin into the oven.

14. Cook this cake for 45 minutes. If you used a deep cake tin, the cake may take longer to cook. If you used a muffin tin rather than a cake tin, the muffins cook more quickly.

15. Get help to turn the cake out of the tin. Sometimes, cake sticks to the tin and then getting it out can be tricky!

Here's how you make chocolate icing for your cake:

1. Get a big bowl.

2. Look at this list of ingredients and put them all on your table before you begin:

    8 tablespoons of powdered sugar

    2 tablespoons of unsweetened cocoa

    2 tablespoons of melted butter

    2 tablespoon of water or milk

3. Pour all the ingredients into the bowl and stir them together.

4. To make the icing more runny, add more water or milk (a bit at a time so that it's not *too* runny). Make it runny so that you can pour it over the cake. Put the cake on a big plate first! To make it more chocolaty, add more cocoa. Experiment!

5. Wait until the cake has cooled completely (about an hour) before pouring the icing on it.

Football and fashion

Millions of people read newspapers and magazines. If your child likes sports, make sure that you have the newspaper sports pages on hand for her. Support a team with her and keep track of that team's progress. Establish the whole culture of being a supporter so that you can promote your child's interest through newspapers, magazines, and the Internet.

Uh oh, not everyone loves sports! Let your child enjoy fashion magazines, if that's what she's interested in. Later, she may branch out to books about favorite TV characters or pop singers, and then she feels better about trying other books, too. Keep plenty of books around the house so that your child can reach for a book anytime she wants to. Make sure that she sees you reading books, too. You're more successful in getting your child to read if you're a reader than if you're asking her to do something that you plainly don't do yourself.

Surfing and chatting

It's here. The Internet. Your child can go here for information and for pleasure. You and your child can find plenty of useful things on the Internet, but you have to keep the trash at bay in the process. Try to get friendly with the Internet yourself so that you can keep an eye on your child's Internet activities. If you don't have that option, but you do have the Internet at home, have someone set it up who knows what they're doing. A computer-savvy person can put a filter on information that comes through the Internet and let you limit the sites your child can access. Most of all, don't fear the Internet. Computer-wise parents out there in cyberspace keep a watchful eye on things. As quickly as people develop new scams and intrusions, these parents think up new ways for ordinary parents to protect their children.

People use e-mail more than anything else on the Internet. If your child likes passing notes to friends, he can have great fun using e-mail. As you have to do when surfing the Internet, watching TV, and renting movies, guide your child and monitor what he's doing. Even if you know next to nothing about computers, you're just as able as the next person to peer over your child's shoulder!

Big boys read less

Boys generally read less than girls, across the board, and they read still less as they get older. All sorts of things contribute to this gender gap. If you know something about the issues that influence your son, you're better prepared to support him (and advocate for him in school if you have to). Here are some trends and traits that recent research has uncovered about Western culture:

✔ Boys get more ear infections than girls in the important early years of language development.

✔ Boys develop language skills later than girls.

✔ In school, boys are more restless, boisterous, and loud than girls.

✔ Boys get into more trouble in school, which can deflect attention from reading problems.

✔ In reading tests, boys consistently score lower than girls.

✔ Most people see reading as a mostly female activity.

✔ Boys enjoy reading less than girls do.

✔ Boys have lower expectations of success in school than girls.

You can easily see from these few points that you should keep a watchful eye on your son's progress with reading and provide him with encouragement, support, and some respected role models. Your daughter needs all these things, too, but she's a little less vulnerable.

You're probably used to taking precautions when your child goes to other people's houses. You're probably fine about asking routine questions: Do you own a gun? Do you use seat belts? Does your car have an air bag? Will an adult be in the house the whole time? Is there a phone my child can use at any time? Now you also have to think about the Internet. You should establish your family's rules on Internet use before your child ventures into new households. Remember to tell him clearly, but without frightening him, that some adults tell children lies over the Internet and he should never give out his name, address, telephone number, or e-mail address.

Hanging out

At around three o'clock, librarians around the country make sure that they've had their break, used the bathroom, and finished important phone calls. They brace themselves. School ends and hundreds of high-school children flock to public libraries to do their homework. These kids know that the library is safe, free, and a place where they can just hang out with friends. Hooray for libraries! From the time that your child can hold a book, take her to your local library for story time and children's events. Take her regularly and help her use books, computers, and comics.

If your child knows your public library before she starts school, she's already comfortable when she gets to her school library. Children learn a lot of useful things in school libraries. And if ever your child goes through a friendless time at school, the school library can give her sanctuary.

Play dates and sleepovers

Don't ruin a perfectly good play date by suggesting some reading. Instead, be subtle. Create cozy reading spaces for children who are tired of racing about outside. Provide hot chocolate, fruit, magazines, comics, and stories on tape. Kindergarten teachers know a lot about this sort of nest-making, and children's librarians know about it, too. They appreciate that beanbags, cushions, sheepskin rugs, and soft toys invite readers almost as much as books do.

When you're decking out a reading nook, get your child's guidance. Get the cushions and rugs that he likes and let him put books in boxes and baskets, and cuddly toys on bookshelves. After he's cast his nook-making eye over things, show him that he has an inviting space by going into it with him.

The cozy nook

My house has a lot of room but needs a hefty measure of *TLC* (tender, loving care), so my kids can hang posters all over their walls and use markers with impunity. The house is perfect for us, and the kids love it. But a few weeks ago, we had a bedroom crisis. My daughter declared that her bedroom was unfit to live in. It was boring and everybody else had better. When I asked my daughter what we should do about this dilemma, she treated me with royal disdain. My child was certain that I wouldn't know a cool bedroom if I fell into one (which wasn't likely in *our* house). I retreated. I have precious little idea of style at the best of times and certainly not in the face of a hostile almost-teenager.

Some thumps and bangs later, my daughter emerged with a triumphant glow. Her room was transformed. She had hung clothes and scarves across the walls, stuck photos in the gaps between scarves and rearranged the furniture. And it really did look quite different. I bought her one small bedside lamp for mood, and she had completed her cozy nook. In pre-cozy nook days, my daughter did far less reading than she does now. Now, she always has a tape story playing and likes to nestle down among the cushions. So do I. I often snuggle in there with her, reading magazines about the latest styles and look. There's not much hope of a "look" for me, but that's the good thing about reading — you don't need dress sense to do it.

Guided Reading

When teachers listen to your child read out loud they call it "guided reading." You can easily see how they guide your child when they help him correct his mistakes, but before they even get to that stage, they've guided his reading in a couple of other ways. They've helped him choose a reading book that's just at the right level for him, and they've talked about the book to prepare him for what will be in the text. I go into the three parts of guided reading; choosing a book, preparing to read the books, and listening to your child read the book out loud so that you can do guided reading at home:

- ✔ **Helping your child choose a book to read out loud:** When you read books to your child or he browses them, he can have any book that he likes. It doesn't matter if a book has hard text because your child doesn't have to figure the text out for himself.

  But with books your child reads mostly by himself, you have to take a different approach. You don't want your child to be frustrated and put off by hard text, so help him select books that he can cope with. Look for books with not too much text, helpful illustrations, and not too many new and tricky words. Use this formula for gauging whether a book has too many hard words: Over 5 unknown words within any 100 words puts your child in the frustration zone. Aim for books with only three or four new and tricky words per page. If the whole page only has about 20 words on it, you want only 1 tricky word among them.

- ✔ **Preparing your child for reading a book out loud:** Scan through the to-be-read book with your child before he tries to read it so that he's well prepared for reading it. Show your child words that look too hard for him to figure out before he comes to them in the text. Point a hard word out and help him sound it out and look carefully at its shape. Jot it on an index card. Show your child the index card again after reading the book so that he has a better chance of remembering it whenever he comes to it again. Talk to your child about the pictures in the book, too, so that he gets an idea of probable plot and vocabulary.

  Beware of taking over! Keep your child in charge of his own books and resist the temptation to choose or hold his book or turn the pages. Every subtle intrusion like this one makes your child view reading as really your thing and not his.

- ✔ **Listening to your child read out loud:** Remember that when you listen to your child read, you need to make it a positive experience for him. Correct him in a supportive way that makes him feel he's progressing and impressing you.

For different ways to correct your child's reading mistakes, flip to Chapter 22, where I talk about helping your child sound out a word, telling him a word to avoid frustration, helping him find words within words, and helping him use contextual cues.

Going to Aunt Maud's

This simple car game sharpens your kid's reading and visual discrimination skills (which I talk about in Chapter 4). To play, begin by saying this sentence:

> I'm going to Aunt Maud's and I'm taking a ***** with me." Your children take turns replying by saying, "I'm going to Aunt Maud's, can I bring a *****?"

Your kid needs to guess the word rule that you're using. For instance, you may decide that only words with a double letter can be used in the game, so you're taking your *boots.* Your child can take things like *mittens, eggs, apples, cheese, glasses, books,* and *balloons,* but she can't take things like *milk, socks, shoes,* and *chocolate.* Your dialogue looks something like this example (your hints are in bold):

> **I'm going to Aunt Maud's and I'm taking my boots with me.**
>
> I'm going to Aunt Maud's too, can I bring a bag?

Sorry no, you can't bring a bag.

I'm going to Aunt Maud's and I'm taking some cheese with me.

I'm going to Aunt Maud's too, can I bring a blanket?

Sorry no, you can't bring a blanket.

With little kids, use easy rules. You can use rules like all words must start with the letter *t* or the word must be the name of a vegetable. As your kids get better at the game, you can get trickier. If you give your child a pen and notepad and have her write down every word, she can figure out the rule better and get a lot of spelling practice, too.

Achieving a Good Book-to-Child Fit

Helping your child read probably sounds pretty easy. You go to the library, get a lot of good stuff to read, make regular time to help your child, and presto! Well, I don't want to douse your flame, but I have to give you one little cautionary reminder.

When you help your child, remember to help, not dominate. Start with his interests, not your best intentions. Find out what he likes to read and in what form. You may be dying to introduce him to the stories that you loved as a kid, but those stories may not be the right thing for him. Take his interests and personality into consideration when you help him choose books.

Making maps

Kids read things that interest them. Be sure to start any mission to improve your child's reading, with your child's interests, rather than with things you think he should be interested in. Find out what he likes to do and build on that interest.

One parent told me that she attributes her son's current interest in reading to her creativity when he was younger. When he was only 6 or 7, she discovered that he liked reading maps. She bought him a decent sketchpad and some rulers and turned his interest into a hobby. She asked him to draw a map for each of their many car journeys, reading her road maps to identify town and street names, and drawing his own versions with labeled towns and roads. He became confident reading the small amounts of text this task required and was then more comfortable with tackling bigger pieces of text.

The big "Barbie" blunder

If your child loves reading books with questionable themes, don't worry too much about it. Let him make his own choices, but keep reading him stories that you like, too.

A short-haired, flat-shoed feminist girlfriend of mine has a wonderful story of when her daughter, Ashley, loved to read the girl stories *Bratz, Cinderella,* and most of all, *Barbie.* My friend says that at first she was fine with Barbie, but only because she planned to share other things with Ashley later. She planned to read good books and discuss strong characters with Ashley and, without even realizing it, built a picture of how things would be. Meanwhile, Ashley brought home *Barbie* books and books filled with ultra feminine characters. My friend tried to gently steer Ashley into other things. Wasn't Barbie just a little silly? Did Ashley realize that real women weren't like that? Couldn't she gravitate to stronger role models? No. Ashley liked (no, *loved*) and wanted to be Barbie. She wanted Barbie dolls, a Barbie birthday party, and Barbie books. Her friends loved Barbie, too. Barbie was cool.

Ashley's mom wondered what to do with her own feminist principles. Should she go underground? Be firmer? Ignore Barbie mania? Then, another feminist mom with the same dilemma wrote an article about Barbie. The journalist explained that it's okay for your daughter to love Barbie. She's trying on one of the many roles that she'll experiment with and knows that women in the real world don't look or behave like Barbie. She's trying styles out, and that's healthy. She'll eventually find her own style, and it will probably be much like her parents. For generations, Barbie has been loved by strong, independent, and yes, feminist women the world over. None of them are any the worse for it. Some of them even admit to their Barbie background.

Chapter 24

When to Get Help for Your Child

In This Chapter

▶ Recognizing a problem

▶ Putting your child's reading ability in perspective

▶ Taking practical steps quickly

▶ Getting help from a few places (including yourself!)

▶ Identifying signs of a struggling reader

Sometimes, it's easy to see when your child needs extra help. When he cuts his hand, chips a tooth, or pushes his head between the bars of a neighbor's fence, you lavish him with your help. But when it comes to reading difficulties, things may not look so clear to you. What exactly *is* a reading problem? How can you tell a reading delay from a full-blown problem? Who should you go to for help? This chapter gives you practical advice. In short and clear terms, it tells you how to spot a problem and start fixing it.

How to Tell When Your Child's Struggling

With hindsight, parents of children who struggle with reading identify things that signaled a problem early on. Their child

✔ Started to walk late

✔ Started to talk late

✔ Had trouble articulating words (when other kids her age spoke clearly)

✔ Had ear infections

✔ Had trouble following simple instructions

✔ Had trouble remembering stories

✔ Had trouble doing simple puzzles

✔ Seemed not to see as clearly as other kids

✔ Seemed more restless than other kids

✔ Didn't show much interest in books

The trouble with lists like this one is that you can easily find some of these indicators in most kids. Also, a parent can easily recall or imagine that these indicators popped up when he's thinking about them at a later date (even though they didn't seem a big deal at the time). If your child shows unusual behaviors with vision (like tilting her head, rubbing her eyes, or squinting), see your doctor.

If your child shows unusual behavior with hearing (she can't hear when you whisper, talks loudly *all* the time, or can't filter out background noise), see your doctor. Have tests done.

If you're worried about your child's coordination, restlessness, or interest in books, watch how she behaves in her kindergarten year, when she's 5 or 6.

If you think your child is noticeably different from other kids and may not be within the normal range for restlessness, coordination, or any other part of her development, get medical advice.

If your child isn't interested in reading in kindergarten, or struggles with work there, keep reading to her. Help her in practical ways, like moving her finger along lines of text and playing word games with her. Watch her progress. At the end of kindergarten, if she's lagging behind her peers, talk to her teacher and draw up a practical, measurable plan for improving her reading. For more on getting your child's teacher involved in extra help, check out the sections "Getting help from your child's teacher" and "Modifying School Work" later in this chapter.

Three Ways to Gauge Your Child's Relative Reading Ability

Your child isn't doing as well with reading as you thought he would. His friends are ahead of him. His sister started reading much earlier than he did. Should you be worried? You can gauge where your child ranks, relative to other kids, in reading in three ways:

✔ **Ask his teacher.** After all, she's seen a lot of other kids, she's seen a lot of your kid, and she can compare your child to classmates.

✔ **Make your own observations of his peers, siblings, cousins, and playmates.** The teacher may be reluctant to give you bad (or incriminating) news. You have the keenest knowledge of your own child, and you have the greatest interest in your own child. Finally, you have a parent's instincts (and they're often right).

✔ **Have him tested.** With tests, you get an objective measure. Test results may prompt your child's teacher to give him extra help, or test results may prompt you to get extra help outside school.

How to Tell a Reading Delay from a Reading Problem

Based on the criteria in the preceding section, you can see if your child isn't keeping up with her peers. Does that mean she has a reading "problem?" This topic is pretty meaty, so I give you the essential points in this list:

✔ Educators use several terms to describe kids who have trouble reading. You hear things like reading problems, difficulties, or differences and learning problems, difficulties, or differences. You may hear about specific learning problems, difficulties, or differences and dyslexia. (*Dyslexia* describes an unexpected and enduring problem with reading. It's a term recognized by school districts as a subset of the broader category of disability "Specific Learning Disabilities," which I talk about in the following bullet.) What does it all mean? In the end, these terms all mean much the same vague thing. They mean that your child is having trouble reading.

✔ The mess with terminology gets cleared up if your child has big problems in class. If she performs about two years below her expected level in school, teachers get concerned. They get your permission and have your child tested for *Specific Learning Disabilities* (SLD), one of the 13 or so official categories of disability recognized under federal law.

If you're sure that your child performs way below everyone else her age, but her teacher doesn't get her tested for SLD, you can request this testing yourself.

If school tests show that your child has SLD, that classification has real, practical meaning. Your child is now eligible for special education services at school.

Only a few kids qualify as having SLD, so don't expect your child to qualify just because she isn't keeping up with her peers.

If an independent consultant tells you that your child has dyslexia, or any other learning disability, it doesn't necessarily count at school. Your school district has to run its own tests or approve the tests that you get. If you want to have your child privately tested, be sure to check with your school district first.

When You Should Deal with the Problem Quickly

Your child's not so bad at reading that he qualifies for special help in school, but he's still lagging behind. Should you wait a while to give him a chance to catch up?

If your child's getting left behind his peers when he's between age 5 and 7, pay attention to his difficulties. Help him every night. Keep the mood light but help him catch up to his peers.

The very best years for learning to read are between ages 5 and 7. In these years, your child makes the quickest progress he ever makes. If he's struggling and you don't give him extra help at this critical time, you miss your best window of opportunity.

If your child is older than 7 and falling behind, get onto it. Help him every night so that he can close the gap. If he's older than 9, you need to get super serious. Only 25 percent of kids 10 and older ever catch up. Older children need frequent, ongoing, structured help to catch up with their peers.

Getting Help

When you decide that your child needs extra help with reading, a few people and organizations can help you. The main ones are

- ✔ Your child's teacher
- ✔ Your child's school
- ✔ A private tutor or leaning center

Getting help from your child's teacher

Even if your child is a preschooler, she probably goes to a play center or play group. Teachers and group leaders know masses of stuff. They have ideas for motivating and tutoring kids and know where to send you to find out more. Ask for simple, practical advice that you can use over several weeks or months. If your child's at school, ask if the teacher can lend you books or materials to use. Write a *simple* plan describing what you will do with your child each night and arrange to meet the teacher in a few weeks time to see if you have made progress.

Chatting with someone about your concerns can comfort you, but remember to use the short time you get to chat with the teacher wisely. Talk to friends before you see the teacher so that you've had time to get worries off your chest. Then briefly describe your concerns to the teacher. Spend most of your time asking her about a plan of action. What kind of things can you do to help every night? When can you meet again for a follow-up? How do you know if your strategies are working?

Getting help from your child's school

Schools have ways of helping kids who struggle with reading. You may not find as much help as you want, but you should find that your child's school runs helpful programs. A *program* is just a plan of work. Teachers do a plan of work with kids, which usually lasts for a limited time. Programs that can help your child include reading programs, homework programs, tutoring programs, and social and personal development programs.

Reading programs

If the reading program at your child's school is a widely available one that thousands of schools use, you may hear names like Reading Recovery, Orton-Gillingham, or Lindamood-Bell. (The last two are named after the people who wrote them.) If the program's a small one, run just by your school, they may call it something like Race Forward with Reading. Ask about reading programs in your school and get your child included in one.

Homework programs

Another kind of program run in schools is a homework program. In homework programs, kids do their homework with other kids and some helpers. The helpers are usually a mix of teachers and older kids. Most kids like homework programs because they get to hang out with friends and get their homework done in a supportive environment. Parents love these programs. I guess it's obvious why.

Tutoring programs

Many schools run tutoring programs. They get volunteer tutors to give individual and regular help to kids. Kids on these programs usually know they're lucky to get this personal attention. If your child's struggling, this kind of program may be just what he needs.

Social and personal development programs

These programs have nothing much to do with reading, but they're worthwhile, all the same. If your child isn't all that confident, or isn't the most popular kid in class, she can get a lot from this kind of program. Even though it's not directly what you're looking for, ask about social programs. They can make your child happier in school. And kids who are happy in school have a better chance of being good readers.

Jim, the wonder librarian

Not long ago, I gave a talk in a school. A lot of people came, and the school principal described the audience as "riveted." Of course, I was very happy. But one thing troubled me. Jim, the teacher librarian who'd invited me to the school, hadn't raved about the book I'd just written, the one the talk was based on. I'm not (much of) an egomaniac, but things didn't add up.

I chatted with Jim, waiting for my opportunity, and then asked, "Did you like the book, Jim?" "I loved it," he said, but I could sense there was an underlying "but . . . " "Go on, Jim, I'm tough," I lied. "What was wrong with it?" "Well there

was just one thing," said Jim. "You didn't say enough about teacher librarians." And in a rare flash of insight, I could see what he meant. Jim's library was like Aladdin's cave. You could see that kids loved going there. For months, he'd been running a family reading time on Wednesday evenings. Of course, he felt I'd given librarians scant attention.

So, Jim, I hope you read this sidebar. And for all the librarians everywhere, thanks for helping our kids! To parents, don't forget that teacher librarians can help you turn your child into a reader.

Getting help from a private learning center or tutor

Learning centers are pretty thick on the ground these days. Some of the big names you hear are Kumon, Sylvan, and Score. They all offer individual or small group instruction, but each has its own angle. For example, Kumon gives your child progressive at-his-level worksheets that get marked by trained teachers; Sylvan boasts that all its instructors are trained teachers and that they have a cool system for motivating kids; Score is the place for computers and young instructors (said to be good role models for your child). If you want to make use of a learning center, visit a few to find a good match for your child's personality.

Prefer a local tutor? You can find tutors through the telephone directory or by word of mouth. Check out their experience and credentials. Tutors can be competent college students or fully trained ex-teachers. They can also be nervous types who can't make it in the classroom. So make sure that you get a winner for your child!

Giving Help Yourself

To help your struggling child at home, you need a simple and realistic plan. Otherwise, you get bogged down and overwhelmed. Decide what you can do with your child and think in real terms. Picture your other kids, your other obligations, and the growing pile of odd socks that you really have to sort through. Is your reading plan workable? If it is, jot it down.

Here's what you should have in your plan:

✔ Sight Words

✔ Phonics

✔ Guided Reading

Sight words

In Chapter 11, I talk about sight words. Teachers call them sight words because they're a bunch of words that occur so frequently in regular text that your child has to have instant, or sight, recognition of them. If she doesn't, she becomes a stop-start, frustrated reader. To see whether or not your child has a firm grip on sight words, look at the list of 220 sight words in Chapter 11. Have your child read through it and highlight the words that she can't quickly tell you. Stop when she has ten words highlighted. Play games with these ten words every night for a week. Then do another ten. Keep going through the list together, focusing on ten words at a time, until you've worked your way through all 220 words. Chapter 11 also has good games to play with those ten words.

Phonics

Kids don't like it when you say things like "spl-ice; spl-iii-ce; sssspl-iii-ccce." But they like being able to read all by themselves, and unless you teach them some phonics, or how to sound out words, they never can read on their own. So find the balance — when to make your child sound out, when to just tell him the word, and when to read a fun book and give the sounding out a rest for a while. Here's the drill with phonics:

✔ At first, focus on the sounds of single letters.

✔ Spend extra time making sure that your child knows short vowel sounds, as in *cat, pen, pig, hot,* and *bun.*

✔ Talk about the special sounds of *ch, th,* and *sh* and mention *ph* and *wh,* too.

✔ Read short vowel + special sound words like *chick, thin,* and *shop.*

✔ Talk about long vowels, as in *ape, weed, ride, hope,* and *cute.*

✔ Get a grip on *Bossy e* in words like *ape, Pete, ride, hope,* and *cute.*

✔ Make sure that he masters the *When two vowels go walking, the first one does the talking* rule.

✔ Whenever you come across a word family, take time to have a good look at it. The *all (all, ball, call, tall)* and *ight (might, right, tight, fight)* families give you a good place to start.

- ✔ Point out that some words, like *who,* aren't worth sounding out. Write them out a few times, pin them to the wall, and remember how they look.

- ✔ Some words, like *what,* only sound out in part. Sound out where you can (the *wh*) and then remember the look of the rest.

- ✔ Take rests and have fun!

- ✔ Have your child read phonetically controlled books (books with limited vocabulary). I suggest some good ones in Chapter 20.

- ✔ Keep reading good books to your child so that he knows what he's working toward.

Guided reading

Guided reading in schools generally means that a teacher helps your child select a reading book and then listens to her read the book out loud. If you want pointers about doing guided reading with your child at home, flip to Chapter 22. It tells you things like how to prepare your child for reading her book out loud to you.

If you want to try different ways of reading out loud with your child, like reading out loud along with her, or joining in with the reading out loud every now and then, flip to Chapter 22. It gives you a full rundown of these "paired reading" techniques.

Twenty or more minutes reading every night really helps your struggling child get better at reading.

Things Struggling Readers Do

Struggling readers aren't happy to be struggling. They want to be like their peers. They don't want people to think of them as "dumb." But the hard truth is that kids quickly classify other kids in school. Those kids who can't read fall into the *dumb, possibly dumb,* or *dumb but still nice* categories. Imagine that you're in one of those categories and imagine how you'd react. You'd be stressed — and that's exactly how your child feels. You need to know how stress can manifest itself and how you can deal with it. The following sections present some common ways kids behave when they're struggling and give practical advice to help them.

Focus on solutions. If your child breaks a pencil, hand him another; if he loses his instructions, help him call a school friend to get them; if he's distraught, sympathize. You can help your child feel better and, from your level-headed example, get better at finding his own solutions. If you berate, nag, and complain, you both have a miserable time. That time doesn't get any shorter as a result of your disapproval, either.

Your child behaves badly in class

Why it happens

Your child wants to deflect attention from her reading difficulties. Or she's bored because she can't read most of the work. Or she wants attention but can't get it for good work. She believes (unconsciously) that bad attention is better than no attention.

Your child may behave badly in class for exactly the opposite reasons to those I've just described. She's bored because she's a fluent reader and things in class progress too slowly for her. Ask the teacher, nicely, if she would give your child "open ended" activities, activities like making posters and writing reports, that allow your child to be creative and follow her thoughts in directions that she chooses herself.

What to do about it

See these behaviors for what they really are — reactions to stress.

Make practical plans to improve your child's reading skills. Set up a regular routine for guided reading and activities like reading word lists or word puzzles and games. Help your child do all her homework or be close at hand to help her when she calls you.

Your child keeps a very low profile in class

Why it happens

Your child wants to deflect attention from his reading difficulties, or he feels that no attention is better than humiliating bad attention.

What to do about it

Make sure that your child has friends for play dates, friends and family outside of school, and sports or interests to take part in. He needs to feel good and capable in other areas of his life.

Your child dislikes school

Why it happens

Put yourself in your child's shoes. Wouldn't you feel the same way if you were having trouble reading, and as a consequence, school was a constant struggle?

What to do about it

Meet the teacher and pinpoint ways to make school easier for your child. See if she can give your child special responsibilities and jobs; see if she can pair your child with a helpful and friendly kid whenever the kids have to work in pairs; ask her to modify your child's work to make it easier for her.

Your child tries too hard to excel in other areas

Why it happens

Your child wants to show you his strengths.

What to do about it

Acknowledge your child's effort and success in sports, music, or whatever else he does. Meanwhile, keep in touch with his teacher so that you do structured and ongoing reading activities at home. Assure your child that he's making progress with reading and that his perseverance will pay off.

Your child is bad tempered and behaves badly at home

Why it happens

Your child is aware of her low status in class. She's not showing it directly (with a big sign that says *I'm stressed*), but she's under stress. She can't indefinitely bottle up that stress. It seeps out as frustration, anger, and despair.

What to do about it

Do three things to help your unhappy child:

- ✓ Listen to her talk about her unhappiness. Be nonjudgmental and noninvasive. Encourage her to tell you more and to figure out her own solutions, if she can. If she asks for your advice, give it to her in simple, practical terms.

Help your child get better at figuring out solutions for herself, so that she gets more confident and able, but watch out for big problems. If your child has a big problem, like being bullied, intervene. She can't manage issues like bullying, racism, or theft all by herself. When you sense or hear that she's struggling with a big problem, see her teacher. Work out with the teacher some immediate, practical ways to help. Make sure that the teacher treats the problem with discretion by, for example, not asking your child to talk to her in the presence of a bully if your child's being victimized by that bully. (Regrettably, this kind of thing can happen.)

✔ Have distractions to take your child's mind off her problem for a while. Organized sports, social clubs, outings to friends' houses, and even playing board games at home all give your child a fun time so that she forgets her worries for a while and feels emotionally stronger.

✔ Keep focusing on practical solutions that will help your child be a better reader. Work out a plan of practical reading activities to do at home and meet often with the teacher to make sure that the plan's working. If it isn't, revise it.

Your child is forgetful and disorganized

Why it happens

Most kids aren't naturally blessed in these areas. It may be that your child is worse than most, but be careful not to lose perspective. Your child may be no more disorganized than most kids in his class.

What to do about it

Help your child out with organizing his school bag, work, and routines. Give him checklists. Give him a special place to keep his bag and books at home (so that he's not always hunting for them at the last frantic minute). As soon as he comes home from school, help him unpack his bag. Help him pack it again when it's time to go back to school.

Troubleshooting Common Problems

If your child reverses letters, leaves them out here and there, and puts them in where they shouldn't be, don't panic. Memory aids in the next few sections, like the *bed* strategy and the picture of *Polly,* can help him fix the reversals. And other errors improve with regular practice.

Have your child read the same text to improve his reading accuracy and fluency. To sharpen his writing skills, give him regular dictations (when you read text to him and he writes it):

✔ Choose short paragraphs with only one or two new words in them.

✔ Help him write the easy words perfectly and figure out the new words.

✔ Dictate the same paragraph again, this time giving no help.

What to do about b and d reversals

A lot of parents worry about letter reversals. Their child reads or writes *b* for *d* and vice versa. At one time or another, most kids reverse letters, especially *b* and *d.* If your child has trouble, try using the simple *bed* strategy. Take a look at Figure 24-1 and then read the instructions that follow to see what it's all about.

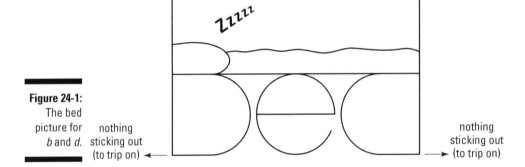

Figure 24-1:
The bed picture for *b* and *d.*

nothing sticking out (to trip on) ←

nothing sticking out (to trip on) →

1. Explain to your child that the bed picture can help her remember which way *b* and *d* face.

2. Draw this simple shape: l__l

   Have your child do the same.

3. Draw a pillow and blanket on top of yours and have your child do the same with her picture.

4. Write the word *bed* in the bed picture, using the sides of the bed as the vertical lines in your *b* and *d,* and sound it out so that your child hears the *b* and *d* sounds. Have her do the same on her picture.

5. Tell her that when she can't remember *b* (buh) or *d* (duh), she can just make her bed! Be sure that nothing is sticking out — that's the big secret. (If letters face the wrong way, they stick out and someone may trip over them.)

6. Show your child how to make her bed with her hands. Figure 24-2 shows you how.

7. Explain that she's making a big bouncy bed as a quick way of remembering the orientation of *b* and *d*.

Nothing can stick out at the ends of the bed — everything goes inside.

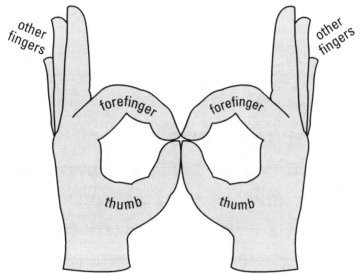

Figure 24-2:
Making a
bed with
your hands.

Having trouble with 9 and P?

Some kids have trouble distinguishing between the number 9 and the letter P. Here's a way to iron it out:

1. Ask your child which direction he reads and writes in. Get the answer left to right from him and have him point to the right.

2. Ask him to tell you a name that begins with P, like Peter, Paul, or Polly.

3. Tell him to draw a face onto the circle part of P, the nose pointing in the reading and writing direction.

4. Ask your child to add features like hair, a cap, and glasses and write the person's name above him.

5. Tell your child that whenever he's not sure about P, he can draw his character, facing in the reading and writing direction. You can see a sample P drawing in Figure 24-3.

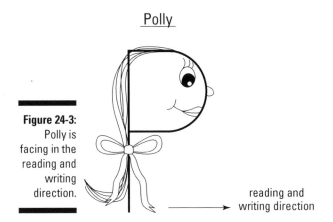

Polly

Figure 24-3:
Polly is
facing in the
reading and
writing
direction.

reading and
writing direction

Modifying Schoolwork

Teachers can alter your child's work in small ways that can help her a lot.
They can ask for different kinds of work from her, too. Here are some practical modifications that your child's teacher can make:

✔ The teacher gives your child text that has key words highlighted. That
way, your child can read the key words to get the main idea.

✔ The teacher buddies your child with another helpful student. The
teacher shows your child's buddy specific ways to help. These help
methods can include

• Reading instructions to your child and having your child highlight
key words as she follows the text.

• Doing paired reading with your child.

• Being on call for answering your child's questions.

✔ Your child sits close to the board so that she can read and hear better
(as long as your child doesn't feel picked-on).

✔ The teacher asks for less written work from your child. Your child can
hand in labeled diagrams, graphs, and pictures in place of some written
work.

✔ The teacher can let your child hand in typed sheets for homework. Your
child dictates the work for you to type.

✔ The teacher grades your child's work with an emphasis on effort, not
output.

Part VI
The Part of Tens

"Hi! We're in the kitchen learning to read
words that start with 'Th'."

In this part . . .

This part gives you all the best stuff in bite-sized pieces that you can digest in minutes. In a few easy lists, you get word families to keep your child talking in rhyme for ages, phonics rules to help him sound out words like *shoal,* tips that you can use to keep your child reading (even on short attention span days), and resources worth putting your hand into your pocket for (and, believe me, you get good value from a shopping list written by someone as cheap as me).

Chapter 25

More Than Ten Word Families

In This Chapter

▶ Recapping on word families

▶ Taking a look at common word families

You've nearly reached the finish line! You don't have much farther to go now, and I'm leaving you on a high note. In this chapter, I give you families of words that you should introduce to your child. And, for easy reference, I put in a table of words for each family.

Families (of people) have similar characteristics. (I'm talking about how everyone in your family has that cute nose or sticky-out ears.) Word families are the same. Words in a family all have a common sound and spelling pattern. Knowing word families can be really handy because your child can more easily remember a family of words with a pattern to it than individual and unalike words. Whenever you come upon a word that belongs to a word family, show your child the family. Start with *all*. Your child can tackle the *all* family pretty easily, and he may run into it often.

The Very Easy all Family

Show your child the word *all*. Does she have it? If she has, she can easily read the words in Table 25-1.

Table 25-1	The *all* Family	
ball	call	fall
gall	hall	mall
pall	small	stall
tall	wall	y'all!

Shall doesn't belong to this family. It's a loner with its own sound.

The Pretty Straightforward *ight* Family

Although this family has a scary appearance (what do *those* letters say?), it's down-to-earth and no-nonsense. All these family members look and sound the same. As soon as you're introduced to one of them, you're comfortable with them all. So let me introduce you. Please meet the *ight* family, in Table 25-2.

Table 25-2	The *ight* Family	
blight	bright	fight
flight	fright	light
might	night	plight
right	sight	slight
tight		

Show your child the *ight* part in each word and marvel at how quickly he reads this whole hard-looking bunch. If you want to explain the way *ight* sounds out to your child, tell him that the *i* is long and the *gh* is silent.

The *oi* and *oy* Families

Here's where I tidy up words like *coin* and *coy* (instead of tidying up my house, desk, or lifetime supply of plastic bags). Explain the *oi* sound to your child and have her spot (and circle or highlight) the letters *oi* and *oy* in the words in Table 25-3. Then read through the table together.

Explain to your child that the *s* in *poison* and *noise* sounds out as *z*.

Table 25-3	*oi* and *oy* Words
Oi	*Oy*
avoid	annoy
boil	boy
broil	coy
coin	destroy
foil	enjoy
hoist	joy
join	Roy
moist	royal
noise	soy
oil	toy
point	
poison	
soil	
spoil	
voice	

The *ou* and *ow* Families

The sound of *ow,* or what you'd scream if I kicked you, is made by *ow* and *ou.* Explain this fact to your child and have him spot (and highlight) all the *ow*'s and *ou*'s in Table 25-4. Then read through the table.

Your child can remember the *ow* (*you hurt me*) sound if you give him, or (jokingly) threaten to give him, a gentle pinch to remind him of the sound.

Table 25-4	Words with the *Ow* (*You Hurt Me*) Sound
Ou	*Ow*
about	bow
aloud	brow
amount	brown
cloud	clown
count	cow
doubt	crown
flour	down
foul	flower
found	frown
ground	gown
hound	growl
loud	how
mouse	owl
out	power
pound	shower
proud	sow
round	tower
scout	town
shout	vow
sound	wow

Watch out for the silent *b* in *doubt!*

Your child can easily learn one sound and a lot of common words with that sound in them. He finds the task harder if you introduce too many variables. When you remember, for example, that *ou* sounds like *aw* in the words *bought, fought,* and *ought* and like short *u* in words like *cousin, trouble,* and *enough,* don't worry about it! Your child can get to know these words later. When he becomes better at reading, he can figure out these words more easily in context than by laboring over them now.

What about words like *blow* and *glow?* Should you teach your child this other *ow* sound, or will that just confuse him? Take time to teach this family when you come across it. But move steadily. Spend time practicing one sound at a time. You can easily show your child words like *blow* and *glow* if he's already very sure of words like *growl* and *howl* (or vice versa). He becomes confused if you pile everything on him at once. Table 25-5 gives you some *blow* and *glow* type words to introduce to your child.

Table 25-5	The Odd *ow* Words	
barrow	blow	blown
borrow	bow	crow
flow	flown	glow
grow	low	mow
owe	own	row
stow	tomorrow	tow

The *er, ir,* and *ur* Families

Sometimes, a number of letters or letter combinations make the same sound. The next two tables, Tables 25-6 and 25-7, show just what I'm talking about.

All three ways to make the *er* sound are pretty common. You most commonly spell the sound out as *er* because *er* is a word ending or suffix. You can write long lists of words, like *bigger, fatter, taller,* and so on, if you want. If you do, remember that when a word like *fat* turns into *fatter,* you should remind your child that she has to double the letter to keep the vowel short.

Even though they don't appear as often, *ir* and *ur* still play an important part. Two common words that use *ir* are *girl* and *first.*

The way you pronounce *er* depends on your accent. If you think some of the words I've included in Table 25-6 don't seem to fit in this sound family, that's okay. With all the rules and words I give you in this book, take what you need and skip over the things you're not comfortable with.

Table 25-6	The One Sound of *er, ir,* and *ur*	
er	*ir*	*ur*
brother	birch	burglar
clever	bird	burn
computer	dirt	curl
farmer	fir	curse
faster	firm	fur
father	first	hurl
fern	girl	hurt
germ	shirt	nurse
her	sir	purr
mother	stir	purse
never	third	suburb
perch	thirsty	surf
sister	whirl	turf
stern		turtle
teacher		urn
term		

The *or, aw,* and *au* Families

Table 25-7 shows three ways to make the *or* sound. The most common way is with the letters *or.* Show the word *or* to your child and then run through column one of Table 25-7 with him. Save the other two columns for later. After he's good at *or* words, show him the *aw* and *au* ways of making the same sound.

Table 25-7	The Sounds of *or, aw,* and *au*	
or	**aw**	**au**
airport	bawl	auto
born	claw	caught
chore	draw	Claus
cord	lawn	faucet
cork	paw	laundry
corn	raw	pause
for	saw	sauce
fork	shawl	
form	straw	
fort	yawn	
horn		
horse		
more		
morning		
normal		
or		
orchard		
order		
porch		
short		
sort		
storm		
torn		

When you're starting out with word families, you should read Dr. Seuss's *Hop on Pop*. It's a good story and has several easy and common word families written on its inside cover. Practice them before reading the story and your child can read it all, himself.

That Smooth *oo* Family

I'm about to do something shameful. I reached my limit of ten word families (in fact, I reached it a couple of families ago), and I still have one more family on my mind. So I'm plunging ahead with unlucky family 13! Ooh, this family is the *oo* family. The *oo* family is so nice that you just have to teach it to your child. *Zoom* through all the *cool* words in Table 25-8 and later, when your child's got the hang of them, show her the look-alike words in Table 25-9. These words look just like the *moon, spoon,* and *soon* bunch of words but have a very different sound. Say the words out loud with your child so that she hears the new sound. Take special notice of *book, look, took,* and *good,* which are words your child will see often.

Table 25-8	Some *oo* Words	
boom	boot	broom
choose	cool	food
fool	goose	groom
loose	mood	moon
noon	pool	school
shoot	soon	stool
tooth	zoo	zoom

Table 25-9	More *oo* Words	
book	brook	cook
crook	foot	good
look	shook	soot
stood	took	wood
wool		

Chapter 26

Ten Phonics Rules

* *

In This Chapter

▶ Knowing what rules to know (and what rules aren't worth your time)

▶ Running through a few really useful rules

* *

Sometimes, people go overboard with rules. They find rules for figuring out words that you can best remember by the look of them. They say things like, "The word *who* has a silent *w*. Sound out the *h* as normal but pronounce the *o* as *oo*, as in moon." What a long-winded and boring rule! Luckily for you, I'm one exciting gal. And I say these words of wisdom about *who*: "*Who* is tricky. Write it down a lot. Remember how it looks." Electrifying, huh? This chapter gives you ten rules that you can easily remember, that really work, and that have wide application.

Bossy e

When your child knows words like *bag* and *hut*, he can move on to words like *tame* and *fume* that have one vowel in the middle and an *e* on the end. Words like this pop up all over the place, and you use the Bossy *e* rule to pronounce them.

Bossy *e* sits on the end of words. It makes no sound itself but makes the earlier vowel say its long sound. It turns *hat* into *hate* and *rat* into *rate*.

Table 26-1 gives you some Bossy *e* words.

Table 26-1		Bossy *e* Words		
ape	compete	bike	bone	brute
ace	complete	bite	broke	cute
bake	Eve	bride	chose	flute
base	Pete	crime	code	fume
blade	stampede	dice	cone	fuse
blame	Steve	dime	cope	plume
blaze	Theme	dive	dome	pollute
brave	these	drive	doze	rule
cake		file	drove	salute
came		fine	froze	

When Two Vowels Go Walking, the First One Does the Talking

I love this rule. You can remember this rule so easily because of the rhyme in this section heading, and the rule applies to heaps of words. In a word like *meat,* you sound out only the first vowel, and you sound it out as a long vowel. The second vowel stays silent. Take a look at the words in Table 26-2 to see exactly how this rule works. By the way, the most common pairs of vowels in this category are *ee, ea* (both making the same sound), *ai,* and *oa.*

Table 26-2		When Two Vowels Go Walking	
ee	*ea*	*ai*	*oa*
bee	bead	bail	boast
beep	beak	bait	boat
beer	beam	braid	cloak
bleed	bean	brain	coast
breed	beast	chain	coat
cheer	beat	drain	croak
creek	bleach	fail	float
creep	bleak	faint	goat
deed	bleat	frail	gloat
deep	cream	gain	load

y Acting like Long i

The words this cute rule applies to are little words that end with *y*. The *y* in these words sounds out as long *i*. Table 26-3 shows this (small) group of small words.

Table 26-3	*y* Endings that Sound like Long *i*	
by	cry	dry
fry	my	pry
shy	sly	try

y Acting like Long e

You just saw a group of little words all ending with *y,* and now you get a bigger group of words all ending in *y.* These words are longer than those words in Table 26-3; the *y* they all end with sounds out as long *e.* To see this word-sound relationship better, take a look at Table 26-4.

Table 26-4	*y* Endings that Sound like Long *e*	
baby	berry	body
bumpy	bunny	cherry
chilly	cloudy	copy
country	crazy	creepy
dirty	dizzy	empty
enemy	entry	family
fancy	funny	ghostly
granny	happy	holly
hurry	jolly	lady
lanky	lumpy	many

Drop the e When You Add ing

Here's another rhyme to make life easy. Word endings can do all sorts of strange things, but after your child knows this rhyme, she never needs to worry about adding *ing* onto words that end with an *e.* Table 26-5 shows this rule in action.

Table 26-5	Drop the *e* When You Add *ing*
Base Word	*Word with ing Ending*
bake	baking
bite	biting
dive	diving
fake	faking
hide	hiding
poke	poking
ride	riding
shake	shaking
slide	sliding
smile	smiling
time	timing
use	using

i Before *e*, Except After *c*

This rule surely rates as the one parents remember most from their own school days. And this rule is still a good one! The words in this group are hard, though. Don't expect your child to be able to read the words in Table 26-6 now. But come back to them later, when he's ready.

Table 26-6	*i* Before *e*, Except After *c*	
achieve	believe	brief
ceiling	chief	conceit
deceive	field	grief
grieve	niece	piece
priest	receipt	receive
shield	shriek	thief
yield	.	

The *ed* Ending Can Sound like *t*

Here's a rule you should be sure to tell your child. She comes across the *ed* ending often, and it can needlessly confuse her if she doesn't realize it can sound like *t, ed,* or just *d,* too. Table 26-7 gives some easy words to read with your child so that she can hear the way *ed* works.

Table 26-7	Words Ending in *ed*	
ed Has a Slight t Sound	*ed Has the Full ed Sound*	*ed Has a d Sound*
hoped	batted	dreamed
jumped	chatted	liked
peeped	hated	pinned
sloped	panted	planned
stripped	shifted	smiled
	shouted	waved

When you add endings to words, as in Table 26-7, double the letter to keep the vowel short. For example, *strip* becomes *stripped,* but *stripe* becomes *striped.*

s Can Sound like *z*

In words like *friends, hands, hopes, loves,* and *doves,* the *s* makes a *z* sound. This sound swap happens a bit erratically, so simply tell your child to try saying *z* if *s* doesn't sound right. In words that end with *es,* like *foxes* and *lashes,* the *s* always sounds like *z*.

er, ir, and ur All Say er (If You Catch My Drift)

Your child comes across the *er* sound often. Point out to him that this sound can appear as *er, ir,* or *ur* and skim through Table 26-8 to get familiar with this sound.

Table 26-8	*er, ir,* and *ur* Words	
er	*ir*	*ur*
clever	birch	burn
computer	bird	curl
farmer	dirt	curse
faster	fir	fur
her	firm	

Getting to Know ight

The *ight* word family can look imposing to your child. Help her get to know it so she doesn't get delayed every time she comes upon really common words, like *might* and *right.* Table 26-9 shows you some of the *ight* words you should show your child.

Table 26-9	*ight* Words	
blight	bright	fight
flight	fright	light
might	night	right
sight	slight	tight

Chapter 27

Ten Things to Help Your Budding Reader

*T*his chapter isn't where I talk grandly and vaguely about things like "creating a reading environment." Instead, I get down to some practicalities. I tell you in real terms how to prepare fertile ground to grow your reader in. You need to do some soil preparation and light weeding, but not enough that you get dirty or hurt your back.

Physical Movement

How often do you see a harried parent clutching a squealing child by the wrist in the supermarket or mall (and breathe a sigh of relief that it's not you this time!)? The parent expects the child to "behave" in public, but the child just isn't cooperating. Perhaps he wants forbidden candy? Or perhaps he's been physically restrained for too long? Your child (at any age) needs physical movement. Don't expect him to sustain his concentration for much longer than 20 minutes in the supermarket or in front of a pile of books. Have breaks and change tempo and activity often. A good 15 minutes of reading or writing works much better to help your child read than half an hour's whining (from either of you) or cajoling.

Another aspect of physical movement is gross and fine motor skills. *Gross motor skills* are physical skills that require big movements (like kicking or catching a ball); *fine motor skills* are physical skills that require small movements (like writing or threading beads). Your child needs the fine motor stuff to hold his book, follow the print, and write. But he needs the gross motor skills, too. When your child has good coordination in games and sports, he can probably become pretty good with fine motor skills, too. Some educators say that when they give uncoordinated kids more physical activity, like 30 minutes trampolining each day, those children make significant progress in reading. Keep your child active, make sure he gets lots of ball-play, and have puzzles, blocks, and Legos around the house.

Instead of putting blocks and puzzles away, keep them out on a table or tray. Then you're more likely to join your child in play when you have a few spare minutes.

Conversation

I expect that you teach your child to say "Please" and "Thank you," to look at the person she's talking to, and to wait for her turn to talk. That's great. Think, too, about the breadth of the conversations that you have with your child and the vocabulary that you use. Explain things to your child. Don't veto or censor conversations unless you think they may be truly harmful. And remember, when your 8-year-old argues the case for buying a pellet gun with concise and persuasive prose, you only have your own oratorical panache to blame.

In case I sound a little vague, I can give you an example of what I mean by not limiting your child's conversation. A few days ago, my child arrived home from school with some new words. She shares a bus with older kids, and the eighth grade boys had been using some colorful language. My daughter asked me about two choice expletives. She knew they were "bad" words but not why. We talked about older kids, peer pressure, showing-off, and (of course) expletives. What purpose do expletives serve? Should we be scared of them? How do adults react if a kid uses profanity? What about when other kids use it, how should she feel and behave?

My child learned two new expletives (I couldn't undo that learning experience) but also that she could talk to me, that words can mean different things to different people, and that the person using words and listening to them makes a difference in how you react to them. Her vocabulary is extensive, but her understanding of the nuances and breadth of language is good, too. And instead of being afraid or curious about some words, she feels more like a nearly all-knowing little princess of prose.

The other (equally important) side of talking is listening. When your child talks to you, listen. Then she feels confident speaking (she must be good at it because you listen to her) and finds out (from watching you) how to listen. You don't have to drop everything you're doing to show your child you're listening, but make some eye contact and give her a few attentive noises. To help your child grow into a confident and eloquent speaker, give her your attention, example, and unconditional positive regard.

Phonemic Awareness

If you say, *"Cat, hat, bat,"* and your child says, *"Mat,"* he has *phonemic awareness.* He knows (whether he's aware of it or not) that speech is made of units of sound and that he can play with those sounds. Teach your child rhymes, songs, and sayings to develop this awareness. Point out similar sounds, like first letters (*match, music, minestrone*) or endings (*itch, twitch, stitch*) of words. A lot of educational studies have shown that good phonemic awareness provides you with one of the best predictors of whether a child becomes a good reader.

Alphabet Blocks, Tiles, and Puzzles

How easy is this? If you have a preschool or lower elementary school child, give her letter blocks and tiles and help her get to know them well. Sit and play with those toys. Talk about the letter sounds, match identical letters, match upper- and lowercase letters, and point out important letters — like those letters in her name.

Books, Magazines, and Comics

I've pretty much talked about this category for the whole of this book, so I go over it briefly, now: Let your child see you read. Read to your child regularly and frequently. Use fiction and nonfiction. Enjoy pictures and rhymes. Read your child's favorite story often. Have babysitters and extended family read to your child, too. And be aware that boys, especially, need male reading role models.

Controlled Use of TV and Computers

Uh oh, here comes a quick preach about the demon, TV. Are you ready? Enjoy TV and computers, but monitor your child's use. Evidence suggests that as TV watching time goes up, reading skills go down, but only if your child is a top-of-the-line, deluxe, can't-possibly-turn-it-off TV user.

Studies suggest that watching more than two hours of TV a day puts your child in the deluxe viewer category.

A Chunk-by-Chunk Reading Style

Your child needs to be able to sound words out. More than that, he needs to sound out in chunks, not single letters. Word families and sounding out all merge together here. If you started off with words like *at* and *an* and showed your child families like *all, tall, small,* and *ball,* then you have this chunk-by-chunk reading style covered. Good readers read in chunks, but poor readers spend a lot of time struggling with single letters.

A Sight Vocabulary

Check out the 220 sight words I cover in Chapter 11. When your child has those words, or some of them, under her belt, she has a sight vocabulary. She can instantly identify some words, and her reading becomes more fluent because of it. It leaves some of her brainpower free for figuring out other words, too.

A Library Card

Need I say any more? I don't think so. Get on down to the library, where you and your child can get good reading stuff for free.

A Cassette Player

It doesn't need to be new or high tech, but get a cassette player for your child. He can listen to stories from the library, which get him *language enrichment* (exposure to language that uses a wide vocabulary). And you may think the peace-and-quiet fairy dropped by your house!

Chapter 28

Ten Reading Teachers' Resources

*Y*ou have two very good reasons to get your teacher stuff all ready to go. First, having things that you and your child can touch that represent what you have in mind makes the lesson plans go more smoothly; second, you need a few bits and pieces when you teach so that you can keep a varied and upbeat pace. Also, you feel (and look) like a complete ditherer if you spend half your reading time searching for pens and books. This chapter gives you ten things to put in your survival kit. It's all basic stuff — nothing elaborate, high tech, or expensive. (In *my* day you didn't get fancy gizmos; you had to think up 67 ways to use half a cereal box and a piece of shoelace.)

Letter Cards, Blocks, and Puzzles

When you're starting out with the alphabet, it's fine to write your own letters individually on small pieces of paper. But they don't look half as attractive as the letters you can buy cheaply in school supply shops or toy stores.

Buy letter cards, blocks, and puzzles so that your child gets an inside-out and back-to-front knowledge of single letters. He needs this knowledge so that he can identify lower- and uppercase letters, match each lowercase letter to its uppercase counterpart, and join letters together to make simple words, like *cat*. The more he sees and plays with letters, the better. Buy blocks, magnetic letters, letter tiles, games, and puzzles that use letters. Get big and small versions, colorful versions, and versions that your child has to construct or manipulate in some way.

Board Games

Board games usually have a greater life expectancy that other games. For one thing, they're pretty durable. For another, you usually play a board game with your child, so she has a lot of fun playing and spending time with you. Buy board games that have simple rules and pieces, and try to play them with your child often. *Chutes and Ladders* and *Bingo* are perennial favorites, but you can find all sorts of other games.

If a game includes cards of letters and pictures, your child can read them for practice, separate from the game.

Whiteboard and Pens

When your child starts writing letters and words, and when you want to write him a letter or word to read, get a whiteboard. Buy a small one (or, even better, a small one each), and get some pens and an eraser, too. You'll grow to love your whiteboard, believe me.

Flashcards

I can't go without a couple of boxes of flashcards. After your child knows some words, make haste to your school supply store or a large bookstore. My absolute favorite flashcards include

- *Easy Vowels* by Frank Schaffer
- *Easy Blends and Digraphs* by Frank Schaffer
- *Beginning to Read Phonics: Fishing for Silent "e" Words* by Judy/Instructo
- *Beginning to Read Phonics: Word Family Fun, Long Vowels* by Judy/Instructo

These cards come in sturdy boxes that you can take with you everywhere. Be selective when you use them. Don't give your child the whole lot — sort through them. Give her all the short, easy words first (like *hat, bun,* and *peg*), and then give her the harder ones (like *sheet, nail,* and *been*) after you show her how to sound them out. If your child is reading sentences well, use *sight words* flashcards. The Frank Schaffer label has produced good boxes of sight words, the latest versions being

- *Easy Sight Words* by Frank Shaffer
- *Sight Words* by Frank Shaffer

Phonetically Controlled Reading Books

The term *phonetically controlled* means a limited vocabulary. Phonetically controlled books have titles like *Fat Cat, Big Pig,* and *The Hot Pot.* Those titles may not sound particularly inspired to you, but they give your child the chance to read all by himself. Mix these books with the more exciting titles you read to your child, and you get a great balance. To find phonetically controlled reading books, ask your librarian or your child's teacher. In bookshops, you can easily find the *Bob Books* by Bobby Lynn Maslen (Scholastic). And if you're interested in CD-ROMs based on phonics, start by looking at *Reader Rabbit* (The Learning Company). Try to borrow library copies of CD-ROMs before buying them yourself because CD-ROMS can get expensive. Ask librarians and teachers for recommendations on CD-ROMs, too.

Stories on Tape

Never mind my kids; *I'm* addicted to these things. I'm not talking about the bestsellers on tape that I sometimes listen to in my car. I mean the kids' stories I drop into my library to pick up every week (to keep my kids out of my hair). Stories on tape are a brilliant invention. They keep your child happily engrossed, and she soaks up all that good plot, vocabulary, and style that may come in handy later, when she writes school projects and letters to Grandma. If you haven't used stories on tape, do it now. If you get the kind of tapes that come with a book, all the better. Your child can follow the story in the book while she's listening to it, tracking and remembering the appearance of words as she goes. She gets to enjoy good stories that bigger kids rave about, too, like *Lord of the Rings* and *Harry Potter.*

Book Series

One of my children is currently trying to work her way through the entire collection of *Goosebumps* books. Every week, she gathers an armful of them from our local library and orders books from other libraries when her supply at our local library starts to thin. She's already read practically all of the *Bailey School Kids* series, The *Magic Tree House* series, and *A Series of Unfortunate Events.* I thank my lucky stars for those series. They save us hours of time looking for books on their own and are easy to track down. When your child starts to read books either with you or by himself, check out the popular series. A few stalwarts are:

- ✔ *A to Z Mysteries* (Random House)

- ✔ *Amelia Bedelia* (HarperCollins)

- ✔ *Arthur* (Little, Brown and Company)

- ✔ *Bailey School Kids* (Scholastic)

- ✔ *Captain Underpants* (Blue Sky Press)

- ✔ *Clifford (The Big Red Dog)* (Cartwheel Books)

- ✔ *Dr. Seuss* books (Random House)

- ✔ *Junie B. Jones* (Random House)

- ✔ *Magic Tree House* (Random House)

- ✔ *Nate the Great* (Yearling Books)

- ✔ *Secrets of Droon* (Scholastic)

A Few Good Web Sites

I am a wary Internet user. I can't stand the endless wait that I often get stuck with and feel the same way about the advertising that constantly pops up at me when I'm trying to check out a Web site. I'm scared of the Internet, too. When I'm told that I need to download a plofot (or whatever the heck it is) in order to view a screen, I panic. Should I or shouldn't I do it? My husband frequently warns me that, at the touch of a finger, I can download some real nasties. They can take weeks to go away and meanwhile eat up all my work and, worse, address labels. So with the kind of Internet user I am in mind, the following sections give you five *easy* Web sites that you may want to check out with your child.

www.kinderkorner.com

After you get past the writer's attempts to make you buy books, you find useful information here. I especially like the *I Love My ABC's* part. It gives you an alphabet comprised of rhymes, like this one for A:

A is for alligator

A is for ants

A is for apples

On my pants

To find *I Love My ABC's,* click on the `Victoria's Online Thematic Units —` `Complete List` link. You arrive at a page of options and one of the first links takes you to *I Love My ABC's.*

www.essortment.com

This Web site is a database of articles. The articles are clear and straightforward, and you can navigate it simply. From the home page, click on the `Family and Parenting` link and from there, click on the `Children's Education` link.

You don't find advertising, pop-ups, or other annoying stuff on this site. One nice article that I found here explained how to get your reader engaged in books by recruiting your own parent's help. Have Grandma or Grandpa send your child books and get a sort of book club going. Your child reads the book herself and then gets a call from Grandma or Grandpa to discuss it.

www.preksmarties.com

This site is designed for pre-kindergartners, but it has good ideas for kids up to about second grade.

www.ala.org/alsc

This address takes you to the children's section of the American Library Association. Here, you can find book lists of award-winning books. Look in the adults' section for award winners for your own reading, too.

www.literacyconnections.com

This site has literacy ideas, including ESL (English as a Second Language) activities and programs for kids and adults. If you're savvy about buying and downloading stuff from the Internet, you can get songs to listen to and simple reading books here.

The Great Outdoors

A while ago, when I tutored kids in one part of my house, I made a point of stopping for game breaks after about 15 minutes of work. I knew that 15 minutes of good work was more effective than half an hour's difficult work. I knew that kids need to move and zone out for a few minutes in order to return to work refreshed and able to achieve more. I filled my house with board games, darts boards, and throwing-balls-into-boxes type games.

One day, my own child came into my reading room and asked if the child I was tutoring could swing with her on our rope swing instead of playing darts with me. Well, as much as I needed practice in playing darts, I agreed. And a revelation occurred. My student swung wildly on our rope swing (which gave exhilarating swings over a gully that looked, from the rope, like suicide canyon) and returned to our lesson rejuvenated. After that, instead of playing darts, I raced my students to the rope swing and took turns swinging with them.

When you're teaching your child, don't forget about having 15 minutes of good work rather than half an hour of cajoling. Have some physical play. Obviously, you don't want to drag your child from his warm bed to jump rope in the snow because I advised it. But if, for example, it's daytime, you're work-ing on phonics rules, and you see your child's head drooping, head for the great outdoors, or at least the basketball hoop.

You Are Your Own Best Resource

Before I leave this chapter, here's a last (and hopefully sage) message to you: You can buy all the resources you want, but resources don't make you a good teacher. On the other hand, you can be a fine teacher with only a paper and pen to your name. That's because your attitude counts most of all.

Today, I remembered something from my own early years that really brought this point home to me. I was a kindergartener. My teacher was Mrs. Herring. She had gray hair and sat behind a big wooden desk. She called me to her desk and pulled me to stand close to her. She looked at the book I was read-ing and asked me a question that I couldn't answer. She reached out her hand and slapped my bare legs hard. (In those days, little girls wore skirts and nobody sued nasty old child abusers masquerading as teachers.) Mrs. Herring left me only bad memories, and I think it's safe to say that her atti-tude stank.

You, on the other hand, have read this book. You have the positive attitude that sets you miles and miles apart from nasty old Mrs. Herring. You can give your child good memories and a remarkable gift. Because of your joy in her, and attention to her, she will read. (Nya, nya, Mrs. Herring!)

Appendix

A Word Family Tree

If you want to take your child through a word family or two each week, what follows is a huge family tree that grows from easiest words to harder words. Be sure to spend a few days on each family so that your child remembers the words later.

Easiest Families of All

an	*ap*	*at*	*in*
an	cap	at	bin
ban	gap	bat	din
can	lap	cat	fin
fan	map	fat	in
man	nap	hat	pin
pan	rap	mat	tin
ran	sap	pat	win
tan	tap	rat	
van		sat	

ip	*og*	*op*	*ug*
dip	bog	bop	bug
hip	dog	cop	dug
lip	fog	mop	hug
nip	hog	pop	jug
rip	jog	top	mug

(continued)

ip	og	op	ug
sip	log		rug
tip			tug
zip			

Next Easiest Families of All

ack	ank	ell	est
back	bank	bell	best
backpack	blank	fell	chest
black	drank	sell	nest
crack	plank	shell	pest
Jack	shrank	smell	rest
pack	spank	spell	test
quack	tank	tell	vest
sack	thank	well	west
smack		yell	
snack			
track			

ick	ill	ing	ink
brick	bill	bring	blink
chick	chill	cling	drink
flick	drill	fling	ink
kick	fill	king	link
lick	frill	ring	pink
Nick	grill	sing	rink
pick	hill	sling	shrink
prick	ill	spring	sink

ick	ill	ing	ink
quick	kill	sting	stink
sick	mill	string	think
stick	pill	swing	wink
thick	skill	thing	
tick	spill	wing	
trick	will		

ock	uck	ump	unk
block	buck	bump	bunk
clock	duck	dump	chunk
flock	luck	jump	hunk
lock	muck	lump	junk
rock	struck	plump	shrunk
shock	suck	pump	sunk
sock	truck	stump	trunk
unlock	tuck	thump	

ch Words

ch Words	tch Words
bench	batch
branch	blotch
brunch	catch
bunch	catch
clench	clutch
crunch	crutch
drench	ditch

(continued)

ch Words	tch Words
flinch	fetch
hunch	hatch
inch	hitch
munch	itch
pinch	kitchen
punch	latch
ranch	match
stench	patch
trench	pitch
wrench	scratch
	sketch
	snatch
	stitch
	switch
	twitch
	watch
	witch

Other Common Word Families

all	oo	ow	ought
all	boo	bellow	bought
ball	boot	blow	brought
fall	cool	crow	thought
small	food	flow	
stall	moo	glow	
tall	moon	grow	
	room	low	

all	oo	ow	ought
	soon	mellow	
	spoon	mow	
	stool	own	
	too	show	
	tooth	slow	
		yellow	

ay	oo	alk	ight
away	book	chalk	fight
bay	brook	stalk	flight
clay	cook	talk	light
day	crook	walk	might
hay	look		right
may	took		sight
play			tight
say			
stay			
way			

The Double Letters

ff	ll	ss
off	ball	dress
sniff	bell	miss
cliff	bill	kiss
stuff	doll	loss
	dull	less
	fall	boss

(continued)

ff	ll	ss
	small	floss
	tall	moss
	wall	

Same Sound, Different Ways

oy	oi
annoy	boil
boy	moist
employ	noise
joy	oil
Roy	soil
royal	spoil
toy	toil

For the following *ow/ou* sound, ask your child, "What would you say if I pinched you?" When you come upon the sound in text and your child forgets, give him a gentle pinch.

ow	ou
bow	around
brown	bound
cow	cloud
crown	found
down	house
drown	loud
frown	mound
growl	mouse

ow	ou
how	noun
now	pound
scowl	proud
sow	round
town	sound

aw	au
caw	auto
claw	author
crawl	laundry
dawn	sauce
draw	

The Five Vowels Plus r

or	ar	er	ir	ur
corn	art	her	bird	burn
for	barn	herd	dirt	curl
fork	car	nerve	firm	curse
horse	dart	perch	first	hurl
north	far	person	flirt	hurt
or	farm	serve	girl	nurse
storm	hard	stern	shirt	purse
torn	large		sir	surf
worn	marsh		stir	turn
	star		third	

"Bossy e" and "Two Vowels Go Walking" Words

Bossy e Words	"When Two Vowels Go Walking" Words
ape	bee
bake	bleed
base	cheer
blade	creek
blame	creep
brave	deep
cake	feel
came	feet
cane	free
cape	green
case	jeep
crate	heel
chase	keep
date	meet
fade	need
fake	see
flake	seed
flame	seen
game	sleep
gate	speech
gave	speed
grade	steel
grape	steep
graze	sweet
lake	tree
lane	week

Bossy e Words	*"When Two Vowels Go Walking" Words*
late	bead
made	beak
mane	bean
mate	beat
name	cheap
pale	cheat
pane	clear
plate	deal
rake	dream
sale	each
save	ear
scrape	east
shade	eat
shake	fear
shape	feast
skate	hear
snake	heat
state	meal
stale	mean
take	meat
tale	neat
tape	reach
wake	read
wave	real
dive	scream
drive	seal
file	seat

(continued)

Bossy e Words	*"When Two Vowels Go Walking" Words*
fine	sneak
five	speak
hide	steal
hike	steam
nine	stream
bone	teach
broke	team
code	braid
cone	brain
hole	chain
home	drain
hope	fail
cute	mail
flute	main
fume	pain
rule	train
	sail
	tail
	train
	wait
	boast
	boat
	coat
	float
	goat
	road
	roast
	soap
	throat

Words Ending in *tion*

action	motion
correction	notion
dictation	position
direction	promotion
disposition	reflection
fiction	refraction
infection	relaxation
invention	selection
mention	suction

Words Ending in *ed*

For Words Ending with e, Only Add d	To Keep the Short Vowel Sound, Double the Last Letter Before Adding ed	Add t, Not ed
coped	bagged	built
escaped	batted	crept
faced	begged	felt
faded	bogged	knelt
faked	chapped	lent
filed	chatted	slept
fined	chopped	smelt
glided	dropped	spent
grazed	fitted	swept
hated	flipped	wept
hiked	hopped	
hired	mopped	

(continued)

For Words Ending with e, Only Add d	To Keep the Short Vowel Sound, Double the Last Letter Before Adding ed
hoped	patted
joked	pinned
laced	potted
liked	shipped
lined	shopped
mimed	skipped
moped	
paced	
paved	
piled	
pined	
posed	
prided	
rated	
saved	
scraped	
shaped	
shaved	
smiled	
stroked	
taped	
traced	
waded	
waved	
wiped	

Soft c and g

Soft c	Soft g
ace	age
cell	average
cent	bandage
center	bulge
chance	cabbage
city	cage
dance	gem
dice	general
face	gin
fancy	gym
fence	hostage
France	huge
glance	luggage
grace	page
ice	plunge
lace	rage
lice	stage
mice	wage
nice	
pace	
peace	
place	
price	
prince	

(continued)

Soft c
race
rice
since
slice
space
twice
wince

Index

• C •

• *Q* •

• *R* •

Notes

Notes

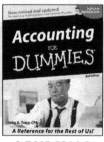

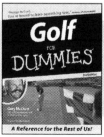

FOR DUMMIES®

A world of resources to help you grow

HOME, GARDEN & HOBBIES

Feng Shui
0-7645-5295-3

Gardening
0-7645-5130-2

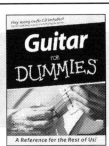

Guitar
0-7645-5106-X

Also available:

Auto Repair For Dummies
(0-7645-5089-6)

Chess For Dummies
(0-7645-5003-9)

Home Maintenance For
Dummies
(0-7645-5215-5)

Organizing For Dummies
(0-7645-5300-3)

Piano For Dummies
(0-7645-5105-1)

Poker For Dummies
(0-7645-5232-5)

Quilting For Dummies
(0-7645-5118-3)

Rock Guitar For Dummies
(0-7645-5356-9)

Roses For Dummies
(0-7645-5202-3)

Sewing For Dummies
(0-7645-5137-X)

FOOD & WINE

Cooking
0-7645-5250-3

Cookies
0-7645-5390-9

Wine
0-7645-5114-0

Also available:

Bartending For Dummies
(0-7645-5051-9)

Chinese Cooking For
Dummies
(0-7645-5247-3)

Christmas Cooking For
Dummies
(0-7645-5407-7)

Diabetes Cookbook For
Dummies
(0-7645-5230-9)

Grilling For Dummies
(0-7645-5076-4)

Low-Fat Cooking For
Dummies
(0-7645-5035-7)

Slow Cookers For Dummies
(0-7645-5240-6)

TRAVEL

Italy
0-7645-5453-0

Hawaii
0-7645-5438-7

Las Vegas
0-7645-5448-4

Also available:

America's National Parks For
Dummies
(0-7645-6204-5)

Caribbean For Dummies
(0-7645-5445-X)

Cruise Vacations For
Dummies 2003
(0-7645-5459-X)

Europe For Dummies
(0-7645-5456-5)

Ireland For Dummies
(0-7645-6199-5)

France For Dummies
(0-7645-6292-4)

London For Dummies
(0-7645-5416-6)

Mexico's Beach Resorts For
Dummies
(0-7645-6262-2)

Paris For Dummies
(0-7645-5494-8)

RV Vacations For Dummies
(0-7645-5443-3)

Walt Disney World & Orlando
For Dummies
(0-7645-5444-1)

FOR DUMMIES®

Plain-English solutions for everyday challenges

COMPUTER BASICS

0-7645-0838-5   **0-7645-1663-9**   **0-7645-1548-9**

Also available:

PCs All-in-One Desk Reference For Dummies (0-7645-0791-5)

Pocket PC For Dummies (0-7645-1640-X)

Treo and Visor For Dummies (0-7645-1673-6)

Troubleshooting Your PC For Dummies (0-7645-1669-8)

Upgrading & Fixing PCs For Dummies (0-7645-1665-5)

Windows XP For Dummies (0-7645-0893-8)

Windows XP For Dummies Quick Reference (0-7645-0897-0)

BUSINESS SOFTWARE

0-7645-0822-9   **0-7645-0839-3**   **0-7645-0819-9**

Also available:

Excel Data Analysis For Dummies (0-7645-1661-2)

Excel 2002 All-in-One Desk Reference For Dummies (0-7645-1794-5)

Excel 2002 For Dummies Quick Reference (0-7645-0829-6)

GoldMine "X" For Dummies (0-7645-0845-8)

Microsoft CRM For Dummies (0-7645-1698-1)

Microsoft Project 2002 For Dummies (0-7645-1628-0)

Office XP For Dummies (0-7645-0830-X)

Outlook 2002 For Dummies (0-7645-0828-8)

Get smart! Visit www.dummies.com

- **Find listings of even more *For Dummies* titles**
- **Browse online articles**
- **Sign up for Dummies eTips™**
- **Check out *For Dummies* fitness videos and other products**
- **Order from our online bookstore**

Available wherever books are sold. Go to www.dummies.com or call 1-877-762-2974 to order direct.

FOR DUMMIES®

Helping you expand your horizons and realize your potential

INTERNET

0-7645-0894-6

0-7645-1659-0

0-7645-1642-6

DIGITAL MEDIA

0-7645-1664-7

0-7645-1675-2

0-7645-0806-7

GRAPHICS

0-7645-0817-2

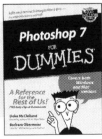

0-7645-1651-5

0-7645-0895-4

FOR DUMMIES®

The advice and explanations you need to succeed

SELF-HELP, SPIRITUALITY & RELIGION

0-7645-5302-X

0-7645-5418-2

0-7645-5264-3

Also available:

The Bible For Dummies
(0-7645-5296-1)

Buddhism For Dummies
(0-7645-5359-3)

Christian Prayer For Dummies
(0-7645-5500-6)

Dating For Dummies
(0-7645-5072-1)

Judaism For Dummies
(0-7645-5299-6)

Potty Training For Dummies
(0-7645-5417-4)

Pregnancy For Dummies
(0-7645-5074-8)

Rekindling Romance For Dummies
(0-7645-5303-8)

Spirituality For Dummies
(0-7645-5298-8)

Weddings For Dummies
(0-7645-5055-1)

PETS

0-7645-5255-4

0-7645-5286-4

0-7645-5275-9

Also available:

Labrador Retrievers For Dummies
(0-7645-5281-3)

Aquariums For Dummies
(0-7645-5156-6)

Birds For Dummies
(0-7645-5139-6)

Dogs For Dummies
(0-7645-5274-0)

Ferrets For Dummies
(0-7645-5259-7)

German Shepherds For Dummies
(0-7645-5280-5)

Golden Retrievers For Dummies
(0-7645-5267-8)

Horses For Dummies
(0-7645-5138-8)

Jack Russell Terriers For Dummies
(0-7645-5268-6)

Puppies Raising & Training Diary For Dummies
(0-7645-0876-8)

EDUCATION & TEST PREPARATION

0-7645-5194-9

0-7645-5325-9

0-7645-5210-4

Also available:

Chemistry For Dummies
(0-7645-5430-1)

English Grammar For Dummies
(0-7645-5322-4)

French For Dummies
(0-7645-5193-0)

The GMAT For Dummies
(0-7645-5251-1)

Inglés Para Dummies
(0-7645-5427-1)

Italian For Dummies
(0-7645-5196-5)

Research Papers For Dummies
(0-7645-5426-3)

The SAT I For Dummies
(0-7645-5472-7)

U.S. History For Dummies
(0-7645-5249-X)

World History For Dummies
(0-7645-5242-2)

Available wherever books are sold. Go to www.dummies.com or call 1-877-762-2974 to order direct.

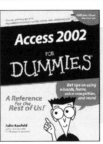